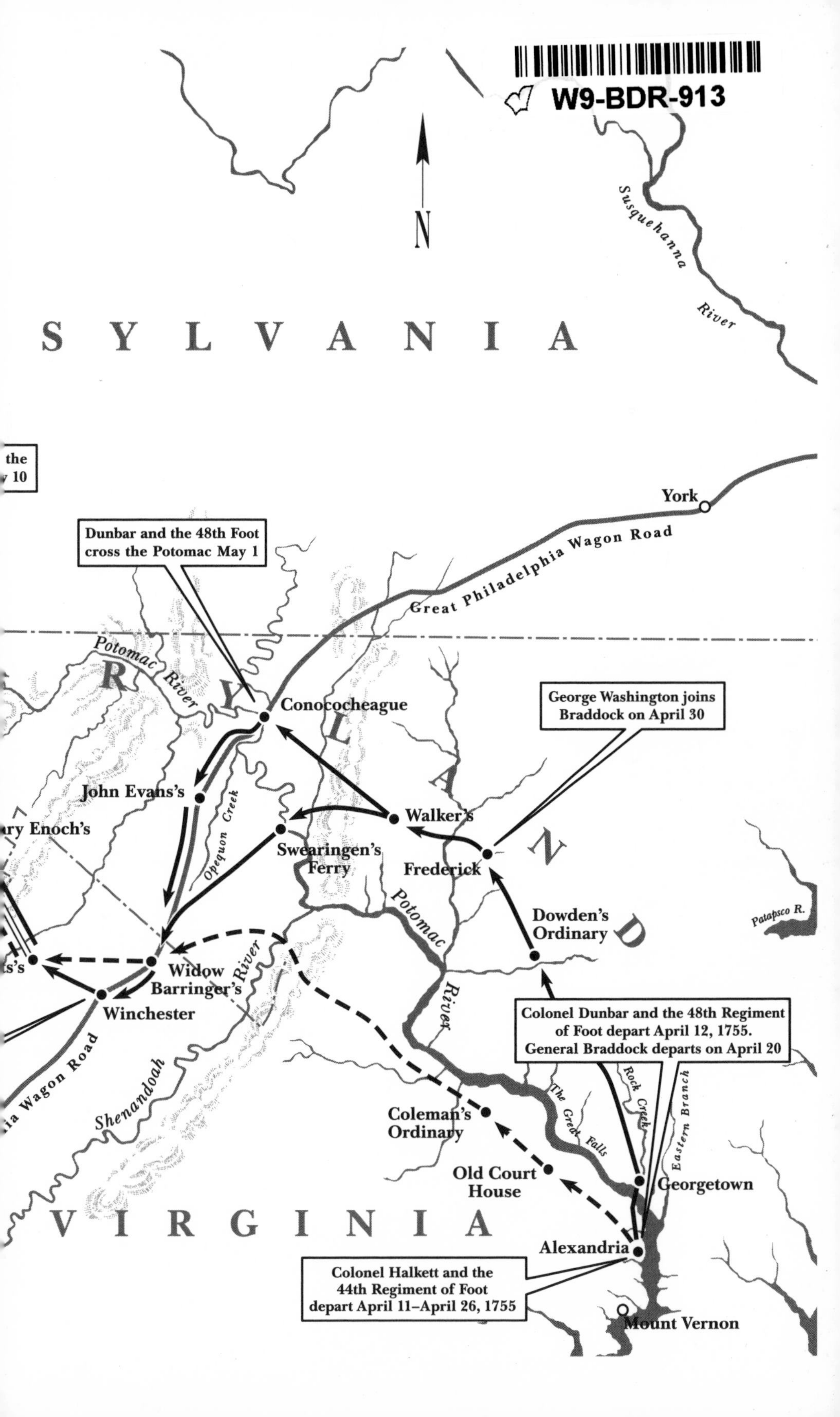
W9-BDR-913
N
Susquehanna River
SYLVANIA
the
10
York
Great Philadelphia Wagon Road
Dunbar and the 48th Foot cross the Potomac May 1
Potomac River
Conococheague
George Washington joins Braddock on April 30
John Evans's
Opequon Creek
Walker's
ry Enoch's
Swearingen's Ferry
Frederick
Potomac
Dowden's Ordinary
Patapsco R.
Widow Barringer's
River
Winchester
River
Colonel Dunbar and the 48th Regiment of Foot depart April 12, 1755. General Braddock departs on April 20
ia Wagon Road
Shenandoah
Rock Creek
Eastern Branch
The Great Falls
Coleman's Ordinary
Old Court House
Georgetown
VIRGINIA
Alexandria
Colonel Halkett and the 44th Regiment of Foot depart April 11–April 26, 1755
Mount Vernon

SARATOGA SPRINGS PUBLIC LIBRARY
DONATED BY THE
EX LIBRIS
SOCIETY

Braddock's March

Braddock's March

How the Man Sent
to Seize a Continent
Changed
American History

Thomas E. Crocker

WESTHOLME
Yardley

Frontispiece: "Braddock's March," an engraving from Washington Irving's *The Life of George Washington*, 1855.

Maps by Tracy Dungan

Westholme Publishing, LLC
Eight Harvey Avenue
Yardley, Pennsylvania 19067
Visit our Web site at www.westholmepublishing.com

First Printing September 2009
10 9 8 7 6 5 4 3 2 1

ISBN: 978-1-59416-096-7

Printed in United States of America

For Edward and Thomas

It was long a subject of hot dispute among men whether physical strength or mental ability was the more important requirement for success in war. Before you start on anything, you must plan; when you have made your plans, prompt action is needed. Thus neither is sufficient without the aid of the other.

–Sallust, *The Conspiracy of Cataline*

Contents

Prologue

On September 24, 1754, William Augustus, the Duke of Cumberland, third son of King George II, and Captain General, or commander-in-chief, of the British army, huddled with his aides at the British army's general staff headquarters at Horse Guards in London. The fine white stone Palladian building had been completed only the year before. With its three-story wings surmounted by a central arch bearing the royal arms of His Majesty, the capacious edifice provided a fitting and modern command post for the organized and reform-minded Cumberland. Built on the site of King Henry VIII's tilt yard, or jousting ground, the elegant and imposing building served both as the London home of the Foot Guards who protected the King at his residence at nearby St. James's Palace and as the nerve center from which Great Britain administered its far-flung military empire. And what more appropriate venue could there be than a royal jousting ground, as Britain squared off one more time against France?

The Duke of Cumberland knew both his own troops and his enemy from first-hand experience. Just nine years before, on May 11, 1745, at Fontenoy in the Low Countries, the duke had ordered the Coldstream Regiment of Foot Guards to wheel into position on the marshy meadows before the River Scheldt. The English troops marched forward as if on parade, while the elite French Guards waited. The English officers led their troops with light rattan canes. As they drew near the French line, they raised their hats in salute to their adversaries. The French politely saluted, declined the English commander's invitation to fire first, and returned the compliment by themselves inviting the English to fire.

And they did. During the course of the battle the Coldstream Foot Guards' officers directed the men's muskets with their canes, first to the left and then to the right, a nudge here, a wave of the wand there, as if they were symphonic conductors. The duke's regiment mowed the elite French soldiers down like ripe grain before the sickle.[1]

The battle already had entered the annals of British military history as a model of discipline and efficiency.

Now, nine years later, the joust was about to begin again. The Captain General's desk was piled high with entreaties for assistance from Governor Dinwiddie in Virginia, with reports about an obscure acting colonel of the colonial militia named George Washington who had single-handedly brought the two great European empires to the brink of war, with intelligence reports about the mineral wealth of the Ohio River valley and the fluid dispositions of the various Indian tribes that inhabited it and with maps procured from the Board of Trade, which was charged with the administration of the North American colonies.

The Duke of Cumberland had done his homework. He had read the reports, and he had studied the maps. He knew the geopolitical grounds, the high stakes, and the urgency as he was about to mount the largest armed expeditionary force ever sent to North America.

On the very maps unrolled on his desk before him it was plain for all to see that the westernmost projection of Anglo-American force, at the combined trading post and fort at Wills Creek in Maryland, was but a mere fifteen miles from France's Fort Duquesne at the Forks of the Ohio River. It would be short work to paddle up the Potomac River to its junction with Wills Creek and then from there to pounce on the French unexpectedly. Were not the western reaches of British America but little more than fifteen miles wide? The maps, after all, said so.

Of course, there were the Indians to contend with. They were a fickle and confusing lot, one day siding with the English and the next with the French. Hardly worth trying to figure out. Almost one hundred and fifty years of British colonization in America, however, had brought home the one irreducible fact about the Indians: their brutality. They did not fight like the British or the French. They skulked, they scalped, they murdered men, women, and children indiscriminately. Cumberland knew he needed to have a tough and driven commander.

As he looked down at the freshly signed commission on his desk, the Captain General had no question that he had just the person for the job: His Excellency Major General Edward Braddock of the Coldstream Regiment of Foot Guards, Generalissimo of All His Majesty's Troops in North America.

LONG OVERSHADOWED BY THE ENSUING DRAMA of the American Revolution, Braddock's march survives today only in traces. Dozens of "Braddock" sites are taken for granted, faded into the everyday landscape like the memory of what caused them—Braddock Road, Braddock's Rock, Braddock Heights, Braddock's Run, Braddock Avenue, Braddock Hills, North Braddock, Mount Braddock, Braddock's Field. They punctuate the map of the twenty-first-century East Coast of America from the suburbs and back roads of Tidewater Virginia and suburban Maryland to downtown Washington, D.C., to the outskirts of Pittsburgh, Pennsylvania. Drivers pass by them; shoppers barely register their existence; even residents take them for granted as part of the everyday landscape.

In the 1750s, it was another story. A British general at the command of some two thousand British soldiers and American militia—at the time the largest professional army ever assembled in

North America–mounted one of the most ambitious and remarkable marches in history. As in later wars, they arrived with high intentions, cocksure confidence, and such woeful ignorance that they were swallowed up and destroyed by the reality of the country they had come to save. Their aim was to oust the French, win over hostile Indians, and claim a continent. The British troops who made the march were the first that England had ever sent to America in force. Their route of march slashed like a scar across the center of the American colonies. They blazed a road where only wilderness had existed. They hauled dozens of cannon across mountains that are formidable even now. They faced an enemy whom they did not know. And they were all but wiped out in one of the most humiliating defeats British arms was ever to suffer.

The Braddock campaign has been underrated in the past as a one-shot loss by an arcane British general. In fact, nothing could be further from the truth. The arrival of the expedition unwittingly provided a tabula rasa, an empty slate, on which the expectant and all-too-willing American colonists wrote their own story. If the British side of that story is infused with folly and laced with irony, much of it attributable to the complex and contradictory character of the commanding general Edward Braddock, the American side is marked by lessons from that experience that are limned deep in the American self-conscious. It is rare that a single battle–and a defeat at that–has had such profound military and political consequences for America.

The important facets of the Braddock campaign treated in this book fall into two interrelated broad categories–military and political.

The military significance lies in the campaign's unique assemblage of then-unknown persons, both in Braddock's "military family" and in the extended officer corps, who came to forge a nucleus of the Continental Army out of their shared experiences and personal relationships, as well as individuals who were later to play important roles on the British side during the American

Revolution. The military significance of the expedition also includes what appears to have been the first effective use of rifles in combat, the launching of the American myth of the superiority of irregular warfare, the birth of special forces, the revelation to Americans of the vincibility of British redcoats, and the redemption of the shattered military career of an officer named George Washington.

The political dimensions were even more far-reaching. They included the first framing of the burden-sharing and taxation issue that divided America from England and directly led to the American Revolution, the first successful organized congress of the American colonies that at once cooperated with the British and resisted British demands, the birth of George Washington as a national political hero, a new American self-reliance forged in desperation in the face of terrorism unleashed by the defeat, the exile of the Acadians from Nova Scotia, a shift in policy that led to the outright seizure of French Canada and the virtual annihilation of the remaining Eastern Indians, and the opening of the single major road for Western expansion in America. These are not mean accomplishments for a single expedition that is now all but forgotten.

It is perhaps not out of place to posit that the Braddock campaign rivals in importance General James Wolfe's seismic seizure of Quebec four years later in 1759. The geopolitical reality of a united British North America–from Canada to Georgia–born on the Plains of Abraham in that *annus mirabilis* lasted only seventeen years, whereas the uniquely American geopolitical reality launched by Braddock's expedition has lasted over 250. It is, at the very least, time to focus a glint of light on the Braddock expedition and recognize it as one of the most important military engagements in the American colonial period.

But first a word on a key to help unlock the mystery of the Braddock campaign: it is a profoundly *human* story. If common wisdom is that Braddock's march is today "inaccessible," it is perhaps best to approach these events of 250 years ago as a pilgrimage of people great and small, a pilgrimage in its broadest and original meaning of the term: a wandering in a strange land. Braddock's march was not a pilgrimage of grace but a pilgrimage of destiny, equally so for the British soldiers who came to the American wilderness as for the Americans who fought at their side and in so doing were set on their own quite separate pilgrimage. Like all great pilgrimages, from the journals of the penitents on the road to Santiago de Compostela to Chaucer's Canterbury Tales, there were tales to tell. And what a tale it was: "Generalissimo" Edward Braddock riding in his sleek chariot, a young and ambitious George Washington, a resourceful Benjamin Franklin, an Indian ally known as the Half King, a wagoneer named Daniel Boone, the young Pontiac, fifty women camp followers, and the host of then-obscure officers who were later to play leading roles on both sides in the American Revolution. And there were the events along the pilgrim's road: a hard-drinking, hard-driving commander, floggings ordered to impose rigid discipline, the scheming of the staff officers, the near rebellion of the troops, passage through the Shades of Death, the first wheeled vehicles ever to cross the Appalachian Mountains, rumors of buried treasure, the pageantry of forty regimental drummers and fifers playing "The Grenadiers' March" as the column advanced through the deepest wilderness under bayonets glistening in the sun, and, at the end of the pilgrimage, a horrific defeat that transformed America.

This is the story of the men and women who were the pilgrims on Braddock's march and how that march changed their lives and helped to make America.[2]

Chapter One

The Proximate Cause

IT WAS PROBABLY NOT A GOOD THING to be a twenty-two-year-old colonial army officer who had caused an international incident, abandoned his unit's colors, been the subject of official inquiry, and had his name made known to the King of England. Such was the inauspicious position in which George Washington stood by late summer 1754. King George II had read or heard of a dispatch from Washington in which he had written: "I have heard the bullets whistle; and believe me there is something charming in the sound." The King wisely commented, "He would not say so if he had been used to hear many."

"Fanfarol," hurrumphed the London gossip Horace Walpole in direct reference to Washington's dispatch.[1] What were these whistling bullets that had "charmed" the young Washington and earned the contempt of the King of England?

Just as a flash in the pan of a Brown Bess preceded the ignition of a musket shot, a small incident in the wilderness ignited what was to become the epic struggle for control of a continent known in America as the French and Indian War and, more broadly in Europe, as the Seven Years' War.

By late 1753, France had created a string of forts from Montreal to Rivière aux Boeufs near present-day Erie, Pennsylvania, aimed at asserting its claim to the Ohio River valley. Alarmed at the militarization of the frontier, Lieutenant Governor Robert Dinwiddie of Virginia dispatched a twenty-one-year-old major of the Virginia militia, George Washington, to Rivière aux Boeufs to request that the French retire.[2] The ambitious Washington leapt at the chance to become the bayonet point of Dinwiddie's policy. As an officer in the Virginia militia Washington wore a gilded brass gorget inscribed with the colonial arms and presumptuous motto of Virginia "En Dat Virginia Quartum" or "Behold! Virginia Yields the Fourth," meaning that Virginia was the fourth kingdom of the British empire after the united kingdoms of England and Scotland, France, and Ireland.[3] At any rate, Virginia under Dinwiddie, if not a kingdom, had its own foreign policy.

Washington met up with a guide named Christopher Gist, who was an educated man, originally from England, and, at forty-five, twice Washington's age. He was as tall as Washington but of a swarthy complexion. He was not a backwoodsman but a trader and entrepreneur who was equally at ease on the mountain trail and in Tidewater society. Together, Washington and Gist traveled almost one thousand miles from Williamsburg to the shores of Lake Erie and back through winter blizzards, icy waters, and Indian ambush. When they arrived at the French fort Washington presented the commander with a letter from Dinwiddie which asked, "By whose authority [have the French] invaded the King of Great Britain's territories? It becomes my duty to require your peaceable departure." The French commander, a one-eyed old officer named Legardeur de St. Pierre, received Washington politely and with respect but returned him with the answer: "As to the summons you send me to retire, I do not think myself obliged to obey."[4]

The "civil" French had underestimated the determined Scots-born lieutenant governor of Virginia. Washington returned to Williamsburg not only with the answer but also with intelligence which Dinwiddie forwarded to London. At Rivière aux Boeufs, Washington, an ardent gatherer of intelligence even at this young age, dined with the French garrison officers, recorded the indiscretions of their wine-loosened tongues, and observed fifty birch bark and one hundred and seventy pine canoes drawn up on the shore awaiting the spring thaw to carry a large French reinforcement downstream toward the Ohio. Washington also kept a journal on the expedition in which he presciently noted that the Forks of the Ohio, which he had passed en route to Rivière aux Boeufs, were "extremely well situated for a fort."[5] Indeed, a detachment of forty Virginia militiamen under Ensign James Ward was already at work at the forks constructing a fortified storehouse.

Immediately upon Washington's return to Williamsburg on January 16, 1754, Dinwiddie resolved to mount an expedition to march to the Ohio to reinforce Ward's outpost.[6] The French had not yet ousted the Americans when Dinwiddie conceived and ordered the plan. Even as the French flotilla was descending from Rivière aux Boeufs, the Virginia Assembly voted £10,000 for the expedition. A small army of Virginia militia, including George Washington, augmented in June by an Independent Company of the King's regulars from South Carolina under Captain James McKay–some four hundred men in toto–constituted the strike force. Their orders were to fortify the Forks of the Ohio and destroy all persons who should impede their mission. The colonel in command was Joshua Fry. However, Fry died on May 31 from injuries sustained in a fall from his horse, and Washington, as second in command, took charge.[7]

Dinwiddie supplied them with small arms and ten small 4-pounder cannon, drawn from thirty pieces of ordnance that the King had earlier presented to the colony of Virginia. The colonial force proceeded from Alexandria in northern Virginia overland to Winchester to Wills Creek, a tributary of the Potomac River, in western Maryland and thence westward along the Nemacolin Trail, a narrow Indian path that was the main route west over the mountains.

With the spring thaw of 1754, Washington's suspicions of French intentions noted in his report to Dinwiddie proved justified. On April 16, a flotilla of three hundred and sixty canoes and bateaux led by Legardeur St. Pierre's successor, Claude Pierre Pecaudy de Contrecoeur, appeared at the Forks of the Ohio to claim the valley for the King of France. The overwhelming French force of a thousand men with eighteen pieces of artillery sent Ward and his forty Virginians home "with great civility."[8] Contrecoeur proceeded to fortify the Forks with palisades and earthworks. He dubbed the new French fortification Fort Duquesne.

While still at Wills Creek Washington learned that the French had ousted Ward and the Virginians from the Forks of the Ohio. Washington knew his small force was incapable of dislodging the French without reinforcements. Therefore he resolved to march forward to the mouth of Redstone Creek, fortify that location, and await anticipated reinforcements. The expedition was a logistical nightmare. The Virginians were inadequately supplied by their quartermaster, an Alexandria merchant named Major John Carlyle. Wagons, horses, reinforcements, and Indian allies all failed to materialize. Throughout April and into May Washington and his men hacked their way through the wilderness along the overgrown trail toward Redstone Creek.

On May 27 the Virginians made contact with Washington's comrade from the previous year, Christopher Gist, and on the twenty-eighth the men arrived at a large clearing called the Great Meadows. About three-quarters of a mile in diameter, the field was a bowl carpeted with marsh grass and goldenrods. The Virginians cut forage for their horses and set up a temporary field camp. Washington, studying the location from a military perspective, declared it a "charming field for an encounter."[9] It seemed that the young Washington was easily charmed.

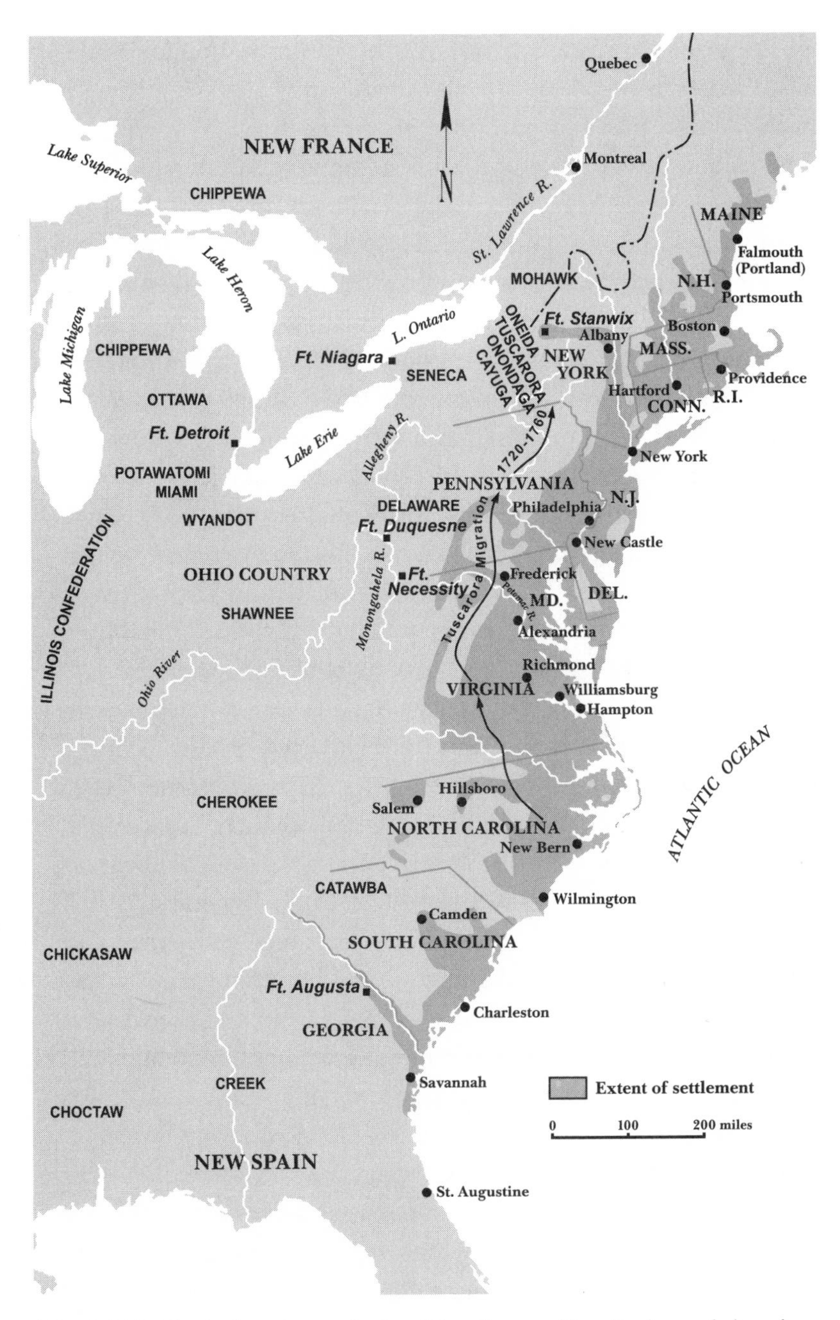

The British North American colonies, New France, New Spain, and American Indian groups in 1755.

While the men rested at the Great Meadows an Iroquois leader allied with the British named Tanacharison, or the "Half King,"[10] brought news that a force of thirty-five French soldiers sent from Fort Duquesne was encamped only seven miles away on the east side of Chestnut Ridge. The Half King was a Mingo Iroquois born about 1700 near Montreal. He held a high position within the Six Nations, but the origin of his exact position was unclear. He represented the central governing body of the Six Nations, the Onondaga Council, but he frequently disagreed with it. He appeared to have authority over some of the Mingo tribes but not all of them. He ruled not by fiat but by diplomatic maneuvering and consensus building. The British never could figure out his authority and thus accepted his appellation of the "Half King." Despite attempts by the French to turn him to their side, he was staunchly pro-British. With his brass gorget from King George, trade blanket, tricorn hat, and canoe bedecked with a Union Jack, he was no doubt a man of incongruous but significant dignity.[11]

Fired up by the intelligence, Washington and a contingent of forty men immediately left with the Half King in pursuit of the French. All through the night they groped through darkness, rain, and undergrowth along the ascent of Chestnut Ridge. At seven in the morning they spotted the French encamped in a glen beneath a great outcropping of gray stone. The damp fern-infested glen remains to this day an out-of-the way cockpit unchanged since that fateful day in 1754. Washington and his troops crept up on the French from the top of the stone ledge. No one knows who fired the first shot, but in the ensuing fifteen-minute firefight and bayonet charge the Virginians killed ten Frenchmen, including Ensign Joseph Coulon de Villiers, the Sieur (or Lord) de Jumonville, a French nobleman. Legend has it that the Half King descended upon the wounded Jumonville, split open his skull with his tomahawk, scooped out his still-warm brains, and "washed his hands" in them in a pagan ritual that horrified Washington and the Americans.[12] In any event, the Virginians captured twenty-one prisoners, but one French soldier escaped to

Tanacharison, left, the "Half King," an Iroquois leader allied with the British. Colonel George Washington, right, as painted in 1772 by Charles Wilson Peale in the uniform of a Virginia militia officer of the 1750s. This is the earliest known portrait of Washington. The gilded brass gorget worn as part of his uniform bears the Latin motto: En Dat Virginia Quartam, "Virginia Yields the Fourth." (*Washington & Lee University*)

tell the tale to his countrymen at Fort Duquesne. Only one Virginian was killed.

Washington boasted of his victory. The French were outraged. They claimed that the party was only a mission of emissaries sent to ask the Virginians to withdraw. On the one hand, such a mission was plausible, given the civil treatment of Washington and Ward by the French commanders in the two prior encounters. French outrage was exacerbated by the fact that Jumonville was the half brother of Captain Louis Coulon de Villiers, a senior French officer at Fort Duquesne. The French reported the engagement as an "assassination" contrary to the rules of war, and, as such, it eventually reverberated through the courts at Paris and London. On the other hand, intelligence and scalps may have been equally on the agenda with diplomacy, and the Half King had perceived a hostile intent.[13]

What is clear is that by the time it became evident that the engagement might become an international incident, the Virginians were nervously back-peddling. Dinwiddie reported to London that the "little skirmish was really the work of the Half King and . . . Indians. We were as auxiliaries to them."[14] Dinwiddie was supported in this assessment by John Davison, an interpreter who took part in the engagement. Davison stated that "there were but eight Indians who did most of the execution that was done. Coll. Washington and the Half King differed much in judgment, and on the Colonel's refusing to take his advice, the English and Indians separated. Afterward the Indians discovered the French in an hollow, and hid themselves, lying on their bellies behind a hill; afterwards they discovered Coll. Washington on the opposite side of the hollow in the gray of the morning, and when the English fired, which they did in great confusion, the Indians came out of their cover and closed with the French, and killed them with their tomahawks, on which the French surrendered."[15]

Matters then went from bad to worse. Spurred by the report of the sole surviving French soldier, the garrison at Fort Duquesne resolved to come after Washington and his Virginians. Coulon de Villiers burned to avenge the death of his brother. On June 28 the commander of Fort Duquesne, the same Contrecoeur who just weeks before had descended in the flotilla of canoes from the north to the Forks of the Ohio, issued orders to Coulon de Villiers to "avenge the attack against the Jumonville detachment and chase the English out of the territory claimed by France (the valley of the Ohio)."[16] A force of six hundred French and Indians under Coulon de Villiers marched from Fort Duquesne. Washington recalled two detached parties of the Virginia militia and dispatched an express rider to summon McKay and his South Carolina Independent Company.[17] The American forces fell back to the Great Meadows, where in two and a half days the Virginians constructed a crude circular palisaded fort with modest entrenchments that mounted seven swivel guns. The South Carolina regulars would not perform fatigue work without extra

Fort Necessity as re-created in the Great Meadows at the Fort Necessity National Battlefield, Pennsylvania. (*National Park Service*)

pay, as eighteenth-century military prerogative allowed. They therefore refused to help clear the road back to the fort. At the center of the fort stood a small cabin which contained the powder and the medicine chest of Dr. James Craik, the militia's surgeon and Washington's Alexandria neighbor who, forty-five years later, was to bleed Washington on his deathbed. There, at the aptly named Fort Necessity, the Virginians and their South Carolina reinforcements waited for the onslaught.

It came on the morning of July 3. The French invested the fort from the north. Washington ordered the superior South Carolina regulars into the trenches as the first line of defense, while the Virginia militia stood behind with the intention of holding their fire until they were certain it could be effective. However, the French were not about to mount a frontal assault. Rather, they moved to positions behind trees that covered a neighboring hill and peppered the fort with musket fire. This desultory firing lasted all day until, by nightfall, the Americans ran low on ammunition. Rain had begun to fall in torrents, and the men stood knee-deep in mud and water. Inside the fort, the militia had broken open the rum casks and begun to get drunk. The situation was not encouraging.

Miraculously, the French called for a parley, and the Americans agreed. Washington negotiated the terms of the capitulation by sputtering candlelight at midnight through Captain Jacob Van Bramm, a Dutch teacher of fencing and languages from Fredericksburg, Virginia, who had accompanied Washington on the Rivière aux Boeufs expedition the year before and who was the only officer in the American force who could speak French, albeit, as it turned out, not well enough. The terms were generous. The guns were to be spiked and abandoned, the force's cattle forfeited to the French. However, the surrender was to be with all honors and the officers paroled were not to take up arms again for one year. Van Bramm and another Virginia officer, Robert Stobo, were to remain with the French as hostages.[18] In the document of surrender Washington, who spoke no French, acknowledged the "assassination" of Jumonville, an admission of culpability that placed the onus for the incident on Washington and caused a diplomatic row between London and Paris.

The next morning, July 4, Washington and his force of Virginians and South Carolinians marched out of Fort Necessity with flags flying and drums beating. In their haste to depart, however, they left behind the colors of the Virginia militia, which the French seized as a spoil of war. Despite the admonitions of the French commander, the Indian allies of the French harassed the bedraggled column as it made the dispirited trek back to Wills Creek.

Washington's career was in ruins. The Half King complained bitterly of Washington's conduct: "The Colonel was a good-natured man, but had no experience; he took upon him to command the Indians as his slaves, and would have them every day upon the scout, and to attack the enemy by themselves, but would by no means take advice from the Indians. He lay in one place from one full moon to the other, without making any fortifications, except that little thing on the Meadow; whereas, had he taken advice, and built such fortifications as he [the Half King] advised him, he might easily have beat off the French. But the French in the engagement acted like cowards, and the English like fools."[19]

So spoke the Half King. The full King, George II, agreed. The young George Washington was literally first in war. However, he had not yet matured to the exalted positions of first in peace and first in the hearts of his countrymen, as stated by his Alexandria neighbor and later comrade in arms Richard Henry Lee.

With the first blood drawn by the unknown colonial militiaman Washington on the margins of empire, and with a crushing French response, it now fell upon London to take the next step.

Chapter Two

Weaving a Web

Deputy Quartermaster General Sir John St. Clair peered down his long nose at the Great Falls of the Potomac and puzzled where to place the gunpowder. The jagged rocks and torrents had not been on the maps from London, at least not as they appeared now before the self-styled Scottish baronet: for as far as the eye could see, thrust-up, craggy bedrock terrace resulting from some unfathomable geological mistake.[1] They dwarfed any brae in the Highlands in their size and violence, islands of rock the size of manors and boulders that would easily crush a tenant house, all protruding at oblique angles and cast about on a shoulder of the earth that shrugged at St. Clair's presumption. And the gorges: deep-cut roaring channels choked with yellowed ice floes and trunks of trees cast down from upriver. The river must have dropped seventy feet or more in the swirling, frothing frigid landscape. However, the orders from London were explicit: to blow up the Great Falls of the Potomac with gunpowder. The intent was to level out the river to permit the transportation of supplies by flat-bottomed boats for the expedition to the interior.

To move one large siege cannon and its attendant ammunition for one day by land required up to forty horses. To move the same cannon by water necessitated only a single small boat and no forage. Once more the reality of America confronted and blocked Sir John St. Clair.

Colonel Sir John St. Clair, Braddock's Deputy Quartermaster General, in a miniature by John Singleton Copley. (*Historical Society of Pennsylvania*)

Just as the ancient Israelites had sent spies to reconnoiter the Promised Land so had the Duke of Cumberland sent forth Sir John St. Clair in advance of the expedition. St. Clair was acting under orders of the duke, the Captain General of the British army, and held the unusual privilege of being authorized to correspond directly with the duke while he was in America, even while he served under Major General Edward Braddock's field command.[2] Like a spider, his mission was to traverse the country, up and down, sideways and forward, in order to weave a web of infrastructure–supplies, roads, and transport–to receive the troops when they arrived. And like a spider the tall, spindly St. Clair moved quickly, almost frenetically. Since leaving Flanders, pausing in London, and debarking at Hampton Roads, Virginia, on January 9, 1755, he had visited Williamsburg to confer with Lieutenant Governor Robert Dinwiddie of Virginia. From there he had raced to Wills Creek (present-day Cumberland, Maryland) to engage Lieutenant Governor Horatio Sharpe on the need to upgrade fortifications. He had then convinced Sharpe to join him in a five-day two-hundred-mile descent of the Potomac by dugout canoe from Wills Creek to Alexandria.

As the baronet surveyed the Great Falls of the Potomac some sixteen miles above Alexandria, his high balding forehead and naturally arched eyebrows gave his elongated visage a quizzical look. How would he be able to explain the failure to eliminate the Great Falls of the Potomac to General Braddock? What indeed would he tell His Excellency?

Like any good advance man, the deputy quartermaster general appreciated the context of his mission. British North America was no more than a strip of littoral covering the Eastern Seaboard between the Atlantic Ocean and the Appalachian Mountains. However, it was a well-populated fringe of the American continent, with over 1.2 million inhabitants by 1755. Pennsylvania alone boasted more than 300,000 people. And more were coming all the time. With the fertile Tidewater plantations already claimed and the Piedmont farmland rapidly filling up, younger sons and newer emigrants had no place to go but west, into the mountains. Therein lay the problem.

The western boundaries of Virginia and Pennsylvania had never been established. The state-of-the-art reference was the 1754 "Map of the Inhabited Part of Virginia" drawn by Peter Jefferson (the father of the future President) and Joshua Fry–the same Joshua Fry who originally commanded the Fort Necessity expedition. St. Clair undoubtedly carried the map in his baggage.[3] It shows the familiar coastline of the Eastern Seaboard, the tracery of the Chesapeake Bay and the Tidewater rivers–the Delaware, the Susquehanna, the Patapsco, the Potomac, the Rappahannock–and then . . . nothing.

The question of the open western boundaries had been the source of competing claims and considerable ill-will between the two large British colonies of Virginia and Pennsylvania. Settlers did not know which colony could deliver good title to the land beyond the Appalachians. Consequently, the land west of the Alleghenies,[4] including the confluence of the Allegheny and Monongahela Rivers that formed the mighty Ohio River, had been penetrated principally by English nomads–traders and trappers.

To drive home, and at once complicate, Virginia's proprietary view of the Western lands, the Old Dominion had a stalking

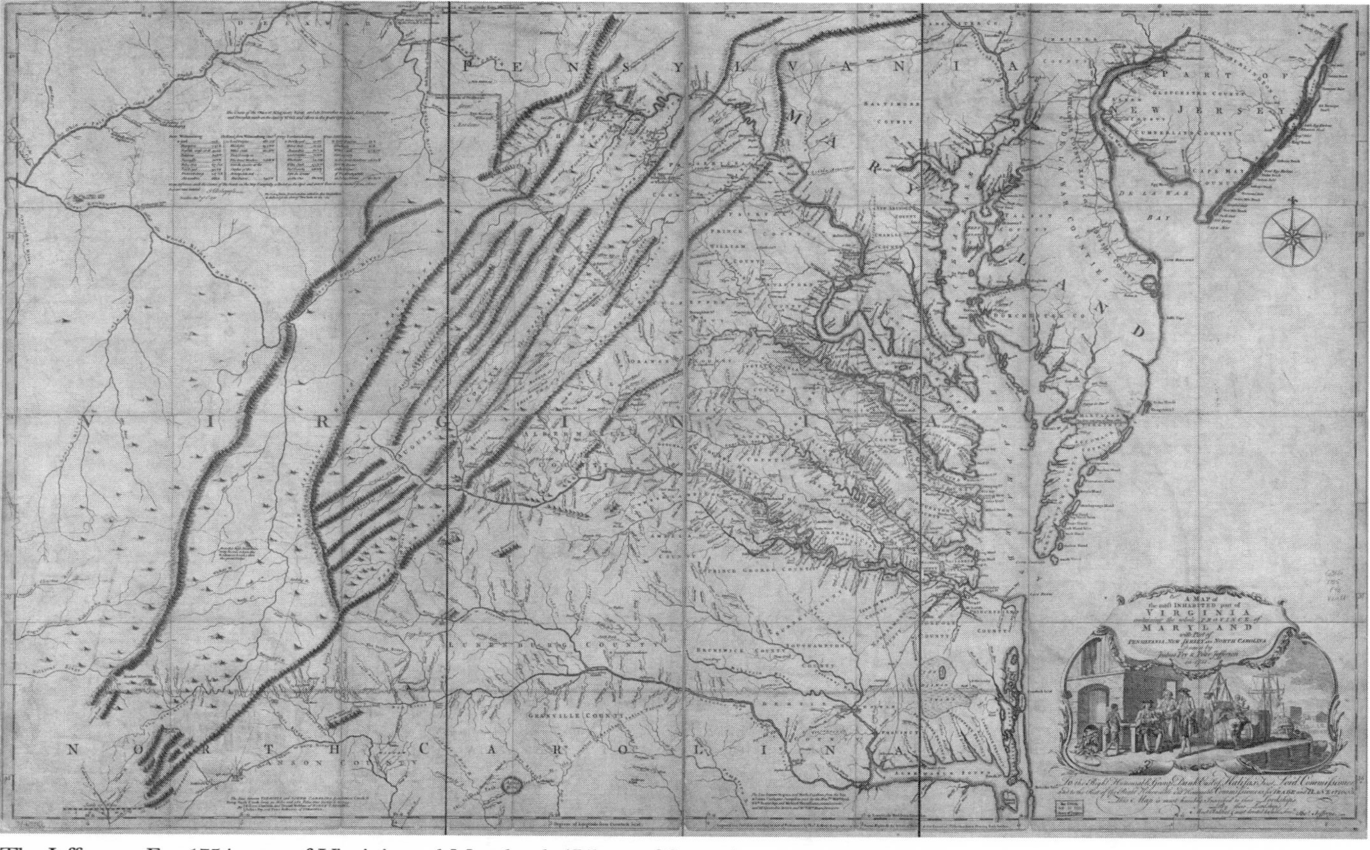

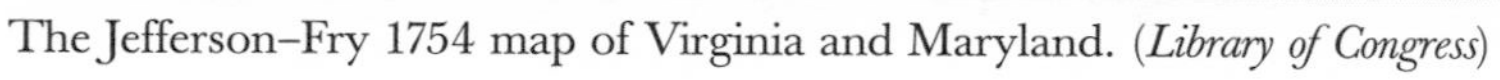

The Jefferson–Fry 1754 map of Virginia and Maryland. (*Library of Congress*)

horse in the form of the Ohio Company, a joint venture company to trade and to settle Virginians beyond the mountains. Established by an oligarchy of Virginia gentry in partnership with a London merchant, the membership of the Ohio Company read like a who's who of Virginia society and included, among others, Lieutenant Governor Robert Dinwiddie, the executors of the estate of former Governor Thomas Lee, the executors of the estate of George Washington's half-brother Lawrence Washington, Augustine Washington, Richard Lee, Thomas Cresap, John Mercer, Robert Carter, and George Mason. The Ohio Company had procured a vague royal charter in 1749 to the very same lands claimed by both Virginia and Pennsylvania.[5] Notwithstanding the niceties of the original patents and crown charters, neither Virginia nor Pennsylvania nor the Ohio Company had purchased the land from the Indian inhabitants. As a result, the aboriginal inhabitants bitterly resented and resisted the claims of both English colonies and the Ohio Company.

There was no mistaking the intentions of the Ohio Company. The instructions given by the committee of the company to their agent Christopher Gist on September 11, 1750, reveal an intent to seize land: "You are to go out as soon as possible to the Westward of the great Mountains . . . to search out and discover the Lands upon the River Ohio. . . . When you find a large Quantity of good, level Land, such as you think will suit the Company, You are to measure the Breadth of it, in three or four different places. . . . You are to fix the Beginning and Bounds in such a Manner that they may be easily found again by your Description; the nearer in the Land lies, the better, provided it be good and level, but we had rather go quite down to the Mississippi than take mean broken Land. . . . And you are to take an exact Account of all the large Bodies of good level Land . . . that the Company may the better judge where it will be most convenient for them to take their Land."[6]

As if the competing claims of Virginia, Pennsylvania, and the Ohio Company did not present a complicated picture, the French, even more threateningly, also claimed the land west of the Appalachians. Nowhere was this French claim pressed with more ardor than in the cockpit of the continent at the confluence of the Allegheny and Monongahela Rivers.

Robert Dinwiddie, Lieutenant Governor of Virginia. (*National Portrait Gallery, London*)

From their ice-bound citadel at Quebec City, the administrators of New France knew they had a problem. With a population of only 80,000 people, far-flung territories, and a bankrupt economy, New France was not a viable colony. It was populated by simple poor people, largely farmers and fishermen who had emigrated from the western French provinces of Brittany and Normandy. Many were organized under a semi-feudal seigneural system, and all were subject to the strictures of a strongly established church. The more ambitious had taken to the woods to trap and trade furs and lead a lifestyle that blended into that of the Indians. However, most fatally, New France was a two-headed beast, with one capital at Quebec and the other at Louisiana, almost three thousand miles distant.

As early as the 1720s, France had devised a visionary scheme to unite its North American colonies from New Orleans on the Gulf of Mexico to Quebec by a string of posts along the Mississippi and Ohio Rivers and the Great Lakes linked to one another by river transport and trade with the Indian inhabitants. The *coureurs de bois,* the trappers and traders who traveled the rivers, would be the lifeblood of New France. If this plan succeeded, not only would the pelt trade be assured to France, but the Indians west of the Appalachians would fall under French suzerainty. With game rapidly disappearing east of the mountains and the best furs to be found to the west, and with trading posts and forts strategically placed in their midst, it would be easy to prevent the Indians from supplying the English with the coveted hides. The Appalachians would serve as a natural barrier between New France and British North America. By creating a new power to hem in the English settlements, France could destroy a valuable staple of trade that was enriching the English colonists. At the same time, by inserting a clear and present danger, France could draw off a considerable portion of the fittest English male population into defense, thereby depleting production of tobacco, corn, wheat, and other agricultural products that were the backbone of the colonial economy.

Thus, the French "made a league with the Appalachian Mountains" to contain the English. It was unimaginable that the English would pierce this wilderness and conquer Canada. The French knew from experience that it would be a Herculean task for the English to carry troops and provisions through the virgin forests and mountains of America. They well knew that the English had to ascend the very rivers that they descended.[7]

By the end of 1753 a string of French forts studded the water routes that ran throughout New France. In the east, Fort Beauséjour held the isthmus that connected Nova Scotia to the mainland, and Fort Saint Frédéric at Crown Point staked a French claim on Lake Champlain as it thrust its finger down into New York. Further forts marched west from Montreal on the St. Lawrence to Presqu'Isle and Rivière aux Boeufs, named for the buffalo that grazed the meadows near present-day Erie, Pennsylvania, on Lake Erie. Bordering the Great Lakes, Fort Niagara was the linchpin. It controlled the passage from Lake Erie to Lake Ontario. Similarly, but of secondary importance, Fort Detroit guarded the link between Lakes Erie and Huron and Fort Michillimackinac protected the strait between Lakes Huron and Michigan. To the south, in the American interior, a strand of small wooden outposts guarded French passage along the Maumee, St. Joseph, and Wabash Rivers. Further downstream on the Mississippi, near present-day Prairie du Roche, Illinois, stood the much stronger stone Fort Chartres, a key link in the north-south chain reaching to New Orleans.[8] Sparse settlements of subsistence farmers and fur traders had sprung up around the forts and provided what passed for settlement in the interior of New France. They grew corn for the New Orleans market and sent semi-annual trade missions downriver by oared barge.[9]

As stated on the floor of the House of Commons at the time, the French held the English colonies within their range of posts as if "in the two ends of a net," which, "if tightened by degrees, would get them all into its body and drown them in the sea."[10]

The French, moreover, could count on the support of a wide swath of the Indian population, including such warlike tribes as the Ottawas, who acted as veritable shock troops of French policy, as well as the Wyandots of Lake Erie, the Caughnawaga or French Mohawks of Canada, and the host of smaller tribes of Algonquians who lived between the Ohio River and Great Lakes.[11] They also counted as allies the "praying Indians" from Canada, recent converts to Christianity. For their part, the English looked for support, albeit uncertainly, to the Six Nations consisting of the Mohawk, Oneida, Onandoga, Cayuga, Seneca, and Tuscarora.

In many instances intra-Indian warfare and the pressure of European colonization had begun to push elements of the Eastern tribes westward into the Ohio country, further complicating the mix. Thus, the region was increasingly populated by displaced tribes, including breakaway Seneca and Cayuga called Mingos. The Shawnee and Miami shared the Ohio Valley area with them at the time, as did the Lenni Lenape or Delawares, who had been subjugated by the Iroquois, forced by their conquerors to dress as women, and pushed out of Pennsylvania into Ohio.[12] There also were the Shawnee, originally from Virginia and Pennsylvania, as well as the Wyandots and Twightwees of the Miami River area of Ohio. These tribes were on the front line of the English-French encounter and subjected to constant blandishments and threats from both sides. All of these Indian groups were nominally subject to the authority of the Iroquois League, but the distances were great and the temptations to wander strong.

On June 21, 1752, French troops leading a mixed force of Ottawas and Chippewas attacked an English trading mission at Pickawillany in the Ohio country, killing or capturing the half dozen or so English merchants present. They made an example of the Indian chief who traded there with the English, who was known to the Anglo-Americans as Old Britain and, with a hint of irony, to the French as La Demoiselle. They boiled and ate him.[13]

As aggressive as it was, the policy of fortifying the French trade and communications routes and warning off the encroaching English was nonetheless successful, not least with the pivotal Indians. Before leaving his post to return to France, Governor General of Canada the Marquis de Duquesne held a covert conference with the leaders of the English-allied Six Nations at Montreal. He chided them on their willingness to surrender control of the Ohio to the English rather than the French. "Are you ignorant," he asked, "of the difference between the King of France and of the English? Look at the forts which the King has built; you will find that under the very shadow of their walls the beasts of the forest are hunted and slain; that they are in fact fixed in the places most frequented by you merely to gratify more conveniently your necessities. The English, on the contrary, no sooner occupy a post than the woods fall before their hand–the earth is subjected to cultivation–the game disappears–and your people are speedily reduced to combat with starvation."[14]

Though they played from weakness, the French sometimes spoke the truth. And increasingly they were winning the struggle to hem in the English east of the Appalachians.

If Sir John St. Clair understood the stakes in the battle for a continent, there was another factor that he did not understand, either by temperament or choice: the frontier settlers, the backwoodsmen. However, he had heard tales. They held no distinction of rank or fortune. They married young and for love. They danced three- and four-handed reels and jigs, well lubricated by home-distilled corn liquor swigged from a jug known as "Black Betty." They ate venison and bear with scalping knives that they carried in sheaths at their belts. They lived by a code of distrust of outsiders.[15] Perhaps, one might observe, they were not so far removed from their French Canadian adversaries.

Now creatures just such as these, distant countrymen of the baronet, though he'd probably never dare admit it, were huddling in jerry-built blockhouses and pouring in from the mountains in fear of Indian attack. They brought with them tales of capture, of being sent into slavery in the French lead mines at Galena on the Mississippi River, of scalpings, of babies' brains dashed out against trees, and, worse yet, of young boys carried off as slaves to serve the priests in Quebec.[16] The colonial governors, men like Dinwiddie and Sharpe, were in a state of alarm verging on panic.

What indeed would Sir John St. Clair tell His Excellency Major General Edward Braddock, who was due to arrive in Williamsburg any day? The plan to blow up the Great Falls of the Potomac and transport the heavy cannon, men, and horses by flat-bottomed boat was impossible. The expedition would have to march overland, dragging its equipment every inch of the way. His Excellency would not be pleased. What pearl of advice, what strategem, could Sir John St. Clair offer that would distract His Excellency and relieve the disappointment?

St. Clair thought in his lateral spidery way. He alone of the regular British officers had seen the country. He would advise His Excellency on disposition of the two regiments of troops, somewhat less than two thousand soldiers, he was bringing with him. There would be need to take account of the security of the army's magazines, forage for the horses, the convenience of the inhabitants, and the desirability of minimizing countermarches. A plan began to take shape in the baronet's mind which he would formulate in a letter to greet His Excellency on his arrival. He would split up the troops. The transport ships would stop at Fredericksburg, in Virginia, and the troops would disembark. Three and a half companies from the first regiment would march six days to Winchester, Virginia, and encamp. One half of a company would proceed north of Winchester for an additional two days' march to hold the crossing of the Potomac River at Conococheague (present-day Williamsport, Maryland), a narrow and shallow crossing of the river with a stretch of placid current studded by islands downstream. The other regiment would be divided: five companies at Alexandria, Virginia, with the artillery and supplies; one company at Dumfries, Virginia, two days' march from Alexandria; one company at Upper Marlboro, Maryland, one day's march; one company at Bladensburg, Maryland, one day's march; and two companies at Frederick, Maryland, six days' march.

It was a brilliant plan, so the baronet might have speculated, that would weave a web to cover all bases and which would allow him to ingratiate himself with His Excellency and even, with luck, his closest advisors, his "military family."

However, unknown to the baronet, another aide–and an Englishman at that–had already stolen the ear of the snuff-dipping, hard-drinking Coldstream commander Major General Edward Braddock. And, in the general's leather order satchel, embossed with the lion and unicorn, were spirited top secret orders that would change the map of North America.

CHAPTER THREE

His Excellency's Secret

FOR MANY YEARS MYSTERY SHROUDED the origins of Major General Edward Braddock, the man Great Britain sent to seize a continent. Vague rumors abounded that he was an Irish or Scottish adventurer of uncertain origin and repute.[1]

In fact, Edward Braddock was a creature of the old world. He was born in the winter of 1694–95 while black bunting draped Westminster Abbey to mourn the death of Queen Mary, the second to last of the Stuart monarchs. Edward Braddock was himself the third in a line of Edward Braddocks stemming from an old Staffordshire family of the minor gentry but with more recent London roots. Improbably, Braddock's paternal grandfather, Edward Braddock I, had been a candle maker in the fashionable parish of St. Martin's-in-the-Fields, London. Equally improbably, this Edward Braddock also played the harpsichord and sang sufficiently well that he obtained an appointment as a chorister in the King's Chapel Royal at Whitehall.[2] An uncle by marriage was the composer and organist at the Chapel Royal John Blow, whose

Song of Simeon and *Teach Me Thy Way, O Lord* are sung to this day in Anglican churches. The Braddocks were members of one of the outer rings of the concentric circles of courtiers who attended the royal family: connected but on the margins. However, those tangential connections proved crucial, for Edward Braddock the chorister was able to procure a commission in the Coldstream Regiment of Foot Guards for his son Edward Braddock II.

Edward Braddock II the soldier served during the later Stuart monarchies during a period of constant campaigning in the Low Countries and even more constant intrigue in the royal court. It was the age of King James, the Glorious Revolution, Godolphin, and the Churchills. However, Edward Braddock II survived both war and politics to work his way up the officer ranks and, on January 1, 1710 at the age of forty-six, received promotion to major general.

Fifteen years earlier, while he was still a mere captain, Edward Braddock II's second wife Mary bore him a son, Edward Braddock III. The boy was baptized at St. Margaret's, a parish church near Westminster Abbey. He grew up in a family of two full brothers and two full sisters, Henrietta and Frances, as well as an older half-sister from his father's first marriage. Of uncertain education, he probably learned most of life's lessons around the court and parade ground that his father inhabited. No sooner had his father assumed the office of major general than he petitioned Queen Anne for an ensign's commission in the Coldstream Foot Guards for fifteen-year-old Edward Braddock III. The Queen signed the commission on October 10, 1710.[3] The elder Braddock had probably purchased the commission for the then-current rate of £450.

Most of Ensign Edward Braddock's early military career consisted of guard duty for the monarch, first Queen Anne and later King George I, as they rotated between their palaces at St. James's, Windsor, and Hampton Court. One of his principal duties was acting as usher to the strangers who held tickets to watch the royal family dine. The transition from Braddock's familial roots in sacred music to the sacred clockwork of military life–professionalism, discipline, and punctuality–was not great, and, at least at the early stage of his career, the young Braddock excelled at his calling. On August 1, 1716, Ensign Braddock received promotion to lieutenant in a grenadier company of the Coldstream Foot Guards. It was a desirable posting.

However, all was not ceremony and spit and polish. In May 1718 Braddock fought a sword-and-pistol duel for unknown reasons with one Colonel John Waller. Both men survived.

In the meantime, his father the major general had resigned his commission and retired to fashionable Bath in 1715 with his wife and two unmarried daughters. There he bought a new Palladian house designed by the noted architect John Wood on Trim Street, just outside the old city wall. The elder Braddocks joined in the social whirl of Bath, taking the waters, playing cards in the Pump Room, dancing at balls presided over by the dandy and social arbiter Beau Nash, and trying to arrange eligible matches for their daughters.

In October 1724, the major general's wife Mary died. The major general followed her the next April. Both were interred in the magnificent Perpendicular Gothic ediface that is Bath Abbey. The elder Braddocks provided well for their daughters, with the considerable inheritance of £6,000 between the two of them. Their son Lieutenant Braddock, still on guard duty in London, received no known inheritance other than his father's red silk officer's sash, twelve feet in length and some thirty inches wide, with tassels at either end. Woven into the sash at each end was a row of standing human figures–almost Indian-like in appearance–and the date 1709, which was the year, old style, that Queen Anne issued the elder Braddock's commission as a major general. This sash was to prove significant in both the life and death of Edward Braddock III. It also is one of only three known possessions of Braddock to survive to the present day, the others being one of the brace of flintlock pistols that he carried into battle and his leopard skin saddle pad.[4]

Edward Braddock's sister Henrietta died in 1729. His surviving sister Frances or "Fanny" Braddock, as she was known, was a pretty, generous, and witty girl of nineteen when her parents died. But she was unfortunate in love and, broken hearted, gambled away her entire inheritance. No longer a belle, Fanny fell in with one Dame Lindsey, a dilapidated former opera singer, who used her as a decoy for her gaming table at one of the assembly rooms at Bath. This employment gave Fanny the reputation of a loose woman. Beau Nash, to his credit, intervened and obtained a position for her as governess to the architect John Wood's children. Her instability only increased, and in 1731 she hanged herself. According to the coroner's inquest, her first attempt was unsuccessful. She had noosed and knotted a red "girdle," or belt, and placed it over a closet door which she then closed. The belt broke. Her second attempt, with a gold and silver "girdle," was successful. When a servant found her and had her taken down, it was discovered that she had bitten her tongue clean through.[5]

No one claimed Fanny's meager personal effects.[6] Beau Nash helped dispose of them. The only recorded reaction by Edward Braddock on hearing of the suicide of his sister was his curt exclamation: "Poor Fanny! I always thought she would play till she was forced to tuck herself up." This unfeeling remark earned Braddock the disapprobation of his contemporaries and laid the foundation for a reputation, deserved or not, as a brute.

However, life went on for Braddock. Now in his late thirties and with over twenty years of service in the Coldstream Regiment of Foot Guards, he had received only one promotion.[7] His life continued to rotate around royal guard duty, with summers spent encamped at Hyde Park and winters in quarters at the Tower of London. He took his meals at coffeehouses like White's in St. James's Street and frequented the theater at Covent Garden. Braddock, who never married, reportedly was kept for a time by a Mrs. Upton, of whose money he made free use.[8] Frustrated at advancement, the first hints of compensating pleasures had entered his life.

Why Braddock failed to advance is unclear. He was evidently well suited to the military calling. He had grown up on the parade ground and instinctively knew the rhythms and mechanisms of military routine. As a professional, he was a perfectionist, impatient and bent on discipline. In the barracks room he was known as something of a Tartar whose exactitude was in inverse relation to his experience as a field commander. But the 1720s and 1730s were a time of peace, and he had no prospect of obtaining battlefield experience. Alternatively, the purchase of commissions provided a route to advancement. Braddock apparently could not afford the price of a captaincy, however. Perhaps more to the point for advancement in the eighteenth-century British army, he, like his forbearers, remained in an outer circle of concentric rings. Thus, he rubbed shoulders, and in a sense competed, with the many members of the peerage in the service. He even socialized freely with these sons of privilege, but when opportunities for advantageous postings arose there was no contest between the commoner Braddock and the baronets and lords who were the novae in the galaxy through which Braddock's own rather dim star moved.

On February 10, 1736, twenty-six years after joining the army, Braddock was finally promoted to captain.[9] His responsibilities continued to consist of guard, and occasional riot, duty in London. Even with the outbreak of the War of the Austrian Succession in 1740 and the disposition of substantial bodies of British troops to the Continent, including many elements of the Coldstream Foot Guards, Braddock remained on home duty. Other than a short trip to Ostend to assess defenses and an expedition to Flanders under the Duke of Cumberland in which Braddock saw no fighting, he remained in London. Even as the Duke of Cumberland led the regiment at the major battle of Fontenoy, Braddock stayed at home. He remained a mere captain at age forty-six, the same age his father was promoted to major general. Nonetheless, a general shifting of responsibilities among the officer corps caused by the war in Flanders at last provided the opportunity for Braddock later in 1741 to put his career into play by purchasing promotion to second major of the Coldstream Regiment of Foot Guards for the going rate of £3,600.

Nor did the uprising of Bonnie Prince Charlie the Young Pretender in 1745–46 greatly disturb the routine of Major Braddock. His unit saw no action. In the unlikely event Braddock had read Milton, he might have appreciated the poet's immortal line "They also serve who only stand and wait." It must have been a frustrating exercise for Braddock, who was not known, even then, as a patient man. He knew he could lead in battle with the best of them. Better in fact. But that was Braddock's secret, unshared by his superiors.

Perhaps the Scottish campaign spurred Braddock into action, for in 1745, he secured promotion to lieutenant colonel of his regiment at the cost of £5,000. As lieutenant colonel, Braddock became senior officer and acting brigadier of the Guards brigade. The Second Earl of Albemarle, titular governor of Virginia but in fact ambassador to France, was the Coldstream Foot Guards' equally titular colonel.

This new assignment saw Braddock back in the Low Countries under the command of Albemarle, and ultimately the Duke of Cumberland, for a second campaign in 1746–47. A surviving set of correspondence from this period (published in a limited archival edition more than one hundred years ago but never before cited in the context of Braddock scholarship) sheds light on Braddock's personality, character, and standing among his military peers in what was otherwise a rather opaque career in the years before he stepped onto the stage of history. Braddock's immediate deputy, Colonel Charles Russell, wrote the letters to his wife during the approximately fourteen-month period that Braddock and Russell were on campaign together.

First, even allowing for the occasionally tremulous tone of a subordinate officer, the letters establish that many of his peers viewed Braddock as uncouth and to be avoided. Thus, Russell wrote to his wife on September 26, 1746: "Lord Bury goes from hence in a man of war, being glad to get rid of Brad[dock] as his principal reason. . . . In short Brad[dock's] behaviour is so excessive bad that everybody shuns him and hates him. He is extremely civil to me, which I encourage, and can always keep him to his good behaviour by keeping him always at a distance, being as little with him as I possibly can, doing my duty, and as much of his, with as little trouble to him as he can wish."[10]

Remarkably, Russell peppers almost every letter with surprised and pleased asides that Braddock treats him well. For example, he adds a postscript to his September 28, 1746, letter to his wife: "Nobody so immensely civil to me as Colonel Braddock."[11] Russell observes that Braddock's reformed behavior may be attributable to rebukes he had received from his superiors: "Braddock and Lord Bury are to be together again, but the former, by having been now and then taken down, is greatly reformed, behaves well, and, to me, continues to be the most polite, civil creature imaginable."[12]

May 1747 found Braddock and Russell encamped at Flushing in Flanders with their troops while the war swirled around them but did not engage them. They quickly found lodging together and set up a mess with several other senior officers: "Colonel Braddock came on shore the day before we disembarked, and took very good quarters for himself and me in one house, and which is one of the best public houses in the town [where they enjoyed] exceeding good claret at 16d. per bottle, and fish in plenty."[13] Russell was most pleased with the ménage: "My mess is much more agreeable than I expected, and the one I most feared [Braddock] is, if anything, the best of the whole; never a disagreeable or impolite expression coming from him, not only to me but to any of the mess. His behaviour is so surprisingly well, and appears quite natural to him, I must say I can attribute it only first to his good sense, and next to the good company his whole mess happens to consist of. We have no gaming of any kind and drinking but moderately."[14] And Russell paid it the highest compliment of male society: "No private house, without women, could be pleasanter."[15]

The comfort of the arrangements was apparent: "The weather is very hot, but ours is like a country house, with green trees before it, and the sea, that is the mouth of the Scheldt, open to the south."[16] Russell several times commented on the salubrious effect of a lack of cards and heavy drinking and felt confident enough in his relationship with Braddock toward the end of their deployment to chide him for becoming ill as sickness swept the camp because "he has lived too abstemiously."[17] The implications were that the normally bibulous Braddock had been behaving out of character while on campaign and, implicitly, that drinking brought out the worst in Braddock.

Still, Russell found one fault with Braddock on which others would comment later: his perceived laziness. In describing the lodgings Braddock had arranged, he noted that Braddock had taken a ground floor room over a superior room up a flight of stairs "through indolence."[18] In other words, he did not want to be bothered with walking up the stairs. This same perceived indolence came through on another occasion when Russell described the handling of a shipment of much-needed food from England: "The whole is consigned to Colonel Braddock to distribute, receive the money for, and make return to the Treasury of the Navy, and as this gives no small trouble, you may be sure it falls upon me."[19]

Notwithstanding this gripe, Russell spent increasing time in Braddock's company, calling with him on the Prince of Orange, joining the Dutch on their yachts[20] and going for rides with him about the countryside, "which is all a perfect garden, and, as Braddock says, very like Buckinghamshire."[21] On one occasion six officers in the mess "drove to Middleburgh in one of the phaetons of this country, having three seats besides the coachbox, and a covering, but all open at the sides. We went to taste wines at a merchant's, who made us very welcome and has supplied us well."[22] On another occasion, the increasingly happy duo of

Braddock and Russell took "a chaise to see a most delightful place about two miles off, the owner of whom we met in a shady walk, when he begged leave to show us his gardens and plantations, and persuaded us to drink a bottle of excellent champagne under a shady tree." They had such a good time that they later reproached themselves for not having learned their host's name.[23]

Then there were surprise revelations about Braddock. One evening two Swiss officers dined with the mess, and, while Russell "ventured to chatter French," Braddock, "who is a refined Frenchman," intervened to help place Russell "on a footing with the Swiss officers."[24] Evenings in the mess were also musical, with "the German flute and fiddle."[25]

Moreover, Russell esteemed Braddock as a good writer. In one memorable scene that cut to the better side of Braddock, Russell sat writing to his wife on a hot August day, while Braddock, roused from his indolence, focused like a laser on the job to be done: "1747, August 5, Wednesday. Flushing,–As Braddock (who continues to behave with great politeness) is in the room with me, sending off returns, and writing a very good letter to Lord Albemarle, of which nobody is more capable, and as he continually interrupts me to hear it, which, it being for the good of the regiment, I must do with patience, I shall have to wait until he has done before I can collect my thoughts."[26]

Eventually, while Braddock and Russell remained on their idyllic island at Flushing, the British lost the pivotal siege of Bergen-op-Zoom, and Braddock and Russell and their troops were ordered to evacuate to Bois-le-Duc. Albemarle invited Braddock and Russell to dine at his headquarters soon afterward. At dinner at Albemarle's "fine chateau," which had belonged to the "old ras[cal] governor of the town,"[27] the commander questioned both officers closely with a view, as they subsequently learned, to promoting Braddock to brigadier general. However, just four days later the promotions list was published, and all the brigadiers were made major generals, but no one was promoted to brigadier general. Instead, Braddock was ordered to lead the

Georgian townhouses on present-day Arlington Street, London, of the kind Braddock may have occupied. His original house was probably destroyed by bombing in World War II. (*London Development Office*)

English retreat of wounded and ill men from the hospitals, plus some twenty pieces of heavy artillery.

The campaign was over. But Russell still wrote to his wife on November 6, as if to reassure himself: "Braddock and I continue very good friends, and I flatter myself he has a very favourable opinion of me, which is *a little uncommon*."[28]

Whoever won or lost the war, Braddock, newly returned to London, had now arrived socially as well as professionally. It was at this point that his life became noticeably Janus-faced. George Washington, who was later to play an important role in Braddock's final days, wrote approvingly of a "man bent against himself." In Washington's case, it meant a man struggling to challenge himself in order to grow, a dynamic illustrated by Washington's own life. In contrast, in Braddock's case, the "man bent against himself" meant a conflicting and dual nature. Ever the perfectionist on the parade ground–impatient, punctilious, the purveyor of harsh discipline–Braddock in his private life and associations had become dissolute, perhaps not more so than many of his contemporaries in the senior ranks but dissolute nonetheless. A short and stocky figure in his early fifties, the snuff-dipping lieutenant colonel was a regular fixture in London. He purchased a townhouse in fashionable Arlington Street, a two-block row of mansions near Jermyn Street and Piccadilly and accessible to St. James's and the gaming clubs of Mayfair. His neighbors included such luminaries as Horace Walpole, the Earl of Bath, and the Duke of Richmond.[29] He was attended by a manservant, a free black named Thomas Bishop

Major General Edward Braddock, left, engraving after a lost portrait by an unknown artist. George Anne Bellamy, right, engraving published in 1785 after a lost portrait by Francis Cotes. (*National Portrait Gallery, London*)

who had long served in the Coldstream Foot Guards and whose personal loyalty and culinary talents Braddock especially valued. The perquisites of office included a coach and four and government-purchased table plate bearing the Braddock family crest–argent a greyhound courant with a bordure engrailed sable–supported by the official lion and unicorn.[30]

Braddock became a regular at the coffeehouses and gaming rooms of Mayfair. He was a "joyous, rollicking soldier of the old fashioned type, rather popular in London as a good companion and good fellow, who loved his glass with a more than merely convivial enthusiasm."[31]

One establishment that Braddock frequented with special dedication was that of George Anne Bellamy, a leading Covent Garden actress more than thirty years his junior. Braddock had known her since her birth. Beautiful, blonde, and buxom, the fashionable Bellamy moved in the highest society of Mayfair. She was ostensibly the illegitimate daughter of Braddock's old friend, the rakish, wealthy Irish aristocrat John O'Hara, Lord Tyrawley. Known familiarly to Braddock as "Pop," Bellamy had by her twenty-first birthday rebuffed the advances of Lord Byron, given birth to an illegitimate child by the Yorkshire baronet Sir George Metham, and become a "confirmed woman of the world."[32] Despite running a constant dodge from creditors, she kept two servants and a coach and four at her home in Frith Street, Soho, and, between acting engagements, entertained at cards for profit. She hired a chef to prepare dinners for her guests and on borrowed money set up a faro bank with two diplomatic friends of Tyrawley, the Spanish minister and the Bavarian ambassador in London. She and a French nobleman always dealt the cards. The faro bank was a rousing success and became a favored spot of the demimonde, frequented by officers and diplomats.[33]

Among the habitués were Metham's close friend Major (later Lieutenant Colonel) Ralph Burton, whom Bellamy termed her "dear friend" and who was later to play a key role in Braddock's expedition, and the Honorable Charles Townshend, Third Viscount Raynham, who chided Bellamy on her "want of stability."[34] Bellamy in turn called Townshend "that weather-cock . . . with whom I was a great favourite."[35] Though in her early twenties, Bellamy delighted in passing herself off as sixteen. The fifty-plus-year-old Braddock no doubt found the conceit pleasing. The historian Francis Parkman, writing in the Victorian era, rather primly described Braddock as her "elderly adviser and friend."[36] However, given the personalities and motivations of both Braddock and Bellamy, one must wonder if there were more to the story. Although the evidence is inconclusive, Braddock and Bellamy possibly were lovers during the late 1740s. It also is possible that Braddock, not Tyrawley, was her father. The evidence is at once complex and elusive.[37]

However, Bellamy's utility to Braddock was not limited to the bedroom or daughterly affection. By the early to mid-1750s Bellamy had taken up with John Calcraft, a young former army paymaster who had set up as a commercial army agent. It was the practice of the time for army colonels to receive and disburse cash received from the army paymaster to furnish their troops. Most colonels employed a professional business agent, who would charge a commission of ten pence per pound, to assist. It was a lucrative business. Bellamy served as a procuress for Calcraft's agency, socializing and flirting with carefully targeted senior army officers, a fact she readily acknowledged in her 1785 autobiography, *An Apology for the Life of George Anne Bellamy*.[38] Calcraft promised marriage to her within six or seven years in a marriage contract into which they entered. They moved in together in a house on Brewer Street, St. James's, halfway between her former residence on Frith Street and Braddock's own house on Arlington Street, and Bellamy bore another illegitimate child, this time by Calcraft.

Meanwhile, Braddock had determined to buy a colonelcy, which he did in early 1753, resigning his commission in the Coldstream Regiment of Foot Guards in one of the frequent games of military musical chairs among acquaintances and neighbors, to become colonel of the Fourteenth Foot.[39] In a bid to help Bellamy, he promptly appointed Calcraft as his agent.

Braddock's new commission resulted in his second extended absence from London in forty-three years of service. In his new position he was appointed commandant and acting governor of the British garrison at Gibraltar. "The Rock" was a hardship post, known for its isolation, disease, and cramped quarters. Rank-and-file soldiers would desert rather than serve at Gibraltar. Once at post, Braddock consoled himself with the intimate company of Mary Yorke, the wife of one of his lieutenants. Although his tenure on the Rock lasted less than two years, Braddock's contemporaries, including Walpole, viewed it as successful. On April 2, 1754, Braddock, at age fifty-nine, was promoted to major general.

Less than six months later came the offer of supreme command of all His Majesty's troops in America. How did he obtain the commission?

The Duke of Cumberland recommended Braddock to the king for the chief command.[40] It is likely that the duke remembered him from his service in the Low Countries and in the

Jacobite Rebellion of the 1740s. Perhaps the Earl of Albemarle, his former commander in the Coldstream, also played a role in positioning him. Or even George Anne Bellamy might have helped.[41] She had friends in high places–she was now consorting with Henry Fox, the Secretary at War, and named her second illegitimate child, by Calcraft, after Fox, to the titter of London gossips. Or perhaps no other suitable senior general was available for or disposed to accept the job. By virtue of his status as a major general, Braddock was viewed as "qualified."

However, there are hints that it was not an obvious or unanimous choice. In particular, Braddock's reputation as a brutish roué appears to have given some concern. Sir Thomas Robinson, reporting to the Duke of Newcastle on a conversation with the king the day before the latter signed Braddock's commission, observed: "His Majesty has a good opinion of Mr. Braddock's sense and bravery and has heard he has become very stayed."[42]

In a similar vein, Braddock's old neighbor in Arlington Street Horace Walpole stated that "Braddock is very Iroquois in disposition. However, with all his brutality, he had lately been governor of Gibraltar, where he made himself adored, and where scarce any governor has endured before."[43]

Why an old soldier who had never in his career commanded troops in combat and who had barely served outside London consented to command the British expedition to North America is a mystery. On the one hand, Braddock was safely ensconced in what was viewed as a retirement post and by all accounts was succeeding as well there as might reasonably be expected. Certainly, he had little apparent motive to seek out the mission, and there is no surviving evidence that he did. At age sixty, he had nothing in his background to hint at the inclination to chase glory over comfort, a predilection almost certainly reinforced in his advancing age. On the other hand, one could look on his long career as a series of frustrations and the North American command as a chance late in life to break free of the confines of Gibraltar and at long last command troops in battle. He might even attain a knighthood or other preferment and at last rise to distinction in the eyes of the peerage in whose orbit he had for so long rotated.

In any event, tracked down while on holiday in Italy, Braddock sped back to London to receive his commission as "Generalissimo of All His Majesty's Troops in North America," dated September 24, 1754. Braddock now had the command of a lifetime. Hastening back to England, his first stop was, of all places, the country whose possessions he was about to attack–France.

Chapter Four

Minuet

William Anne Keppel, the Second Earl of Albemarle, was a man who served his King and country in a multitude of ways. He descended from a Dutch courtier who accompanied King William III from Holland to England, and his middle name honored his godmother Queen Anne, in whose coronation year of 1702 he was born. In addition to serving as titular colonel of the Coldstream Regiment of Foot Guards and governor of Virginia, he was the British ambassador to France. He also was a reckless spender (Horace Walpole dubbed him "the spendthrift Earl") and an accomplished spymaster.

It was through the Earl of Albemarle that Whitehall chose to recall Braddock from his holiday in Italy to assume command. Sir Thomas Robinson, the Secretary of State for the Southern Department (in charge of southern or "Catholic" Europe as well as the New World colonies), wrote to the earl describing the plans for the expedition and requesting that he contact Braddock and recall him to London.[1] This Albemarle did, but with the caution of a practiced diplomat. Reporting to Robinson on October 9,

1754, Albemarle advised that he had requested Braddock to return to England immediately on receipt of his message, "but without mentioning to him that the public service required it, but only business of the greatest consequence to himself, but thus if my letters should be inspected at the post offices, nothing uncommon might be concluded upon them."[2] By October 23 Albemarle was able to advise Robinson in London that his agents in Marseilles had reported that Braddock had landed at that southern port and departed for Paris on the seventeenth.[3] As he traveled Braddock must have burned with anticipation about what the Earl of Albemarle meant by this mysterious "business of the greatest consequence to himself." Heading straight for the ambassador in Paris, he knew he would find out.

Braddock spent from one to two weeks in Paris prior to his arrival in London on November 10. It was an interesting time to have called on his former commanding officer. Always attentive to matters at the French court, Albemarle had earlier that year reported to Robinson that a certain Mademoiselle Murphy had given birth to an illegitimate son by King Louis XV at Versailles. However, Albemarle hastened to add that the birth of the boy was unlikely to influence the position of the king's favorite, Madame Pompadour, "as the King's affection is only a *fantasie passagère*."[4] A month later he reported to Robinson that the king and Pompadour had returned from Choisy on the death of her only child and that she was "grief-stricken at the loss of her daughter," prompting a postponement of a performance of the *Mousquetaires*.[5] Other morsels from the rumor mill at Versailles that caught the earl's attention at that time included the activities of various Jacobite exiles and the seriousness of the illness of the British Pretender, who was harbored at the French court.[6]

However, all was not palace intrigue for the British ambassador. England and France were slipping inexorably toward war with each other, and both Albemarle and his host government were painfully aware of this fact. Earlier in the year Robinson had forwarded to Albemarle reports from the directors of the East

India Company about the successes of Indian troops supported by the British against Indians allied with the French. On instruction from London, Albemarle discussed the reports with the French Foreign Minister Rouille, "who desires peace and blames [the French East India Company official in India] Dupleix, who is being recalled."[7] On the darker side, Albemarle corresponded extensively with Robinson throughout this period on payment of arrears in a "Royal Pension" granted to the Neapolitan ambassador to France, the Abbé Marquis di Caracciolo, in return for "information." (Robinson ordered Albemarle to pay the Abbé and arranged reimbursement for Albemarle through a bill of "Extra Extraordinaries.") The Abbé, well oiled in the British service, was then dispatched to Madrid to try to ensure the neutrality of the Spanish court in the coming conflict.[8]

Thus Braddock arrived at the heart of the country whose interests he was about to attack. Albemarle's extant papers from late October to early November 1754 are incomplete. Nonetheless, it is inconceivable that he did not meet with Braddock and perhaps even present him at the French court. Albemarle would have explained to Braddock exactly what "public service" had demanded his recall to London. News of the Jumonville massacre and Washington's defeat at Fort Necessity had reached London informally by August, with Lieutenant Governor Dinwiddie's official report following by September 5. The news had reached Paris, probably via London, by the time of Braddock's arrival in the French capital.[9] In his dispatches Dinwiddie urged London to send regular British troops to America to oust the French from the Ohio, a view readily endorsed by Albemarle.[10] Informed by Robinson of developments and his own appreciation of the geopolitical game being played by England and France, Albemarle would have painted the broad picture of what was at stake.

He may have explained how a succession of governors of New France pursued French strategy with aggression. As early as 1731, France erected Fort Saint Frédéric at Crown Point on Lake

Champlain within the territory of the Six Nations and had even earlier seized Niagara. In 1745 the Marquis de la Galissonière was appointed governor general of Canada and lost no time in dispatching Bienville de Céléron, with three hundred men, on an expedition down the Allegheny and Ohio Rivers. Céléron deposited lead plates along the way, claiming the country for King Louis and warning off any English they encountered. In 1750 de la Galissonière's successor, the Marquis de la Jonquière, upped the ante with a further military expedition to the Ohio which seized the property of English traders and sent the traders themselves prisoners to France. However, de la Jonquière lasted a mere two years. His successor, the Marquis de Duquesne de Menneville, left not only his name but a legacy in the New World: the armed occupation of the Ohio by French troops.

William Anne Keppel, Second Earl of Albemarle, titular governor of Virginia and British Ambassador to France. Engraving by John Fabre, Jr. published in 1751 after a 1749 mezzotint by J. Forman. (*National Portrait Gallery, London*)

Moreover, French pressure in North America was not occurring in a vacuum. Rather, it was an extension of European politics, part of a broader picture. Following the Treaty of Aix-la-Chapelle, which ended the War of the Austrian Succession in 1748, England had sought to surround France through a continental "system" of aid to the Netherlands and strategic German states such as Prussia, friendly overtures to Spain and Denmark, and an alliance with Austria. Thus hemmed in diplomatically, France had limited room for military maneuver on the continent. Because of the relative success of this British policy in Europe, France had sought to tighten the screws on England in North America, especially in the disputed Ohio country. Britain's reaction was to seek to mount a quick, decisive action in North America to restore the preexisting balance in the Ohio basin and other "English" areas that had suffered French encroachments without precipitating a general war between England and France.[11] Caught off guard in North America and diplomatically hobbled in Europe, France would be brought to heel through a negotiated solution to the North American problem.[12] The gist of Whitehall's thinking was to reestablish the status quo ante by limited military action and then negotiate.

Moreover, it was a plan of some subtlety. It was to proceed in three stages. The first stage consisted of Braddock's clearing of the French from the Ohio. The second stage would be his continuing on to remove them from Crown Point on Lake Champlain, which they had held for over twenty years but which was well within British North America. The third and final stage would be removal of the French from Fort Beauséjour, which they had recently erected at the juncture of Nova Scotia and the Canadian mainland. (France had ceded Nova Scotia to Britain in 1713, and the latter viewed that province, both legally and practically, as English, even thought it continued to be inhabited largely by French-speaking peoples.) Between each stage there would be time to negotiate with the French so that further military action might not be necessary. If in the interim the French were to learn of the movement of troops to America, they were to be told that this was no different from what France itself had done for many years and was being done solely for defensive purposes.[13]

As Braddock was later to learn, planning in London had assumed a life of its own so as to make this official version of the Whitehall plan only a partial truth.

Moreover, the French had wind of British planning almost from the start. The French ambassador in London, the Duke of Mirepoix, had quickly picked up on the intrigue at Whitehall and by early October reported it to his king, Louis XV. There was some talk of convening a conference to sort out Anglo-French differences. When the French foreign minister demanded an explanation of British intentions from Albemarle, he got the official explanation of defensive measures, even though the French were well aware that it was the first time that London had ever dispatched regular troops to North America. What is more, the centralized and sophisticated French state almost certainly would have known that General Braddock had suddenly appeared in Paris en route to England under secret orders and that he was a guest in their country at that very moment. Indeed, some months later, the French foreign minister confirmed to the British that he was "well aware of the extent of British forces going to North America," as well as of the command of Braddock and the size and composition of the forces.[14] Apparently the British had been deluding themselves that they were proceeding under a veil of secrecy. As events gathered momentum, there was little the French could do to stop Braddock from proceeding to England to assume command. Despite colonial hostilities and strained relations, France and England were not yet at war in the autumn of 1754.

The eventual French response to the British plans took some months to formulate. When it came, it was both military and diplomatic. Militarily, France was incapable of immediately sending reinforcements to Canada to check Braddock because the frozen St. Lawrence River prevented ships from reaching Quebec in the winter. Nonetheless, the French sought to shore up their position in America by dispatching a fleet with six thousand troops from Brest under the Baron Dieskau, scheduled to arrive as soon as the St. Lawrence had thawed sufficiently to receive them the following spring. This massive reinforcement, readily acknowledged by the French foreign minister when challenged by the British,[15] was out of proportion to the two depleted regiments, well less than two thousand men, sent by England to America with Braddock. As noted by one British secret agent in France, "in all these armaments there appeared a plain design to make settlements and to build forts; besides that, it was given out they resolved to augment the fortifications at Louisburg, and to build more forts on the Ohio."[16] Perhaps trying to gain leverage from the size of their expedition, French diplomats opened talks with the British on establishing a neutral zone in the Ohio area. The talks came to naught.

Also on the diplomatic front, the French opened secret negotiations to try to wean Austria away from its alliance with Britain in favor of a new Franco-Russian-Austrian alignment aimed at Britain's ally Prussia. These negotiations bore more fruit and helped lead to a wider European war–the Seven Years' War, of which the North American theater was the French and Indian War–when Prussia invaded Saxony in August 1756 and formal war was declared between Britain and France.

But all of this was in the future and far beyond the comprehension of either Braddock or Albemarle as the two friends met in Paris in October 1754. Sometime in the first week of November, Braddock took his leave of his patron. In less than two months, on December 22, 1754, the Earl of Albemarle died suddenly. He was only fifty-two. December 22 was the very same day that Braddock launched his expedition by setting sail from England to America.

King George specifically ordered that Albemarle's body, together with certain sealed and no doubt compromising letters, go by river to Rouen for shipment to England.[17] However, winter cold had frozen the Seine. Albemarle's efficient but apologetic chargé d'affaires De Cosne spirited the body from Paris, away from creditors trying to stop its removal because of the ambassador's debts, and arranged for the coffin to endure a bumpy carriage ride to the coast. There it was loaded onto a British ship for the journey to the Tower of London.[18] The name of the ship was *Peace and Plenty.*

Chapter Five

Sweet William's Revenge

FIRST BLOOD HAD BEEN DRAWN at Jumonville by an obscure and ambitious colonial militia officer, and the challenge to the crown assumed compelling urgency: the French must be ousted from the Forks of the Ohio. London began to stir.

The mounting of a war effort required simultaneous moves on many fronts. First was the question of overall planning of the campaign. Then the appointment of the commander. Next the assembly of the troops, materiel and logistics necessary to project the force over such a great distance. And not least, the personal elements–the secret instructions to the commander and the fine tuning of his "military family" or senior commanders and aides whose cooperation would be essential to the success of the enterprise. Each element influenced the others.

The first–and in many ways foremost–member of Braddock's military family was not someone he had chosen. Rather, it was the individual, twenty-six years his junior, who recommended him as commander, Prince William Augustus, the Duke of Cumberland.

The Duke of Cumberland was the third son of King George II. From an early age he had exhibited a fascination with things military. He grew up a parade-ground youth, well steeped in the Prussian school of military science. By his early twenties, when he first rode off to fight in the War of the Austrian Succession, he was a victim of his Hanoverian genes, a pop-eyed young man with a bullet head and the torso of a whale. After the Battle of Dettingen, which was the last time a king of England led troops in battle, the monarch handed over command to his son Cumberland. He became commander of the allied forces in the Low Countries in 1745 and directed the costly, unsuccessful, but gloriously disciplined performance of the British troops on the field of Fontenoy on May 11, 1745.

Later in 1745 Cumberland was recalled to England to oppose the invasion by the Young Pretender. Braddock first served in the field under Cumberland during the maneuvers to check the Scots invasion, although the two men undoubtedly knew each other earlier from Braddock's service in and about the palace over the years. On April 16, 1746, Cumberland defeated the Young Pretender at Culloden near Inverness. More than one thousand Scots died. Following the battle his subcommanders asked for orders. He wrote "No quarter" on the back of a playing card, the nine of diamonds. The British troops slaughtered their prisoners and remained in Scotland for months tracking down and executing Jacobites.

For his actions, the Duke of Cumberland gained the epithet in Scotland of the "Butcher of Culloden." In contrast, the admiring English named a flower after him to celebrate his success at Culloden. It was, and is, called the sweet william.[1]

At the time of his return to England in 1745 to oppose the Young Pretender, the king had elevated Cumberland to Captain General of the British army. Cumberland added the reputation of a competent administrator to that of a seasoned, combat-hardened, if not always successful, soldier. He advocated discipline in the army, from top to bottom. His control over his officers was such that he created a new professional officer corps. He opposed, but never successfully eradicated, the practice of purchase of commissions. He did, however, rein in elderly, semi-autonomous colonels with which the army was riddled at the top. He standardized uniforms and equipment and established a universal drill. He advocated light infantry and light horse and even foresaw the utility of rifles in the age of muskets. He proposed a corps of "jaegers," Hanoverian marksmen, both mounted and on foot, to supplement the regular troops. Other Captains General of the British army, such as Marlborough and Wellington, may have gained more glory on the battlefield, but Cumberland's twelve-year incumbency as Captain General was notable for its reforms and emphasis on professionalism.

William Augustus, Duke of Cumberland, the third son of King George II. Portrait by Sir Joshua Reynolds, c. 1758. (*National Portrait Gallery, London*)

Despite his eminence, Cumberland was not vested with responsibility for the North American expedition from the start. Politicians–the Secretary of State for the Southern Department, assisted by the Board of Trade–administered the affairs of the North American colonies. The Secretary of State was Sir Thomas Robinson, who reported to the Prime Minister–at this point the Duke of Newcastle, a political hack of abysmally limited capacities and widespread ignorance of even the geography of the continent that was his charge.[2]

Newcastle also was a political enemy of Cumberland, whom he regarded with some justification as a dangerous militarist. Newcastle therefore looked elsewhere for initial advice on how to meet the French threat in North America. First, he sought the advice of John Hanbury, the Quaker London merchant who was a partner in the Ohio Company. Hanbury not surprisingly advocated operations centered on Virginia. Next, Newcastle spoke with Lieutenant Horatio Gates, a godson of Horace Walpole. Gates, who in later life became an American general and the victor over the British at Saratoga, had served in Nova Scotia under Colonel Edward Cornwallis. Gates demurred on the grounds that his service in Nova Scotia did not qualify him to opine on the middle colonies. The next stop for Newcastle was Arthur Dobbs, who was about to leave England to serve as governor of North Carolina. Dobbs was of little use in providing advice but soon departed with money and promises of arms for Lieutenant Governor Dinwiddie in Virginia, as well as a commission for Lieutenant Governor Horatio Sharpe of Maryland, who was already a commissioned officer in the British army, to serve as lieutenant colonel of foot and commander of all troops raised in the colonies.

Finally, as Newcastle groped for the right military counter to the French moves in North America, he sought the advice of the Captain General. Once consulted, Cumberland rapidly took over the planning of the expedition, leaving Newcastle as little more than a fretting bystander. Deprived of political oversight, such as it was in the mid-eighteenth-century parliamentary system, the expedition became the province of a small clique of like-minded war planners, spearheaded by Cumberland and which included the king. They worked in semi-secrecy, excluded information that did not come from their own sources, and generally acted as if they alone were the repository of competence and knowledge. Realities on the ground were to prove them wrong time and again.

The immediate question was who would fight. Dinwiddie had asked for regular troops. Cumberland favored raising only colonial troops to fight the French and dispatching regular army noncommissioned officers to train them. This was a logical plan, and history would have taken a very different turn if Cumberland's

Colonel Sir Peter Halkett, left, commander of the 44th Regiment of Foot. Lieutenant Colonel, later Major General, Thomas Gage, right, miniature by Jeremiah Meyer 1775 (*National Portrait Gallery, London*)

advice had been followed. However, the king objected, and, after some discussion of sending Scots regiments, a plan was finally devised to send two regiments of British regulars and raise two more of American volunteers.

The plan was significant, even audacious. It would be the first time England had sent troops in force to the American colonies. Moreover, it would be the largest professional army ever assembled in North America by far up to that time both in absolute numbers and in relative terms–one soldier for every six hundred Americans. (A comparable ratio in terms of today's population would entail a force in excess of five hundred thousand men.) The impact of such a force's presence on a small but vibrant colonial society was appreciated in advance by neither the senders nor the recipients.

The two designated regiments were the 44th and 48th of Foot, commanded by Colonel Sir Peter Halkett, Baronet, and Colonel Thomas Dunbar, respectively. The second in command of the 44th was a then relatively obscure lieutenant colonel named Thomas Gage, former aide-de-camp to Braddock's patron, the

Earl of Albemarle, and later of Revolutionary War fame, while that of the 48th was Lieutenant Colonel Ralph Burton, whose wife was a close friend of George Anne Bellamy and who moved in the same Mayfair circles as Braddock.

Sir Peter Halkett's 44th Regiment traced its short history to the recent War of the Austrian Succession. It was neither old nor distinguished. Known originally as the 1st Battalion the Essex Regiment, it was one of seven new regiments raised in 1740. The royal warrant of the regiment called for it to recruit in the southern counties of England. However, the names of the officers commissioned to the regiment were predominantly of northern English and Borders origin. At its formation it ranked as the 55th and took the name of its first commander, Colonel James Long. As such, it participated in Lieutenant General Sir John ("Johnny") Cope's defeat at Prestonpans in 1745 during the Jacobite rebellion. Halkett, then its lieutenant colonel, fought bravely but was captured and held prisoner. Eventually Halkett and his officers were paroled on the condition that they not take arms against the Young Pretender for eighteen months. However, four months later the Duke of Cumberland summoned Halkett and four other officers to rejoin their regiments. They refused to do so on the grounds that "his Royal Highness was master of their commissions, but not of their honor." Despite the duke's displeasure, the government later approved their position. The regiment also later fought in Flanders under the Duke of Cumberland. It was known as "one of the most worthless regiments" in the British army.[3]

Halkett was a Scotsman of some import whose ancestral name was not Halkett. His grandfather, Sir Peter Wedderburn, Lord Gosford, had been a prominent lawyer. His father, also Sir Peter Wedderburn, had married Janet, the daughter of Sir Charles Halkett of Pitfirrane. Wedderburn changed his name to Halkett on his wife's succession to her father's estate. Sir Peter Halkett was born in 1703 and would have been about fifty-two upon his embarkation for America.[4] He had served at least two terms as a member of Parliament, first for Dunfermline and then for

Inverkeithing in the 1730s. But his first love was soldiering. He had devoted most of his career to commanding in various Scots regiments before assuming the lieutenant colonelcy of the 44th. Halkett's wife was Lady Aemelia Stewart, daughter of the seventh Earl of Moray. His eldest son, Francis Halkett, served with him as a captain and brigade major in the 44th.[5] Another son, James, was a lieutenant in the regiment. Peter Halkett was a thin, lean man with an aristocratic nose. He also was a soldier's soldier, a centurion.

Like the 44th, the 48th Regiment also traced its origins to the War of the Austrian Succession. It too had fought in the Jacobite rebellion, including at Culloden under the Duke of Cumberland. Like the 44th, its members were seasoned veterans and somewhat older than the average in the British army.[6] Its commander Colonel Thomas Dunbar, who was to become Braddock's second in command, was known as an amiable career officer of Falstaffian proportions. One contemporary described him thus: "He bears the Character of a hearty, Jolly old gentleman."[7] The reputation of the 48th approximated that of the 44th.

In September 1754 both regiments were stationed between Limerick and Dublin and registered on the Irish establishment. This arrangement allowed their cost to be borne by Ireland, which had no vote in Parliament. The original intent was to send each regiment of five hundred men to America under Braddock and augment it by recruitment in the colonies to a complement of seven hundred. Of the seven hundred names on the roll of each regiment, six would have been fictitious names called "warrant men." Their pay went for allowances for widows of officers, recruiting, clothing lost by deserters, and other sundries. Also several noneffectives called "contingent men" were maintained to keep arms in repair and to cover miscellaneous expenses.[8]

The Crown was also to raise two other regiments of one thousand each in the colonies, to be commanded under Braddock by the Americans Sir William Pepperell of Maine and William Shirley, governor of Massachusetts. In addition to this mixed force of 3,400 British and colonials, Braddock was to take command of the King's Independent Companies in America, plus as many Indians as could be recruited. A British fleet was to hover offshore to intercept any French reinforcements. Together with mobilizations of militia, the planners envisaged a force of approximately twelve to fifteen thousand–an incredible ratio of one soldier to every eighty Americans, the equivalent in today's terms of an army of more than three million.

Of course, reality fell short of intentions. The 44th and 48th were both under strength and could not even meet their projected British complements. Accordingly, drafts went out for men to a variety of regiments, including the 20th Foot at Exeter, the 11th at Salisbury, the 10th and 28th at Limerick, and the 26th and Royals at Galway. The call was not popular, as the prospect was for three years' service in America, and word had already spread of the Indians' depredations. The colonels of these regiments were not anxious to lose their good men and so parted only with their dregs. Halkett picked up a few volunteers in London, and sergeants were sent out to drum up recruits in the countryside. The major qualifications for service were that a recruit be a subject of the king and Protestant. The end result was a force of drunks, felons, and deadbeats that was remarkable even by the low standards of mid-eighteenth-century English soldiery.[9]

On September 26, two days after the signing of Braddock's commission, Cumberland met in London with Newcastle and a handful of others to finalize plans for the expedition. Lord Halifax, the head of the Board of Trade, did not favor the strategy of attacking from Virginia. He preferred an attack on Niagara and Crown Point to cut French communications prior to dealing with the French incursions on the Ohio. He was concerned that the convoying of cannon and equipment through the wilderness was risky. He was overruled.

There were contemporary allegations of corruption in relation to the decision to use the Virginia route and to attack the Forks of the Ohio first. A writer in the *Gentleman's Magazine*, in a possible veiled reference to the role of Hanbury of the Ohio Company, stated that the expedition was "sent to Virginia instead of Pennsylvania to their insuperable disadvantage, merely to answer the lucrative views of a friend of the ministry, to whose share the remittances would then fall at the rate of 2-1/2 *per cent* profit."[10] Such allegations have never been proven, and it is equally possible that the decision to attack the Forks first via Virginia was the natural consequence of all eyes having been turned to the activities of the Ohio Company, Washington's disastrous campaign the prior year, and the erection of Fort Cumberland as the most westward projection of British power.[11]

In any event, by early October, the military machine was in high gear under Cumberland's personal and industrious direction. Armorers at the Tower worked fulltime to assemble ammunition, gun carriages, and Brown Bess muskets. Drums, marquees, and tents were laded aboard advance transports and ordered to Virginia. The inventory of armaments for the expedition included, among other items, the heavy coach to which Braddock was entitled as a Major General and three suits of armor. On October 7 the names of all the officers for the two American regiments were published, and they were ordered to prepare for embarkation.[12] Cumberland ordered Colonel Sir John St. Clair, an officer in O'Farrel's 22nd Foot, to leave immediately to reconnoiter the land.

With the arrival of Braddock in London on November 10 from his interrupted Italian vacation, Cumberland's influence on the expedition became even more pronounced–and more closeted. For three weeks, while cold autumn rains drenched London and fallen yellow leaves accumulated on Braddock's old campground at Hyde Park, the duke huddled with his staff and Braddock at the Horse Guards in Whitehall to plan the expedition. Cumberland held a strong view about the need to check the French in America. Unlike Newcastle, he had bothered to inform himself, at least to a degree, on that faraway land. Probably from

Washington's dispatches, he knew the Ohio was rich in iron, coal, and water transport and would be a far greater plum for France than all of Flanders.[13] He said he himself would oppose the French in America rather than lose one foot of that territory.

Cumberland gave Braddock copies of Dinwiddie's correspondence with London, which contained reports of Washington's exploits and first introduced the major general to the obscure colonial officer. More significantly, he presented Braddock with specific secret instructions. Once in the duke's hands, the plan had evolved considerably beyond the staged approach of military action and negotiations originally proposed by Newcastle. Braddock's orders were to proceed against the French at the Forks of the Ohio and, once that was accomplished, immediately to seize the key French fort at Niagara. Braddock may have sensibly argued for reducing Niagara first and then proceeding downriver to the Forks of the Ohio.[14] However, he, like Lord Halifax, did not prevail.

Simultaneous expeditions under Braddock's command were to take the French forts at Crown Point in New York and Beauséjour in Nova Scotia. The operation at Beauséjour had assumed particular dimensions. Halifax and the royal governor of Massachusetts William Shirley had devised a plan to remove all the French-speaking populace of Nova Scotia and ship them to Louisiana on the pretext that they refused to swear loyalty to the English king.

The expedition thus moved from a three-stage, graduated, and politically nuanced expedition to an essentially simultaneous peacetime assault on four objectives (Forts Duquesne, Niagara, Crown Point, and Beauséjour)[15] that would result in an attack on a position held by the French for over seventy years–Niagara–and the forced depopulation of an entire province, an early run at ethnic cleansing. Negotiations with the French were no longer in the picture.

Although the geographic sweep of the command was great, there was no mistaking the top priority: the ousting of the French from the Forks of the Ohio. Moreover, Cumberland gave

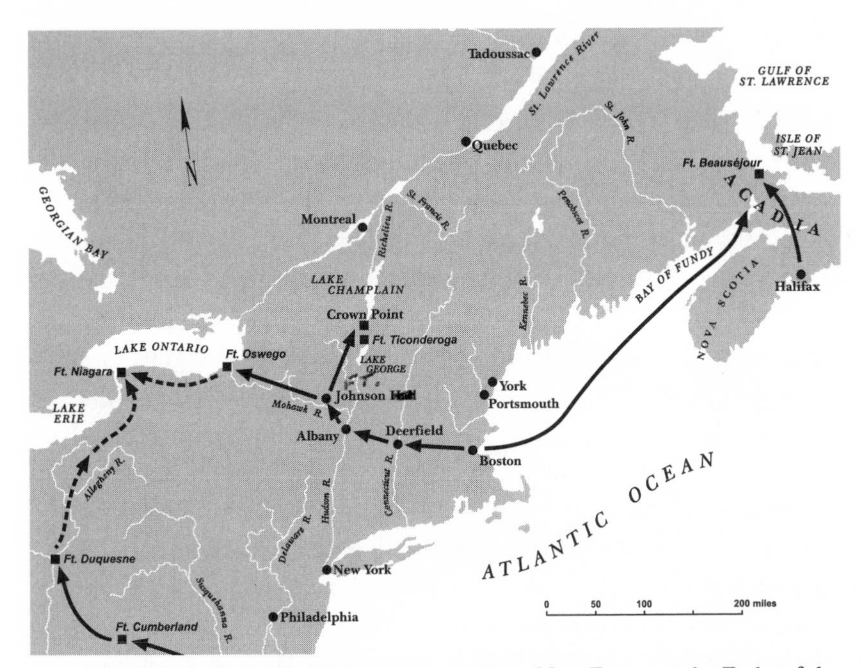

The British plan for a simultaneous assault on New France at the Forks of the Ohio (Fort Duquesne), Fort Niagara, Fort St. Frédéric at Crown Point, and Fort Beauséjour.

Braddock essentially vice regal authority as "Generalissimo of All His Majesty's Troops in America," with the power to command both British regulars and American militia and to commission and decommission officers under his charge. The secret orders provided that if unable to command personally, Braddock could appoint subordinate commanders directly without the permission of the king. It was an extraordinary grant of authority.

The duke reminded Braddock of the necessity of discipline to maintaining order of the troops on the expedition and specifically warned of the need to be wary of surprise and panic caused by the Indians. Cumberland, after all, had dealt successfully with irregulars before in Scotland.

Braddock was to rely on the Americans as loyal subjects of His Majesty. Their undisciplined militias may have been next to worthless, but they knew the terrain. And the colonists would help with supplies and financing.

The duke referred to the government's maps of North America, which showed only fifteen miles from the British outpost at Wills Creek to Fort Duquesne. Cumberland was confident of the distance, the route, and the help to be expected of the American colonists and loyal Indians. He informed Braddock that his personal agent Deputy Quartermaster General Sir John St. Clair was already on his way to America to secure wagons and supplies and to scout the route, which should be by water all the way up to Wills Creek. However, Cumberland may have warned, Braddock had not a moment to lose, as the French were about to reinforce their forts with the early spring thaw. Braddock undoubtedly resolved to see St. Clair first thing when he arrived to get his report.

Finally, the duke may have hinted that there could be a preferment for Braddock if the expedition were successful. It was rumored at the time that they discussed the governorship of New York.

Cumberland thus set both the order and direction of the campaign based on assumptions in which he had a headstrong confidence. Ultimately, he chose Braddock as commander and sent him forth with detailed instructions and implicit promises. Moreover, by selecting the 44th and 48th Regiments, he had placed the senior field commanders Halkett and Dunbar as charter members of Braddock's command. A charter member of Braddock's "military family"–his personal aides–also appears to have been Cumberland's choice: Lieutenant Robert Orme, aide-de-camp to Braddock.

Orme, appointed to this position on November 2, before Braddock even arrived in London on November 10, was a twenty-nine-year-old officer in the Coldstream Foot Guards. He had entered the army as an ensign in the 35th Foot and on September 16, 1745, exchanged into the Coldstream Regiment of Foot Guards, in which he rose to lieutenant on April 24, 1751. On his appointment he assumed the title of captain, although it is unclear whether he ever actually attained that rank. Orme's background and what commended him to Cumberland for so intimate a position to Braddock remain shrouded in mystery. He moved in the same London social circle as Walpole and, for that matter, Braddock. Braddock and Orme were almost certainly at least acquainted, if not more. However, the date of his appointment at a time when Braddock was en route from Italy to London suggests that Cumberland, not Braddock, appointed him. In any event, in his penchant for contentiousness and plotting, Orme was to prove a problematic choice.

Captain Robert Orme, Braddock's principal aide-de-camp, painted by Sir Joshua Reynolds in 1756, depicting Orme on the Braddock Expedition. (*National Portrait Gallery, London*)

The second member of Braddock's military family was Captain Roger Morris, aide-de-camp. It is not known who appointed him or what commended him for the position, other than apparent social rank. The third and eventually final member of Braddock's military family was personally unknown to either Cumberland or Braddock. In fact he was not even a resident of the British Isles. His name was George Washington.

On his last night in London, November 29, 1754, Braddock, accompanied by Lieutenant Colonel Ralph Burton and Captain Robert Orme, dined with George Anne Bellamy at her house in Brewer Street. She was pregnant, probably by Calcraft, possibly by Fox (her daughter Caroline Elizabeth was born some months later). It was a heavy, somber evening, with Braddock full of foreboding. Before he said good-bye Braddock told her he would "never see her again" and that he was "going with a handful of men to conquer whole nations." He showed her a map of North America and pointed out where his troops would have to cut through the wilderness to reach the French forts. "Dear Pop," he confessed, "we are sent like lambs to the altar."[16]

As he departed, Braddock pressed a folded document into her hands, his last personal gesture to Bellamy. After he left she opened the paper. Her hands cradled Braddock's last will and testament.[17] She read. The will divided Braddock's estate between Mary Yorke at Gibraltar and John Calcraft, George Anne Bellamy's supposed husband.[18] The disposition was an attempt to pass the money to her and not have it attached by her creditors.

When Bellamy's front door slammed shut behind Braddock and his aides, he left with the secret of their relationship. Both Braddock and Bellamy carried that particular secret to their graves.

The next day in order to supervise and speed up the departure of the troops, Braddock hurried to Cork aboard the *Centurion*,[19] commanded by Commodore Augustus Keppel, the second son of Braddock's patron, the Earl of Albemarle, whom he had just visited in France.[20] However, bad weather had delayed the arrival of the necessary transport ships in Ireland. Like King Canute, Braddock, despite his willfulness, could not command the forces of nature. Therefore, Braddock returned to England with his staff and a few of the troops in the *Centurion*. Just before Christmas, on December 22, the dirty weather broke, and Braddock was able to slip away for Virginia aboard the *Norwich*, escorted by Keppel's flagship *Centurion*. Accompanying Braddock were Orme, his secretary William Shirley, Jr. (the son of the governor of Massachusetts), Braddock's body servant and chef Thomas Bishop, and Francis Delboux, sous-chef. The troop transports were to follow. Altogether, the expedition consisted of thirteen transports and three ordnance ships, all led by the *Centurion* and three warships under the command of Keppel.[21]

Commodore Augustus Keppel, portrait by Sir Joshua Reynolds, c. 1765. (*National Portrait Gallery, London*)

The main body of the expedition boarded ship on January 8, 1755, at Cove, near Cork, and after five days of loading found sufficiently favorable winds to set sail on January 13. Their departure was some three weeks after that of Braddock and his staff. The fifty-six-day voyage to America, covering 5,254 miles as measured by one ship's log, was rough. Their progress ranged in daily miles from a respectable 178 (on Sunday, February 9) down to zero (on Wednesday, March 5). The ships became separated in the stormy North Atlantic. The lot of the rain-sodden, shivering, and seasick soldiers cramped between decks was not enviable. They got little solace from the sailors. As an old saw went: "A messmate before a shipmate, a shipmate before a stranger, a stranger before a dog, a dog before a soldier." However, only one person was lost overboard on the entire trip, so the officers would have been satisfied.

During the long voyage, Braddock, Orme, Morris, and perhaps Burton would have dined daily together and would have had ample time to form mutual friendships and plot their strategy. The four officers knew each other from London and the social circle in which they moved. They had much in common and tended to see the world through the same or similar optics. Their forced time together during the long passage of the stormy North Atlantic was to create a bonding between these officers that was to have a profound effect on the expedition. In contrast, the senior field commanders, Halkett and presumably Dunbar, were on other transports with their troops. St. Clair was already en route to America, if not actually there. They thus did not break bread with their commander and the other senior English officers for almost three crucial months during which personal relationships and objectives were set. In any event, these three Scots–Halkett, Dunbar, and St. Clair–would have been outsiders to the English "inner four" even though they were gentlemen and their social equals if not superiors.

When the *Norwich* hove in view of Hampton Roads in Virginia in the chill gray of Thursday, February 20, Braddock and his retinue saw a shore far different from England's green and pleasant land. Their new-found land would have been a thin band of gray covered with thousands of naked trees stretching uniformly as far as the eye could see, a vast and undifferentiated wilderness. Their stomachs must have sunk as they realized that this service would be hard indeed.

CHAPTER SIX

The Generalissimo Comes to Town

BRADDOCK AND HIS ENTOURAGE debarked and were rowed ashore at Hampton. No sooner had they stretched their sea legs than they repaired to the King's Arms tavern where they were feted with a feast of ham, turkey, breast of veal with plump Chesapeake oysters, Madeira wine, punch, and cider.[1]

The first item on Braddock's agenda upon his arrival was to review the much-anticipated reports from Sir John St. Clair. These he found awaiting him when he stepped off the *Norwich*. Braddock tarried for several days at Hampton to allow for the arrival of Commodore Keppel with the *Centurion*. Keppel's ship finally limped into port on February 22 with a sprung foremast. The next day Braddock, Keppel, Orme, and Shirley rode to nearby Williamsburg, the colonial capital of Virginia, to meet with Dinwiddie.

The lieutenant governor and the major general warily took the measure of one another, two imperiums of colonial power thrown together by fate. However, the meeting was facilitated by the fact that St. Clair had preceded Braddock to Williamsburg, in effect heralding his arrival. St. Clair was now far to the north in Winchester, Virginia, inspecting recruits. Braddock wanted St. Clair to report to him in person. He therefore asked Dinwiddie to dispatch a rider to recall St. Clair to Williamsburg immediately.

Dinwiddie proclaimed St. Clair to Braddock as "A very good ingineer. . . . A very diligent, good officer. . . . Sensible. . . An amiable man, full of spirits, with discretion and good judgement." St. Clair claimed, in addition to being a baronet, to have fought in Italy with the legendary general Count Browne, an Irish mercenary in the army of Empress Maria Theresa. He had regaled the governor with tales of the courts of Europe (with which, of course, he was intimately familiar). "And his observations of them were very judicious," acknowledged Dinwiddie, the son of a Glasgow merchant who had started his career as a customs clerk in Bermuda.[2] Braddock might have smiled indulgently.

The reports that greeted Braddock were not encouraging: the recruits were indifferent, promised help from Quaker-dominated Pennsylvania was not forthcoming, and horses and transport wagons were scarce. Braddock quickly dispatched two letters to England. The first missive was to Secretary at War Fox (which incidentally would have signaled his safe arrival to his "Pop"). It read in relevant part: "After a passage of seven weeks, in which I had very bad weather, I arrived here where I found everything in great confusion, as I had expected. A great deal of money had already been spent here, though very little done. . . . Pennsylvania will do nothing, and furnisheth the French with everything they have occasion for."

Braddock wrote a letter of similar tenor to Colonel Robert Napier, the Duke of Cumberland's adjutant. He complained, "So little order has reigned among them [the inhabitants] hitherto that much has been spent in doing very little."

Even as he wrote, St. Clair rode in from Winchester. "Sir John St. Clair had arrived at this moment. This man is indefatigable," Braddock observed.[3]

Indeed Braddock was now able to hear at first hand from St. Clair how bad the situation on the ground really was. Of cardinal

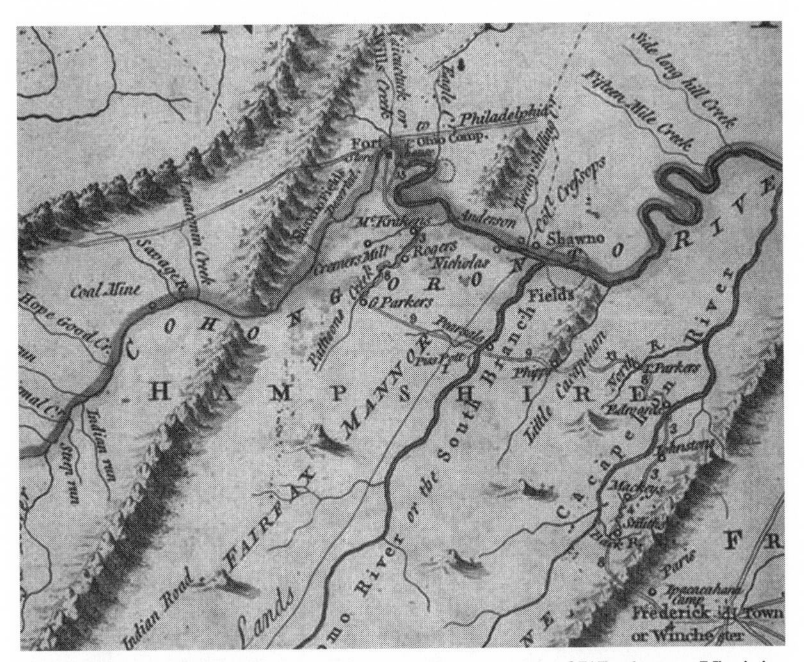

Detail of the Jefferson–Fry map showing the area west of Winchester, Virginia, (bottom right) reconnoitered by Sir John St. Clair. Wills Creek appears at the center top, while the Savage River is at the middle to the left. St. Clair discovered to his chagrin that both the difficulty of the topography and distances between objectives were much greater than previously supposed. (*Library of Congress*)

importance was the topography, woefully underestimated by London. St. Clair explained that not only would it be impossible to move the artillery by boat up the Potomac River but the mountains between Wills Creek and Fort Duquesne were not fifteen miles, as supposed by Cumberland and Braddock, but closer to seventy miles (St. Clair was mistaken; the actual distance was approximately 120 miles). And there were no good roads. Even the road from Winchester to Wills Creek, well within the pale of English settlement, was "the worst road I ever traveled," according to St. Clair.[4] St. Clair had reconnoitered the country for several miles beyond Wills Creek and had peeked over the first intervening mountain range. He recommended the mouth of the Savage River as the place to cross over the mountains into the wilderness.

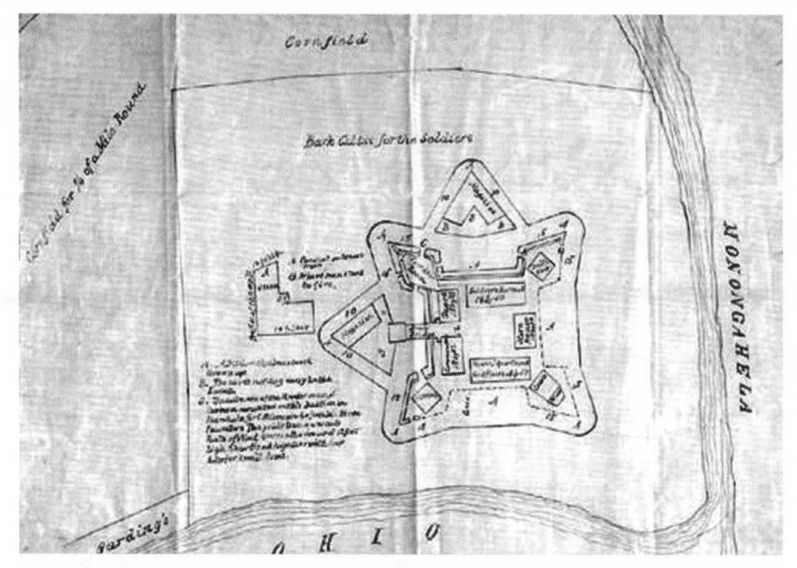

Plan of Fort Duquesne drawn by Captain Robert Stobo during his captivity and smuggled to Braddock. The sketch almost cost Stobo his life because when the French found the drawing in Braddock's baggage they tried and convicted Stobo to death for espionage. He subsequently escaped his captivity at Montreal and returned to the English colonies. (*Chateau Ramezay Museum, Montreal*)

St. Clair and Braddock pored over a smuggled sketch of Fort Duquesne, together with accompanying note, that had been prepared by Captain Robert Stobo, one of the two hostages left at Fort Necessity.[5] The clandestine report showed the fort as situated on the east side of the Monongahela on the promontory formed by its confluence with the Allegheny. The fort was small but stoutly built to European standards, a hectagon with its long sides fifty yards in length and its shorter ones forty. It was constructed of a double row of large squared logs to a height of twelve feet. They were reinforced with compacted earth to a height of eight feet. Three bastions bristled from the landward sides. Although the sides of the fort that paralleled the two rivers and the point were protected by nature and not hardened with bastions, a stockade of logs a foot in diameter and twelve feet high ran the entire perimeter of the fort. Wattled cross-poles laced the stockade in the manner of a basketwork, and loopholes pierced the stockade to permit the men to fire. Some four rods from this all-encompassing stockade ran a ditch protected by a second stockade seven feet high and solidly embanked with earth. The woods all around had been cut down to the distance of a musket shot (about forty yards) to prevent the stealthy approach of any enemy. Downstream cornfields and vegetable gardens provisioned the garrison. The interior of the fort contained barracks, underground magazines, a kitchen, and even a jail. Most of the structures were constructed of the same sturdy logs as the stockade and outer defenses, although bark huts sheltered the enlisted soldiers. However, because canoes and portage had their limitations for the transport of heavy artillery, the fort mounted only eight cannon, mere 3- and 4-pounders, five of which were placed on the northwest bastion to defend the powder magazine. In all, despite its light armament, the fort was a fairly impressive piece of French design and frontier execution.

The garrison at Fort Duquesne fluctuated. It had numbered only about one hundred when an abortive peace mission from Virginia visited the fort after the fall of Fort Necessity. It later stood close to eleven hundred, once reinforcements arrived upon New France's learning of the British preparations for an expedition. In addition, some four hundred Adirondacks, Caghnawagas, and Ottawas had come down from Canada to the fort. However, most of this force had returned to Canada at the onset of the winter of 1754–55 to settle down in winter quarters, leaving behind a garrison of perhaps two hundred and fifty French and Canadians, plus assorted Indians, under Contrecoeur.

Notwithstanding the strength of the position, its relatively weakened garrison would have handed Braddock an almost certain victory if he had struck in April or early May. In any event, St. Clair recommended that Braddock erect a battery on the brow of an opposite hill once he reached the fort and set the buildings in its interior afire with hot shot and thus subdue the fort.

St. Clair also reported on the help that could be expected from Indian allies (not much), but most of his ire was reserved for the wealthy Quakers of Pennsylvania who would not lift a finger to help the expedition. In tidewater states like Virginia and Maryland, St. Clair explained, networks of rivers and creeks facilitated transportation, and there was therefore a dearth of horses and wagons. While Pennsylvania did have a significant inventory of horses and wagons, the Quaker-dominated assembly, together with indifferent German immigrant farmers, had done nothing to help. Even assuming they were able to procure transport, St. Clair was concerned about forage. "I am afraid we will not be able to cross the mountains till the grass begins to shoot," he warned.[6] His words proved prophetic.

Nonetheless, Braddock quickly moved to take charge and make the best of a bad situation. On February 26 he turned his pent-up energies to the issuance of orders. First on the list was the expected arrival of the troop transports. In his initial order from North American soil Braddock issued the following command which showed both solicitude for the well-being of his troops and impatience with slackers: "His Excellency General Braddock orders that . . . a Subaltern Officer of each ship shall see their men safely conveyed to the place appointed at Hampton for their Reception, which Mr. Hunter will shew them; and that the Surgeons or mates of the two regiments and Train shall attend the sick of their own corps. Every commanding Officer is to take particular care that as soon as their sick are sent a Shore all the Hatchways be uncovered, scuttles opened and the Platform thoroughly washed and cleaned, no Officer or soldier, except the sick, to lie on shore upon any acct."[7]

The same day Braddock laid before Dinwiddie a "scheme," as he put it, to form four companies of rangers. These rangers did not have the same mission as later guerrilla units such as the renowned Rogers's Rangers. Rather, they were largely Tidewater volunteers, not backwoodsmen, who covered the main body of the army to protect it from ambush. Braddock also proposed forming two companies of carpenters and a troop of light horse for skirmishing (the last no doubt added as a nod to Braddock's mentor the Duke of Cumberland who, as captain general, had advocated such units). Evidently Dinwiddie concurred, for Braddock issued orders two days later for their mustering. However, Braddock made clear from the start who was to pay. As Orme dryly noted: "The General acquainted Governor Dinwiddie with his Majesty's pleasure, that the several assemblies should raise a sum of money to be employed towards defraying the expenses of the Expedition, And desired he would propose it to his Assembly; And that his Majesty also expected the Provinces to furnish the Troops with provisions and Carriages. The General desired the Governor would use all imaginable dispatch in raising and convening the Levies to augment the two Battalions to 700 each. He also proposed to the Governor to make an establishment for some provincials, amongst which he recommended a Troop of light horse."[8] Dinwiddie's response is unrecorded. Perhaps it was now his turn to smile indulgently.

Also on February 26 Braddock issued an order, pursuant to an act of Parliament subjecting all troops raised in America to the Regulations and Orders of the Articles of War, that the Articles of War be read publicly to all officers and men and that "every man severally shall take the Oath of Allegiance and supremacy; and in consequence of these articles they are to obey from time to time any orders they shall receive from me." In other words, Braddock established himself as supreme commander over both British regulars and American militia, an assumption of authority that was to draw some comment from his American "cousins."[9]

In yet another order issued the same day Braddock charged St. Clair with reviewing the independent companies then at Fort Cumberland at Wills Creek, as well as recently raised Virginia and Maryland levies at Winchester and Frederick, respectively. He further instructed St. Clair to "mark down such men as you think proper for completing the two British Regiments," while taking care to note that "All blacks and mulattoes except the young and strong to be discharged."[10]

At this juncture St. Clair laid before Braddock his cherished plan to disperse the arriving troops about the countryside in a

A 12-pounder naval cannon displayed at Waterfront Park, Alexandria, Virgina. This iron cannon, which is of the type supplied to Braddock from the HMS *Norwich*, is approximately 9 feet long and weighs roughly 2900 pounds. Braddock's expedition began with eight 12-pounders (four brass and four iron naval) in tow along with other artillery. (*Author*)

three-hundred-mile radius. Braddock approved St. Clair's proposal on the spot and issued an order on February 28 to give it effect. However, Orme and his friends were not about to let St. Clair dictate strategy. They apparently got Braddock's ear, and the general quickly reversed the order. Orme smugly recorded that His Excellency had second thoughts because "he knew that much confusion must arise in disembarking at different places; That it would be impossible to cloath, arm and discipline the Levies when so much dispersed, and that soldiers are sooner and better formed in Camps than in Quarters. He therefore, in conjunction with Mr. Keppel, fixed upon Alexandria to disembark and encamp at; and the Levies for the two regiments were ordered to that place."[11] The second thoughts were correct.

However, perhaps the overriding concern that Braddock faced was the expedition's artillery. Arriving on the troop transports were four brass 12-pounders, six 6-pounders, four 8-inch howitzers, and fifteen cohorn mortars. Both Braddock and St. Clair

A 6-pounder cannon, left, and an 8-inch howitzer, right, of the types taken by Braddock on his expedition. This artillery provided Braddock's forces with unprecedented firepower in the American wilderness. (*Fort Ligonier, Ligonier, Pennsylvania*)

were concerned about the need for more and heavier artillery to lay siege to Fort Duquesne. Braddock raised this concern with Commodore Keppel, who agreed to give him four naval 12-pounders, which were removed from the upper deck of the *Norwich* and presented to Braddock along with one thousand balls and fifty barrels of powder.[12] Commencing his overland expedition with eight 12-pounders, Braddock had formidable, indeed unprecedented, projected firepower. By way of comparison, exactly sixty years later, the former artillery officer Napoleon Bonaparte deployed as his main strike force at the battle of Waterloo a battery of twenty-four 12-pounders–affectionately known by their gun crews as *Les belles filles de l'Empereur* (the Emperor's beautiful daughters).[13] And Napoleon's big guns, facing armies that numbered in the hundreds of thousands, did not have to cross an ocean or uncharted mountains.

Keppel and Braddock also discussed the problem of moving such heavy armament over what were now appreciated to be multiple steep mountains. Keppel volunteered rope and tackles, plus thirty seamen to handle them. Braddock was also concerned with the need to cross unbridged rivers too deep to ford. Floats would be necessary to ferry men and supplies. He therefore accepted Keppel's offer, and a detachment of sailors was organized under

Lieutenant Charles Spendelow of the *Norwich* to accompany the expedition. In addition, Lieutenant William Shackerly, also of the navy, was appointed to make maps and take observations of the country through which the expedition was to pass, a sort of official cartographer attached to the army.[14] Orme observed of Braddock and Keppel, with some accuracy, that, "never, I believe, two men placed at the head of different Commands co-operated with more spirit, integrity and harmony for the publick service."[15]

But all was not correspondence and organizational tedium in Braddock's days at Williamsburg. Slowly the troop transports began to arrive. On Sunday March 2 two transports, each with one hundred British regulars, hove in view at Hampton. The *Seahorse*, with five more ships, arrived within the next five days. Braddock rode down to Hampton to get reports on the crossing. By March 13, he was able to report that the three ordnance ships and all but one of the transports, the *Severn* bearing one company of Sir Peter Halkett's regiment, had arrived in a convoy with seven men-of-war, evidently the result of a mid-passage rendezvous.[16]

The ships lay at anchor in the roads with their human cargo strictly forbidden to come ashore. However, troops immediately began to jump ship and desert. Dinwiddie posted a reward for their apprehension, and a few were caught. One deserter was court martialed and given twenty-four lashes with the cat from ship to ship: in other words, he suffered the most exemplary form of naval punishment whereby the sailor was rowed in a dinghy from one ship to another and whipped within view of all hands who had been mustered to witness punishment. Two other deserters from the *Centurion* received 240 and 350 lashes spread out over several days because so many at once would have killed them.

Braddock the iron disciplinarian no doubt approved of Keppel's firm hand. However, as His Excellency was soon to learn, he could command but not all would obey.

Chapter Seven

The Opportunity of a Lifetime

Just as Braddock arrived with orders and an agenda on how to deal with the American colonies, he would have been naïve to think that individual Americans did not have their own agendas for dealing with him. What is remarkable about the Americans' reaction to the arrival of the expedition is how they viewed it as a grand opportunity to improve their own prospects for advancement. The Americans did not hesitate to write their own dreams and ambitions onto the blank slate that Braddock unwittingly presented.

In no instance was this phenomenon more vividly illustrated than by a little-noted exchange of correspondence conducted by George Washington with Braddock through the latter's aide-de-camp Robert Orme. Following the debacle at Fort Necessity, George Washington had resigned his colonel's commission in late October 1754, and returned to civilian life. The motivating factor for Washington's resignation was not so much the stain of his capitulation as the fact that Dinwiddie had reorganized the colonial forces so that officers with a king's commission, even if ranking lower than Washington, would command him. Notwithstanding his resignation and increasing tension between Washington and Dinwiddie over the reorganization, Washington wrote, "My inclinations are strongly bent to arms."[1]

Washington repaired to Mount Vernon, which he had recently inherited from the widow of his half-brother Lawrence Washington, and licked his wounds. However, the arrival of Braddock presented too great an opportunity for Washington to resist. Within a week of Braddock's setting foot in America, the commander of "All His Majesty's Forces in North America" had received a letter from young Washington congratulating him on his arrival. The response that followed, directed by Braddock but written by Orme, was remarkable. It read:

> Williamsburg, 2 March, 1755
>
> Sir: George Washington
>
> The General having been informed that you expressed some desire to make the campaign, but that you declined it upon some disagreeableness that you thought might arise from the regulations of command, has ordered me to acquaint you that he will be very glad of your company in his family, by which all inconveniences of that kind will be obviated.
>
> I shall think myself very happy to form an acquaintance with a person so universally esteemed, and shall use every opportunity of assuring you how much I am, Sir, your most obedient servant.
>
> Robert Orme, aid de camp

Braddock offered Washington the rank of captain by brevet and proposed to place him on his personal staff, to be a member of his "military family." Why would Braddock have behaved so solicitously toward Washington? It is true that Washington knew the countryside over which the expedition was to pass and had actually fought the French. He thus had the valuable commodity of experience. However, he had presided over a defeat and come off the braggart, at least in some stratospheric quarters. More likely, the explanation for Braddock's interest in Washington lay in the references in Orme's letter to "The General having been informed that you expressed some desire to make the campaign" and to a "person so universally esteemed." Although there is no direct evidence extant, Dinwiddie might have been anxious to place "his" man on Braddock's staff for the obvious reasons of acting as the lieutenant governor's eyes and ears and serving as a conduit to ensure that his views were made known to the general as the campaign progressed. Washington might have been equally anxious to work through Dinwiddie in order to restore and enhance his military career. In any event, it is probable that once again Washington became the willing instrument of the lieutenant governor. The extreme solicitousness of Orme's letter can only be attributable to Dinwiddie's having paved the way.

Washington, however, played hard to get. On March 15 he replied to Orme with a rare combination of candor and obsequiousness:

> I was not favoured with your polite letter of the 2nd inst., until yesterday, acquainting me with the notice his Excellency General Braddock is pleased to honor me with, by kindly inviting (desiring my Company in his family) me to become one of his family in the ensuing Campaign. It is true, Sir, I have ever since I declined a command in this Service express'd an Inclination to serve the Ensuing Campaigne as a Volunteer; and this believe me Sir, is not a little encreased, since its likeley to be conducted by a Gentleman of the General's great good Character;
>
> But besides this, and the laudable desire I may have to serve (with my poor ability) my King and Country, I must be ingenuous enough to confess, I am not a little bias'd by selfish and private views. To be plain Sir, I wish

> for nothing more earnestly than to attain a small degree of knowledge in the Military Art. . . . I shall do myself the pleasure of waiting upon his Excellency as soon as I hear of his arrival at Alexandria (and would sooner, was I certain where) till which I shall decline saying further on this head; begging you'll be kind enough to assure him that I shall always retain a grateful sense of the favor he was kindly pleased to offer me.[2]

The negotiations had begun, and Washington was firmly determined to become the final member of Braddock's military family, not only in violation of the stipulations of his surrender at Fort Necessity, which forbade him to take up arms for one year but also–and more important–on his own terms. On March 21 Washington shot off another letter to Orme. Washington asked to join the expedition at Wills Creek:

> I find myself much embarrassed with my affairs, having no person to whom I can confide, to entrust the management with. Yet, under these disadvantages and circumstances, I am determined to do myself the honor of accompanying you with this proviso only, the General will be kind enough to permit my return as soon as the [illegible] . . . or grand affair is over. . . . Or, if there should be any space of inaction long enough to admit of a visit [back to Virginia] . . . to indulge me wherein and I need not add how much I should be obliged by joining at Wills Creek only, for this the General had kindly promised. These things Sir, however unwarrantable they may appear at first sight, I hope will not be taken amiss when it is considered how unprepared I am at present to quit a family, an estate scarcely settled, and in the utmost confusion.[3]

In other words, Washington wanted to join, but only at Wills Creek, and then take leave as soon as there was a lull in the campaign. Braddock had not promised these conditions in Orme's prior letter to Washington, but it is possible that Washington had met the general in Williamsburg through Dinwddie and had the terms offered orally. In fairness, Washington had only recently inherited Mount Vernon and was in fact in the process of taking charge of the estate.

Orme responded on March 22, the day Braddock left Williamsburg, as follows:

> Sir: George Washington
>
> The General orders me to give you his compliments, and to assure you his wishes are to make it agreeable to yourself and consistent with your affairs, and, therefore, he desires you will settle your business at home, and to join him at Wills Creek if more convenient to you; and, whenever you find it necessary to return, he begs you will look upon yourself as entirely master, and judge what is proper to be done.[4]

Washington had negotiated his way onto Braddock's staff and had set the terms and conditions of his service. It was a remarkable achievement by a twenty-three-year-old colonial in dealing with a sixty-year-old major general with the disposition of an Iroquois.[5]

Nor was Washington the only colonial American to exploit the opportunity. Adam Stephen, a Scottish-born, University of Edinburgh-trained former surgeon in the Royal Navy, had worked since 1748 as a rent collector for Washington's patrons, the Fairfax family. The doe-eyed, curly-haired Stephen had accompanied Washington at the massacre at Jumonville Glen and in the debacle at Fort Necessity, where Washington had promoted him to major. As early as February 1755, Stephen, age thirty-four, started recruiting locals for St. Clair to fill out the ranks of Braddock's under-strength regiments. Within a couple of months he had worked his way into a position as head of a detachment of Virginia provincials attached to Dunbar's 48th. Hoping, like

Washington, for advancement into the regular British army, Stephen's life, and American history, were both to be forever changed by his service in the expedition. He became a close associate of George Washington and played a vital role in the American Revolution as a major general.

Other, lesser lights also enlisted in the cause. George Croghan, age thirty-seven, signed up as head of the expedition's Indian scouts. Croghan was a major Pennsylvania Indian trader who eventually became Deputy Superintendent of Indian Affairs in America and conducted the final peace negotiations following Pontiac's rebellion in 1763. At one time he owned over one million acres of frontier land but died in poverty. John Neville was a twenty-four-year-old private from Virginia. He rose to become a colonel in the militia by 1775 and commanded Fort Pitt, built by the British on the site of Fort Duquesne. He later served as a brigadier general in the American Revolution. He was a Federalist and a wealthy man and also served as a member of the Pennsylvania Council that ratified the United States Constitution and of the Pennsylvania Constitutional Convention.

Dr. Thomas Walker was commissary to Braddock's Virginia troops and would almost lose his life in the Braddock campaign. He eventually served on Virginia's Committee of Safety and Executive Council in the Revolution. He was a neighbor of Peter Jefferson, and, when the latter died in 1757, Walker became guardian of his fourteen-year-old son and was responsible for raising and educating the future President of the United States.

The list goes on and on. The men came from the Tidewater, from the Piedmont, from the mountains. They reflected the breadth of colonial society–from the young bloods of the warrior caste to tenant farmers to recent immigrants. Counterparts to these men, who later played active roles in the Revolution, also flocked to the cause in New York and New England to participate in the simultaneous northern prongs of Braddock's strategy.

For many, service in the Braddock campaign was an astute career move. One summary of twenty noteworthy men who participated in Braddock's march and the ensuing battle at the Monongahela found that "four had been at the Battle of Fort Necessity. . . eight were wounded at the Battle of the Monongahela . . . six were with General Forbes at the taking of Fort Duquesne . . . four fought at Quebec . . . six were intimately involved in Pontiac's Conspiracy . . . eight became general officers in the American Revolution . . . one became commander in chief of the British forces . . . two were considered for the post of commander in chief of the revolutionary forces . . . four made major historical contributions through their writings . . . one entered the U.S. Congress . . . and one became the President of the United States."[6]

Adam Stephen. (*West Virginia University Library*)

Their stories, and those of even more famous Americans, as well as British, were just beginning to be written when Braddock folded his tents in Williamsburg and moved a hundred or so miles north to Alexandria, Virginia, which had been designated as the next major staging area for the campaign.

CHAPTER EIGHT

An Army in Alexandria

MAJOR JOHN CARLYLE LOOKED at the pineapples carved in the lintels over the two doors in the northwest large parlor of his grand Georgian stone mansion in Alexandria, Virginia. The carvings had been scrupulously copied from a plate in William Salmon's *Palladio Londenensis*, the latest pattern book from the mother country. The pineapple was the symbol of hospitality. Carlyle could only sigh as he dipped his quill in irony to write in his uniquely fractured–but telling–English to his brother George in England:

> Last fall when Capt. Gilpin left us we was raising men & Money to fill our Virginia Regiment, & waited for Directions from England–Which Came In March Last, with Genl Braddock & the forces under his Comand, the Troops & Men of War All arrived Safe as did Braddock, they was ordered up here (the highest Landing upon the Continent) & were Landed in high Spirits about 1600 men, besides a fine train of Artillery 100 matrosses [in the

> British army a matross was an artillery soldier who ranked below a bombardier or gunner] &c. & Seemed to be Afraid of nothing but that the French & Indians woud not Give them a Meeting, & try their Courage.

In light of this hubris, Carlyle recorded efforts to warn the British and their unexpected reaction: "We that knew the Numbers &c. of the French, Indeavour'd to Sett them right, but to no purpose, they differed us & them & by Sum means or another came in So prejudiced against us, our Country, &c. that they used us Like an Enemy Country & Took everything they wanted & paid Nothing, or Very little for it, & when Complaints was made to the Comdg Officers, they Curst the Country, & Inhabitants, Calling us the Spawn of Convicts the Sweepings of the Goals &c., which made their Company very disagreeable."

What is more, the affront was personal: "The Generall & his Aid de Camps Secretary & Servants Lodged with Me, he took everything he wanted abused my home, & furniture, & made me little or No Satisfaction . . . & paid me 50 L for the use of my house for a Month, but to our Great joy they Marched from hence Abt the 20t of Aprill & with the Greatest parade & Negligence Got up Safe to Fort Cumberland."

And then there was the particular matter of Braddock:

> I Cannot Pass over Braddocks Character Without Sum Notice, As he was Intrusted with a Commission with greater Power, then ever the Duke of Cumberland, or the Late Duke of Marlbrough ever had; he Coud Comand All the Governours on the Continent, & coud When he Pleased Constitute, A new Regiment, Put them on the British Establishment & Give Away the Comissions, A Power Always before only In the hand of the King but On This Expedition Put Into the hands of General Braddocke, A Man (If I am a judge) of Week understanding, Positive, & Very Indolent, Slave to his Passions, Women & Wine, As Great an Epicure as could be in his

> Eateing, Tho' A brave Man, See into what hands So great an Affair As the Settleing the Boundarays in the No America was put.[1]

What had gone wrong? Certainly, there had been little inkling of such ill will when Braddock and his troops headed up the Potomac River for Alexandria to the good wishes of the populace. One eyewitness described the jaunty scene: "We left Hampton and Sailed up the Portwomack [Potomac] River to Alexandria, it Being a pleasant River, having Virginia on the left hand in Sailing up it and Maryland on the Right . . . and having many gentlemen('s) Houses on Boath Sides which we salluted with our Great Guns and answered again from the Gentlemen Houses with their great Guns and Colours flying."[2]

Americans looked expectantly to the hero who was coming to save them from the French and Indians. Though they knew little or nothing of General Braddock, he was the King's chosen appointee, coming all the way from London with a flotilla of ships and a thousand redcoats. Their anticipation and desire to impress was almost palpable.

Nowhere was this more true than in Alexandria, Virginia. Alexandria at that time was a settlement that had been incorporated as a town barely six years earlier, largely by Scots and Quaker merchants seeking a shipping point for tobacco from Tidewater Virginia and wheat from the newly opened farmlands of the Piedmont. Some eight miles upriver from Washington's estate at Mount Vernon, the town was situated on a modestly arcing bay of the Potomac River. Viewed from the river, its two most prominent features were a boatyard at Point Lumley on its southern extremity and a wharf and collection of tobacco warehouses—which had been the inception of the town—at its northern end. Between these two features, the town itself stretched for perhaps a half mile laid out on a grid pattern. Most of its houses were of wood or brick and wood combination with ample space for gardens. The one major exception to this pattern of modest dwellings

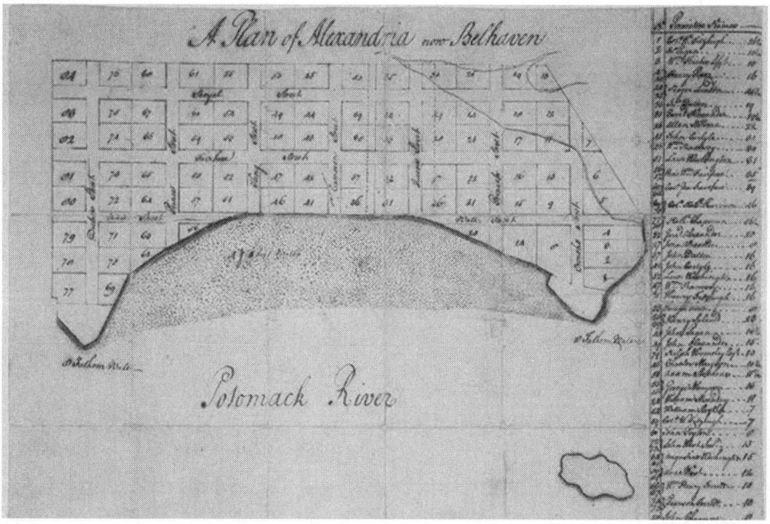

The plan of Alexandria, Virginia, drawn by George Washington in 1749. The plan is divided into eighty-four lots of mostly one-half acre size. John Carlyle's lots are numbers 41 and 42. (*Library of Congress*)

was Carlyle's mansion, which stood, as it still stands today, on Fairfax Street across from the town's marketplace and courthouse. Carlyle was a wealthy merchant who had married Sarah Fairfax, a daughter of William Fairfax of Belvoir, the land agent for five million acres held by his cousin Lord Fairfax, and the most powerful man in the vicinity. Carlyle had erected his elegant home of white sandstone quarried from nearby Aquia Creek. The lintel stone over the front door bore an inscription of his and his wife's intertwined initials and the date 1752. The house stood back from the street, a virtual country seat improbably perched in town. In 1755, the property backed directly onto wharves that ran into the river. Then, as now, it was the dominant private dwelling in Alexandria.

A further eight miles upriver, on the Maryland side, stood Alexandria's archrival Georgetown, a tobacco port also founded by Scots emigrants. A further eight miles beyond Georgetown was the head of navigation, the fall line at Little Falls, and then, beyond that, the Great Falls of the Potomac that had awed and confounded Sir John St. Clair.

Stormy weather delayed the flotilla's advance up the Chesapeake Bay and Potomac River from Hampton to Alexandria. Braddock left Williamsburg March 22, accompanied by Dinwiddie and Keppel, but did not arrive at Alexandria until four days later, March 26. Some of the transport ships had preceded him upriver.[3] The ships docked along the northern wharves and discharged the troops and supplies at the foot of Oronoco Street. The first order of business was to disembark and encamp the soldiers where they could do the least harm to the town. It was the first time the soldiers had set foot on land in three months. As journalist-turned-historian Lee McCardell imaginatively but not improbably re-creates the scene:

> The troops, put ashore by the transport crews, marched up the lane from the river, drums thumping, fifes a-squeal. Frightened hogs and geese, which had the run of the place, scattered. Townsfolk, children, a few farmers, Negro servants watched their first British regulars swing past. Never before had they beheld anything as gorgeous as those yellow faced red uniforms with their big shining buckles and white lace–slightly soiled. Never before had they heard so many drums–twenty to each regiment. The thistle wreathed Roman numerals were another curiosity.
>
> The soldiers, unkempt by months of cramped living aboard ship, their pigtails smeared with a regulation mixture of flour and tallow, regarded the Alexandrians with much less satisfaction. The blacks were the first Negro slaves some of the soldiers had ever seen. But the long confinement of a transatlantic voyage had aroused more interest in the town. The redcoats marched past a courthouse, a jail, a whipping post, and a pillory–grouped around the market square. They looked for alehouses–and saw one small tavern. No cook shops. No pastry

> shops. No coffee houses. No signboards. Along the lane leading to the site of their encampment . . . they passed not more than half a dozen coaches and those with unmatched horses and as plain and dusty as any country carriages they had ever seen in Ireland.[4]

The townspeople of Alexandria would have had good reason to be impressed by the splendid uniforms of the British regulars. Both regiments wore red coats faced with yellow silk (in the case of the 44th) or buff (the 48th) and decorated with gold braid. The soldiers' legs sported red breeches and white spatterdashes, an elongated version of spats that covered the leg from ankle to mid-thigh. Each combatant shouldered a .75 caliber Long Land Pattern Brown Bess service musket with bayonet. The Grenadier units were the elite of each regiment. The Grenadiers were men hand-picked for their height, smart appearance, and bravery. Their original function was to hurl grenades and attack fortified positions in advance of other troops. By 1755, their mission had evolved into performing flanking duty for the regiment. The Grenadiers wore a more ornate uniform than the other troops, a fact noted in the eighteenth-century lyrics to "The Grenadiers' March," which termed them as those "Who carry caps and pouches, and wear looped clothes." However the most distinctive feature of the Grenadiers' uniform was their mitered cap, which was the predecessor to the famous bearskin hat adopted in 1768. In the case of Halkett's 48th Regiment, the cap was red-faced with yellow and bore the royal monogram "GR," together with the Grenadiers' insignia of a running horse and the legend *Nec Aspera Terrent* (Difficulties Do Not Deter). The overall effect was to make already tall soldiers positively looming. The sergeants carried halberds rather than muskets, while officers shouldered spontoons or short pikes as badges of office in addition to their dress swords. Both pieces of archaic weaponry were quickly discarded as the army adjusted to the harsh reality of campaigning in America. In contrast, colonial troops wore blue uniforms faced with red. The redcoats derisively called the colonial troops "bobtails" because of the short cut of their coats. The colonial soldiers had similar, but generally inferior, equipment to that of their British cousins.

The men thus turned out marched up Oronoco Street in Alexandria, past the site of the house where the Confederate General Robert E. Lee was to pass his boyhood some sixty years later. But where the regiments headed no one knows for certain today. Their encampment may have been along a marsh on the then-northwest corner of the town (a somewhat improbable location on which to encamp troops) or possibly atop a ridge known as Shuter's Hill on the western edge of town.[5] Either way, their officers wanted them out of town for reasons of sanitation and order.

At least fifty women accompanied the troops. Most were soldiers' wives, common law or otherwise, who cooked and washed for sixpence a day. All were to march with the troops throughout the expedition, suffering its hardships and adventures.

Also disembarking at Alexandria was Charlotte Browne, a widowed nurse who was accompanying her brother, a commissary, on the expedition. She, as well as an improbable assortment of officers, Captain Robert Cholmondeley's batman, and a sailor, kept journals of their adventures. Charlotte Browne found Alexandria "Extremely hot," crowded, and overtaxed. She lamented that she "Went with Mr. Lake to every House in the Place to get a Lodging, and at last was Obliged to take a Room but little larger than to hold my Bed, and not so much as a Chair in it. Went on Board [the ship] at Night."[6]

While Mrs. Browne cooled off on deck, Braddock installed himself in the ample guest bedroom in the northeast corner of the second floor of Carlyle House (the Carlyles' bedroom was, typically for Virginia, on the ground floor). From there Braddock could watch the rising sun over the Maryland shore and the unloading of the ships. A guard of a lieutenant and thirty privates drawn in alternation each day from the two regiments was posted in the front yard of the house.

Depiction of grenadiers of the 43rd, 44th, and 45th (top) and 46th, 47th, and 48th Regiments of Foot (bottom) by David Morier c. 1751–60, possibly painted for the Duke of Cumberland. (*The Royal Collection, Her Majesty Queen Elizabeth II, London*)

Braddock issued his first order the day after his arrival, on March 27. It confirmed the appointment of Orme as his aide-de-camp. In addition, he appointed Captain Roger Morris, of Dunbar's 48th Regiment, as a second aide-de-camp and Captain Francis Halkett, elder son of the commander of the 44th Regiment, as brigade major.

Then he turned his attention to the men. Braddock acknowledged that the two regiments of regulars were "Acquainted with Military Disciplin" but desired that they "sett the most Soldier like Example to the new lev(i)es of this Country." He therefore ordered that the Articles of War be "immediately" read to all troops. Braddock also issued a series of further detailed orders relating to the organization and conduct of the troops. Tight control and discipline were the underlying themes:

> Any soldier who shall Desert tho he Return Again shall be Hanged without Mercy.
>
> Every man will be allowed every day as much fresh or Salt provision & bread or Flower . . . as it would be possible to provide Them Unless any man should be found Drunk Negligent or Disobedient. In such Case this Gratuity shall be stopped.
>
> Every Offr leaving his Company upon a march to be Cashered. And every Commanding Offr will be Answerable for the men of his Company left behind. And the Commanding Offr of each Regt are to Order to be punished with the Outmost Severity Any Soldier who shall leave his line without Leave, Sickness or Disability.[7]

Braddock further ordered all men to keep their arms in "Constant good order" and that they be issued two spare flints and 24 cartridges. Roll was to be called "morning noon & night." All guards were to be relieved at eight o'clock. The field officer was to visit all guards, posts, and pickets and report to the general by nine o'clock.[8] All guards were to beat two ruffles to honor the general and Governor Dinwiddie whenever they ventured forth. Braddock directed a general muster for seven in the morning on Monday March 31 so that he might review the troops of both regiments and the artillery. All officers were to appear at the muster in boots and with their commissions "in their Pockitts."

One of Braddock's early concerns in camp at Alexandria was the continued effort to augment the five hundred men in each regiment with colonials in order to achieve the optimal troop strength of seven hundred soldiers. The officers culled desirable men from the Virginia, Maryland, and North Carolina militias which had begun to assemble in Alexandria. Recruiting detachments were also ordered into the countryside. The quality of the recruits was disappointing; some were even criminals who arrived shackled in chains.[9] Restrictive recruiting standards resulted in a somewhat shallow pool of talent. According to the Recruiting Instructions, 1755, "You are to inlist no Irish or any other Country unless you are sure that they are Protestants. . . . All your Recruits must be strait and well made, broad shouldered . . . you are to inlist none but shall measure 5 Feet 5 Inches without shoes, from 16 to 20 [years old], and 5 Feet 6 from 20 to 35 [years old]."[10] Moreover, desertions were a constant problem, to judge from the rewards posted in colonial papers for the return of errant troops.[11]

Indeed, the problem with seepage from the ranks through desertion was so bad that on Good Friday March 28, only two days after arriving at Alexandria, Braddock established a general court-martial under Lieutenant Colonel Gage to sit at eight o'clock the next morning. The only recorded act of the court-martial was to sentence one James Anderson of Dunbar's 48th Regiment to one thousand lashes with a cat-o-nine-tails, presumably for desertion. While different from the promised hanging without mercy, the end result for Anderson would have been the same. Fortunately for the soldier, "part of the punishment [was] remitted."[12]

The same day that the court-martial ordered one thousand lashes Braddock ordered "every Regiment in camp . . . to have divine service at the Head of their Colours" the next day, Easter Sunday. Perhaps in celebration of the season, on Easter day Braddock presented the troops who had arrived from Ireland with twenty shillings "for their Incouragement that they may do their duty like good Soldiers." Instead they rewarded their commander with a riproaring drunk that lasted for days. The odd mix of sudden shore leave, lashes, piety, and magnanimity did not appear to be a winning combination.

The soldiers' drunkenness continued unabated, to the point that the officers were helpless to deal with its effects by normal means. On April 2 Halkett issued the following order: "As Soldiers when they are reprimanded or Conversed with by Officers or Serjts. Whilst they are in Liquor often make use of Insolent Expressions which bring upon them heavy punishments And sum times even to indanger their Lives by Words tending to Mutiny, which words are fare from their sober thoughts And Wholy Occationed by the Effects of Liquor, All Commissiond & non Commissiond Officers Are Expressly forbid either to Reprimand or Converse with any Drunken Soldier but immediately to Confine Him, And deal with him when sober as they shall think he deserves."[13]

Nonetheless, the work moved forward. Each morning at six the artillery troops presented themselves at the wharf to unload the stores, Braddock taking note in his orders that "care must be taken that they have their Waggons at the Warfe Exactly at the same time that there may be no Delay." Braddock "recommended" that the officers carry no more baggage than "absolutely necessary" and that they store the remainder in Alexandria. Mindful of the shortage of troops, he further ordered that his officers were not to recruit batmen or servants from among the troops but find them locally "in the best manner they can from the Country people."

Maintenance of order in the camp continued to be a preoccupation during the first week of April. For example, Halkett ordered that "No Soldier is to Cut Wood for the Town people or Suttlers. What they cut for Themselves to be small wood. No large Trees to be felld on any acct. . . . The Officers of the Quarter Guard to send a Corpl: & a file of men every Night at 9 oClock, And to see all lights are Extinguished in the Soldiers Tents . . . to see that every thing is quiet."[14] Braddock admonished men not to use their muskets as tent poles or otherwise encumber their pieces on pain of immediate and most severe punishment. All troops were ordered to apply to the train for paper, powder, and ball sufficient for twenty-four cartridges. As usual, punishment was the motivator: "Commanding Officers of Compys are disered to give perticular Directions to their men to be Carefull of their Ammunition And to inform them They will be severly punished for any abuise or Neglect of it. The Offrs of Compys who call the Evening rolls Are to inspect Ammunition of their severall Compys And are to report the Difficiencies to their Commanding Offr: of the Regt."[15]

Still, the drunkenness continued. By April 3, four days after the twenty-shilling bonus, Orme noted that "The General was very impatient to remove the troops from Alexandria, as the greatest care and severest punishments could not prevent the immediate use of spirituous liquors, and as he was likewise informed the water of that place was very unwholsome."[16]

Nor had relations between the officers and local gentry proven altogether felicitous. The arrival of the spit and polish British regulars was the source of much excitement. The town fathers and their families turned out for the reviews and jockeyed to invite the eligible British officers into their homes for meals, as has so often been the case in a military town. Following one grand review, attended by the local gentry, the ladies of the area feted Braddock with "delicious Cake, and potted Wood Cocks."[17] However, at the same time there was also occurring a strong undercurrent of mutual sizing up and rendering of judgments, if only sotto voce. One unidentified British officer left this vivid memoir from the visitors' point of view:

I reckon the Day I bought my Commission the most unhappy in my Life, excepting which I landed in this Country. . . . What is excessively disagreeable here is, that the Wealth of the Country consists in Slaves, so that all one eats rises out of driving and whipping these poor Wretches; this Kind of Authority so corrupts the Mind of the Masters, and makes them so overbearing, that they are the most troublesome Company upon Earth, which adds much to the Uncomfortableness of the Place. You cannot conceive how it strikes the Mind on the first Arrival, to have all these black Faces with grim Looks round you, instead of being served by blooming Maid Servants, or genteel white Livery Men: I was invited to Supper by a rich Planter, and the heat of the Climate, the dim Light of the Myrtle Wax-Candles, and the number of black half-naked Servants that attended us, made me think of the infernal Regions, and that I was at Supper with Pluto, only there was no beautiful Proserpine, for the Lady of the House was more like one of the Furies; she had passed through the Education of the College of Newgate, as great Numbers from thence arrive here yearly: Most being cunning Jades, some pick up foolish Planters; this Lady's Husband was far from a Fool, but had married, not only for the Charms of her Person, but because her Art and Skill was quite useful to him in carrying on of his Business and Affairs, many of which were worthy of an adept in the College she came from. Among others he made me pay for my supper by selling me a Horse upon Honour, which, as soon as it was cool, shewed itself Dog-lame and Moonblind.

As for eating, they have the Names of almost every Thing that is delicious, or in Fashion in England, but they give them to Things as little like as Caesar or Pompey were to the Negros whom they call by those Names.[18]

In some cases the animosity was reciprocated. Such was the result of an incident, perhaps apocryphal, that occurred with the Lee family. Richard Henry Lee was the twenty-three-year-old son of Thomas Lee of Stratford Hall in Westmoreland County, a former acting governor of Virginia and member of the Ohio Company. The younger Lee had marched to Alexandria with his local militia to tender his services to Braddock. For whatever reason, Braddock declined his offer and dismissed him. However, Lee tarried at Carlyle House and walked down to the river with Braddock, Keppel, and other officers. A lighter was waiting to take the party out to a British man-of-war anchored at midstream. All the British officers stepped into the boat. Although Braddock saw Lee standing forlornly on the wharf, he ordered the rowers to shove off. Keppel sensed that something was amiss, ordered the boat to wait and invited Lee to join them. Lee accepted, but he remembered the incident, and the Lees never forgave Braddock the slight.

Of course, Braddock had little, if any, idea who the Lees of Virginia were. Besides, he already had one Lee, an obscure lieutenant in the 44th named Charles Lee.[19] Lieutenant Charles Lee would, twenty years later, turn against the British and fight as a major general on the American side during the Revolution, serving at one time as second in command to General George Washington, who undoubtedly would have first known him during the Braddock expedition.

Drunkenness, unwholesome water, and testy locals were not the only afflictions that greeted the British in Alexandria. There was also the weather. Early spring in Virginia was not the time of budding daffodils and birthing lambs to which the soldiers from rural England and Ireland were accustomed. Indeed, the spring climate in Virginia in 1755 bore little relation to that prevailing today. Following a boisterous, gale-lashed, gut-wrenching passage of the North Atlantic, the soldiers and their camp followers stepped out into an oppressive late March heat wave that made comfort and sleep impossible. They shed the great coats in which they had huddled on the passage. Because of the rapid change in climate some took ill and were placed in the hospital at Alexandria. However, the worst was yet to come as the weather fluctuated in the weeks ahead between sickening balm and snowy blizzard.

The changeable weather no doubt contributed to a cold that Braddock contracted soon after arriving at Alexandria. Two brothers, Drs. John and Alexander Hamilton, of Calvert County and Annapolis, Maryland, respectively, treated him while he endured several days' "confinement."[20] While attending to Braddock, Alexander Hamilton expressed concern about the secrecy of the expedition in a letter to another brother in Scotland, writing that "the French having many Spies amongst us" because of the proximity of Catholic Maryland to Alexandria.

However, Hamilton also noticed a further affliction: plotting among the senior officers. The three social equals–Burton, Orme, and Morris–had ingratiated themselves with Braddock. The long voyage across the Atlantic and now the leisure time in camp at Alexandria had begun to bear fruit: a plot to form a new regiment after taking Fort Duquesne, with Burton appointed colonel and Orme and Morris as lieutenant colonel and major, respectively–all in advancement over Sir John St. Clair in particular and the two other Scots colonels, Halkett and Dunbar, in general. Dr. Hamilton wrote:

> This Gentleman's [Braddock's] behaviour was austere and Supercilious, rough spoken and in short nothing Engaging appeared in his Conversation. He showed a distant behaviour and Reserve, even towards the governors of our Colonys, as if they had been infinitely his Inferiors; shutting himself up like a Bashaw from the Conversation of his own officers, Suffering none of them to hold discourse with him, more than what was just absolutely necessary, At open variance with some and not in Speaking terms with others. For which behaviour I never could

> learn any reason but his o(wn) haughty and Imperious Temper. Three favorites indeed he had. Some of them were raw and unexperienced. These were Leut. Col. Burton of Dunbars Regiment, Capt Orme & Capt Morris his Aids de Camps. Of these was made a secret Cabal or Junto, who kept their Schemes entirely to themselves, not permitting the older and more experienced officers to have the least insights into their Measures & Consultations. . . .
>
> Coll. Dunbar he had an open difference with and on Sundry occasions used him very ill; and with Sir Peter Halkett, a Gentleman remarkable for his Civility and good nature, he was Scarce in Speaking terms and often spoke to him in a huffing manner. Sir John St. Clair, the Quarter Master General, he show'd no more respect to, than if he had been his Lacquai [lackey], and he was only barely civil from the teeth outwards to Major George Washington. . . . In short, the aforesaid triumvirate Orm, Burton and Morris were his only favorites. . . .
>
> But there was also a plot afoot:
>
> It was said. . . . That as the General made himself absolutely sure of taking the Fort, There was a scheme laid by the Junto, that a new Regiment should be formed there, of which Regiment Burton was to have been appointed Colonel, Orm Leut. Col. & Morris Major in prejudice of the older Officers, particularly Sir John St. Clair, who had as yet no particular Command.[21]

What Braddock's view of the plot was, or whether he even knew of it, is uncertain. Its principal, or at least most vociferous, proponent seems to have been Orme. It was to resurface later in the campaign. The animosity it engendered in relation to Halkett and Dunbar was to corrode the cohesion of the senior command.

Notwithstanding his authority to issue new commissions to the plotters and anyone else, Braddock's preoccupations were properly elsewhere. Despite his unflinching faith in the supremacy of British arms, Braddock knew he was racing against time. Fragmentary reports had poured into Alexandria from the frontier that the French garrison at Fort Duquesne and the other French military outposts would be reinforced as soon as the spring thaws came. British intelligence in Quebec was an amateur affair and far from perfect. (Braddock evinced little apparent interest in gathering military intelligence.) One O'Conner, a British subaltern officer, was hanged as a spy at Quebec in the spring of 1755. Three others shared his end, and on May 1 two more British spies were to be executed in Canada.[22] The latter two agents had in their respective pockets a list of all the cannon cast at Quebec or imported there since 1752 and of all the major fortifications along the St. Lawrence, as well as sketches of the artillery batteries of New France. Despite the loss of these spies, Braddock knew that hundreds of canoes were poised at Montreal to descend the rivers with thousands of French soldiers and Indians with the coming of spring. In effect, Braddock knew that he hadn't a moment to lose.

Chapter Nine

The Carlyle House Congress

The expedition's days at Alexandria were occupied not only by grand parades, unlading of stores, and a race against time but also by the necessity of high politics. Indeed, politics were one of the primary reasons Braddock tarried so long in Alexandria. One of his first objectives on landing in the New World was to convene a summit of the colonial governors to endorse and provide material support to the expedition, consistent with his orders from the Duke of Cumberland and the king. On Thursday April 3, just a week after arriving at Alexandria, Braddock, Sharpe, Dinwiddie, and Keppel traveled to Annapolis for a prearranged meeting with three governors–William Shirley of Massachusetts, James DeLancey of New York, and Robert Hunter Morris of Pennsylvania.[1] Braddock, Keppel, and the two middle colony governors traveled in Dinwiddie's coach. They took the ferry across the Potomac from Alexandria and then drove through Upper Marlboro to Annapolis. Orme, Shirley, and various secretaries and servants accompanied them on horseback. However, a large East Coast snowstorm prevented the other governors from traveling to Annapolis for the meeting, even as Virginia was sweltering under oppressive heat. Braddock and his entourage had no choice but to wait. Braddock refused to allow any of the local gentlemen to be introduced to him in Annapolis, thus earning a reputation for aloofness–"austere and supercilious" behavior.[2] Sharpe entertained the party throughout a long weekend, showing off the greenhouse at his mansion in Annapolis. However, the other governors failed to arrive. Braddock was restless and anxious to conclude the meeting and place his army on the march. By Monday Braddock had had enough. He returned to Alexandria and told Sharpe to bring the missing governors with him to Alexandria as soon as they arrived.

Almost a week later,[3] on April 13, Governor Sharpe of Maryland rode into Alexandria with the three errant governors. Colonel William Johnson, New York's agent for Indian affairs who had long lived among the Indians and was in fact a sachem, accompanied them. They joined Governor Dinwiddie, who was already back in Alexandria with Braddock.

Upon their arrival Braddock convened the first successful pan-colonial conference in American history, the precursor to the Continental Congress that was to meet almost twenty years later.[4] Indeed, the seeds of the issues that led to the later Congress were first sown at Braddock's gathering of the five colonial governors. Months later, Carlyle was to describe it to his brother in England as the "Grandest Congress . . . ever known on this Continent."[5]

The congress met in the large parlor at Carlyle House, starting April 14. The large parlor, with its carved pineapples over its twin doorways, was a fitting venue in which to receive the governors. It was, and is, a room of size and elegance. The paneled walls were highlighted with pier glasses, brackets bearing candelabra and twenty gilt-framed small pictures. The cornices boasted finely carved dentil work alternating with Tudor roses. A Wilton carpet softened the dark wood floor, and a Carlyle family portrait in oil hung over the fireplace faced in gray marble. A coal-burning

The Large Parlor at Carlyle House, scene of the congress of colonial governors convened by General Edward Braddock. (*Erik Kvalsvik*)

grate of brass, as well as a brass fender, and brass-headed fireplace tools provided a gleam and warmth to the high-ceiling room. Typical of colonial Virginia style, a matched set of twelve chairs stood sentinel about the perimeter, with little or no furniture in the middle of the room.

Braddock opened the meeting by reading his letter of authority from the king and his orders for the objectives of the expedition: a common defense fund to be raised by the colonies, recruitment of the Six Nations and their allies to the cause, the appointment of Colonel (later Sir) William Johnson as Commissary or Superintendent of Indian Affairs, a hardening of the garrison at Oswego, New York, and a four-pronged assault on French interests at the Forks of the Ohio, Niagara, Crown Point, and Beauséjour. Braddock proposed that once he seized Fort Duquesne he would

Four of the colonial officials who met at the Carlyle Congress. Clockwise, from top left: Lieutenant Governor Horatio Sharpe of Maryland (*New York Public Library*), Governor James DeLancey of New York (*New York Public Library*), Governor William Shirley of Massachusetts (*Wadsworth Atheneum*), and Governor Robert Hunter Morris of Pennsylvania (*Library of Congress*).

march north to Niagara to join the Anglo-American force that would already have reduced it, rolling up all the French posts along the way. A garrison of some two hundred Virginia and Maryland provincial troops would remain behind to hold Fort Duquesne. Braddock anticipated an easy, if important, victory at the Forks of the Ohio and looked forward to spending a merry Christmas with Governor Morris at Philadelphia.[6]

Colonel (later Sir) William Johnson was appointed by Braddock as Superintendent of Indian Affairs and commissioned as a major general of provincial forces at the Carlyle House Congress. Johnson would lead the attack on Crown Point. (*Library and Archives Canada*)

The question of a common fund to pay for the expedition was crucial. Secretary of State Sir Thomas Robinson had paved the way by sending a circular letter in late 1754 to the colonial governors proposing a union of the colonies to pay for defense–a military union unlike the earlier abortive political union recommended by the Albany Conference in the summer of 1754. The governors of Virginia, Maryland, and Pennsylvania agreed to bear the expense of any additional works at Fort Duquesne, once it was captured, and to maintain the garrison there, as well as pay for any vessels needed to be constructed on Lake Erie. However, this limited agreement for funding part of the cost of the campaign was all the consensus would allow. The governors objected most strenuously to London's proposal for a common fund to be raised in the colonies to pay for the entire expedition. The colonial legislatures, they argued, would not supply the money. The minutes of the conference stated in stark terms: "The Governors present acquainted his Excellency that *they had severally made application to their respective Assemblies for the establishment of the common fund proposed, but had not been able to prevail upon 'em to agree to it, and gave it as their unanimous opinion that such a Fund can never be established in the Colonies without the aid of Parliament*" (emphasis added).

Only an act of Parliament in London could force the issue. The point was plain: the colonial assemblies, not the royal governors, controlled the issue, and it was their position that they had no authority (at least when it was not convenient for them) to establish the common fund without Parliament in London having ordered it. In light of the Revolutionary rallying cry of "No taxation without representation!" it is ironic that the American provincial assemblies, in which the colonists were represented, declined to tax Americans for the cause and explicitly demanded referral of the question of taxation to the British Parliament in which the colonists were not represented. Thus, early on the Americans set up the issue of taxation without representation by their very own actions.

Beyond the question of the common fund, the governors advised that their respective governments would not even meet His Majesty's expectations in helping to defray the expenses of Braddock's expedition in America unless the king's ministers "compelled" them to do it.[7]

Braddock demurred and complained to his superiors in London of "the necessity of laying a tax upon all His Majesty's domains in America" to reimburse the crown, one of the earliest suggestions of Britain taxing its American colonies.[8]

The governors' reluctance at the Carlyle House conference to fund the expedition was the start of the long-simmering dispute over who was to pay for the British efforts to defend the colonies. Ultimately, the refusal of the Americans to pay–and subsequent heavy borrowing by the British government to fund the war, with a consequential rise in the national debt which Britain wanted the American colonies to help pay off–led to the imposition of extraordinary taxes, including the infamous Stamp Act in 1765, and the revolt of the American colonies. It is therefore perhaps not an exaggeration to say that the American Revolution started at Braddock's congress convened in Major Carlyle's large parlor.

Skeptics of the importance of the Carlyle House conference occasionally dismiss it as not being comparable to the subsequent First Continental Congress because it was a gathering of appointed royal governors rather than an assembly of elected American delegates. The truth is that it was not comparable, but it was a direct precursor. The record of the Carlyle House conference makes clear that the royal governors present were highly sensitive to, and indeed constrained by, their elected colonial American assemblies. One might ask, who elected those assemblies? The answer is the same or similar enfranchised fragment of the populace–white, male property owners–who almost twenty years later elected the colonial assemblies, which in turn chose the delegates to the Continental Congress. Therefore the consensus manifest in the electoral base upon which both the Carlyle House conference and the subsequent Continental Congress posited their positions was essentially the same, and it is hard to discern how the opinions expressed at the First Continental Congress were more "democratically derived" than those at the Carlyle House conference by royal governors listening to, and conveying the will of, their elected assemblies. The Carlyle House conference of course had a narrower geographic base than the subsequent First Continental Congress in that only five colonies participated. Nonetheless, there can be little question that it was a predecessor to the later Continental Congress and that it framed the issues that were to rend the Anglo-American political fabric over the ensuing twenty-odd years.

In addition to discord over funding at the conference, there were disputes over military strategy. The northern governors argued for attacking Niagara and the northern outposts first. They thought the projected march across the mountains to Fort Duquesne too risky. They also suspected some plumping by Virginia and the Ohio Company as responsible for setting this strategy. However, the plan to take Fort Duquesne first won out. Braddock's orders from London were clear on the primacy of seizing the Ohio.

In contrast, there was agreement on the strengthening of Oswego to contain the French. Braddock, on the recommendation of the congress, appointed Governor Shirley a major general and gave him responsibility for taking Niagara and strengthening Oswego. He would command two newly raised American regiments, Shirley's and Pepperell's (also known as the 50th and 51st Regiments). In addition, the congress ordered two small warships of sixty tons each to be built and launched on Lake Ontario to defend Oswego, with the expense and direction to be borne by Massachusetts under Governor Shirley. The vessels were ultimately completed in September 1755 at a cost of £22,000.

Colonel Johnson was given command of the Crown Point expedition and responsibility for the mission to the Six Nations on which its success would depend. Johnson at first declined the mission on the grounds that the English had reneged on promises made to these Indians in 1746 and that he did not want to be placed in the position of further deceiving them. However, Braddock prevailed upon Johnson to accept the mission and set straight the dealings with the Six Nations. He prepared a commission appointing Johnson as the sole commissioner for Indian affairs in deference to the Six Nations' uneasiness with the duplicitous commissioners of Indian affairs at Albany. Braddock, who had hitherto paid scant attention to the Indians, advanced £2,000 for gifts to the Indians and ordered two speeches prepared in his name seeking their alliance.

The speeches were exemplars of fair dealing. In them Braddock explained that His Majesty had sent a very considerable body of troops to drive the French from the encroachments that they had from time to time made on his dominions and on their lands and hunting grounds which, by a treaty of 1726, the English had taken in trust to guarantee for the use and benefit of the Indians. His Majesty had invested him with the supreme command upon the continent, with orders to strengthen and confirm the amity which had so long existed between them and the English. Although distance made it impossible for Braddock to meet personally with them, he had appointed Johnson as his representative to meet with them and conclude the strictest and most-lasting treaty of friendship and alliance. The general would confirm and ratify all promises made by Johnson. Braddock in turn instructed Johnson to take special care in all meetings and agreements with the Indians to have in view His Majesty's honor, service, and interest and to report fully and frequently to Braddock personally on his mission.[9]

Finally, a regular officer, Lieutenant Colonel Robert Monckton, was charged with leading a force of New Englanders in execution of the Beauséjour expedition with the close coordination of Shirley, who had conceived the scheme of removal of the Acadians.

The governors hammered out the details over several days and departed on April 17. The congress was a qualified success. It was the first-ever meeting of colonial governors drawn from all regions of America–southern, middle and New England. It had endorsed the first plan for action on a continental basis. If Braddock and the governors departed with some reservations, that would hardly have been surprising. Braddock had little expectation that the governors would arrive with chests of doubloons to finance his army. The question of funding would have to be referred to London, as indeed it was. Braddock wrote to the Duke of Newcastle in the wake of the congress: "As very little assistance has already been offered me by the provinces and still less is to be expected from them, it is necessary for me to apprise your grace that my contingent account will be much greater than I had persuaded myself, or than, I believe, Your Grace imagines."[10]

What was important was that English America was united behind the military aspects of the expedition and, at long last, had the political will to act. Translating that political commitment into results was to prove an altogether different matter.

The reason was logistics, the most boring of topics for many armchair generals. If truth be known, it also is for field commanders. It makes them grumpy. And no one was getting grumpier than His Excellency General Edward Braddock as he dallied in Alexandria, anxious to move his troops but hindered from doing so by a lack of certain critical cogs in his military machine.

Starting with St. Clair's briefing upon his arrival in Williamsburg, Braddock had come to appreciate that there had occurred a top-to-bottom breakdown of logistics for the expedition. With the collapse of the idea of water-borne transport, there was no choice but to secure wagons to move the army. The shortage of wagons and horses to transport cannon, baggage, and food was particularly acute. The ships from Ireland had brought some sixteen specially constructed wagons for the gunpowder, but far more would be necessary to transport all the supplies of the expedition. Moreover, except for the officers' personal mounts, the expedition had brought no horses on the assumption that they could be procured locally in America. His Excellency's heavy coach, the officers, artillery wagons, cannon carriages, ammunition wagons, food transports, baggage train, and even a rolling blacksmith's forge would require hundreds, if not thousands, of horses. The "indefatigable" St. Clair had scoured the countryside for wagons and horses with little result. Dinwiddie had promised 200 wagons and 2,500 horses, but it was becoming increasingly obvious to Braddock that they were not to be had in Virginia.

Governor Sharpe of Maryland, who had come to Alexandria to escort Braddock to the abortive meeting at Annapolis, suggested that Braddock split his command and send some of his troops with their baggage and supplies across the Potomac and northward through Maryland to Fort Cumberland. Sharpe was confident that the Maryland farmers would rally with the wagons and horses that the Virginians had so far failed to deliver. This alternative coincided with the efforts of St. Clair to cut various roads to Fort Cumberland, including one from Shippensburg, Pennsylvania, to intersect Braddock's likely route near the "Turkey's Foot" of the Youghiogheny River in Pennsylvania and another, less documented wagon road that he was cutting on the Maryland side of the Potomac.[11]

Advocates of a purely Virginia route, no doubt hoping to blaze a Virginia road to the West, were critical. Washington wrote to William Fairfax in early May: "You will naturally conclude that to pass through Maryl'd (when no business required it) was an uncommon and extraordinary route for the Genl and Colo. Dunbar's Regiment to this place; . . . the reason, however, was obvious to say that those who promoted it had rather have the communication should be that way than through Virginia."[12]

Nonetheless, Braddock, who was concerned about procuring wagons and horses, listened to Sharpe. Thus, as early as March 28 St. Clair ordered that "a proper person of the Artillery should be sent to Rock Creek to receive the stores sent thither by water and lodge them in the storehouses provided by Mr. Beal, that he is to see these stores loaded on waggons for Conogogee," with eventual transport to Fort Cumberland.[13] The stage was being set for two separate routes to Fort Cumberland and the first of two instances when Braddock would divide his command.

That Braddock was to accompany part of the troops through Maryland while the remainder were to march through Virginia was recognized throughout the command, if only begrudgingly by the Virginia contingent, as evidenced by a letter that St. Clair wrote Braddock on April 6 from Winchester, where he had gone to arrange wagons and transportation of the artillery. St. Clair submitted to Braddock "the disposition for advancing the troops to Will's Creek" and promised to "make your stay at Frederick [Maryland] as short as I can." However, logistical problems, as always, continued to plague St. Clair: "I need not jolt your Excellency's mind, that money is wanting for every thing, if nothing else can be done, paper money or Maryland must be had otherwise . . . our carriages will be at a stop. Please send up as much as is to be had of it."[14]

At the same time that Braddock was working to build a consensus of support for the expedition among the colonial governors with the congress at Carlyle House, St. Clair had struck out for Winchester and Fort Cumberland. His mission was to complete the cutting of an alternative road from Winchester to Fort Cumberland and to secure more wagons, confirm that floats had been arranged for the various river crossings that the troops would encounter, and generally try to arrange for forage and other provisions along the route of march. It was a frustrating mission. On April 13, St. Clair wrote from his camp on the Cacapon:

> I am now to inform you that 53 waggons are immediately wanted to be at Alexandria and 24 teams of horses

> with their harness' besides the 34 teams of horses I ordered Mr. Dick to send down. I would not have the country people plead that they have then ground to plough, this service of the King and country, must be first done.
>
> You are therefore to warn all the waggoners in the country for his majesty's service. . . . Should any one of the inhabitants refuse to go on this service you are to let me know their names that I may apply to Sir Peter Halkett for a Detachment of our soldiers to be Quartered on them, and you may take my word for it that if these people do not go on this service with their Waggons and horses I shall convince them that they had better drawn up our Artillery gratis from Alexandria and been yoaked in place of their horses.[15]

A subsequent order that St. Clair wrote eight days later confirmed that his threat to quarter troops with the Americans without paying was not a one-time pique of anger: "in case the inhabitants refuse to go on this service for the safety of the country, you are to apply to Lieut. Richard Baily of Sir Peter Halkett's Regiment . . . who will send partys of his troops to be quartered on the inhabitants at free cost for their disobedience to his Majesty's orders delivered to them by me."[16]

It is not known whether St. Clair made good on this threat, although it was consistent with the king's orders to Braddock which expressly vested Braddock with discretionary judgment on quartering of troops. In any event, St. Clair's threat was the first mention of the practice of quartering occupying troops with the inhabitants of America that was to prove so hateful that it became an article of indictment of the king in the Declaration of Independence twenty-one years later.

After traveling the rough and bumpy road north from Winchester, St. Clair arrived at Fort Cumberland on April 16. Promised provisions had not arrived, and, as before, the hoped-for wagons were nonexistent. A delegation of Pennsylvania commissioners, led by that colony's foremost Indian trader and frontiersman, George Croghan, met St. Clair at the fort. They had come to discuss the cutting of a road in support of the expedition from Carlisle to the Youghiogheny at the direction of Governor Morris of Pennsylvania. Instead of gratitude for this long-belated offer of support from the reluctant Quaker state, St. Clair, in the words of Croghan, "stormed like a lion rampant." Reporting the scene to Governor Morris, Croghan described the tirade:

> He said our commission to lay out the road should have been issued in January last upon his first letter, that doing it now is doing of nothing, that the troops must march on the first of May, that the want of this road and the provisions promised by Pennsylvania has retarded the expedition, which may cost them their lives because of the fresh numbers of French that's suddenly like to be poured into the country; that instead of marching to the Ohio he would in nine days march his army into Cumberland county to cut the roads, press horses, wagons, &c; that he would not suffer a soldier to handle an axe, but by fire and sword oblige the inhabitants to do it, and take every man that refused to the Ohio as he had yesterday some of the Virginians; that he would kill all kind of cattle and carry away the horses, burn the houses &c and that if the French defeated them by the delays of this province he would with his sword drawn pass through the province and treat the inhabitants as a parcel of traitors to his Master; that he would tomorrow write to England by a man-of-war, shake Mr. Penn's proprietaryship, and represent Pennsylvania as a disaffected province; that he would not stop to impress our assembly his hands were not tyed, and that we should find, ordering us to take these precautions and instantly publish them to our governor and assembly, telling us he did not value anything they did or

> resolved, seeing they were dilatory, retarded the march of troops and hand an arse (as he phrased it) on this occasion, and told us to go to the General if we pleased, who would give us ten bad words for one that he had given.[17]

The Pennsylvanians tried to reason with St. Clair but to no avail. At the same time that St. Clair lashed out at the Americans, he sent up a plea to his fellow officer Halkett for assistance in the form of additional troops:

> Last night I arrived at this place. . . . I found every thing in the situation I left it in, that is to say not any one thing done which I had ordered and what is worse, the Pennsylvanians have disappointed us in cutting their roads and sending us their flour.
>
> I am able to do but little without some of your regiment at this place. . . . You see Dear Sir Peter in what a dismal situation I am, which you can only remedy.[18]

The eventual solution to the logistical problem posed by the lack of wagons and teams was to come from a most unexpected source later in the campaign but not before St. Clair's words and demeanor had reverberated throughout the colonies.[19]

Meanwhile Braddock began preparations to break camp at Alexandria and move out. He was anxious to have his army take the field by May 10. With the congress of the governors over, there was little reason to stay in Alexandria. Forage for such horses as the expedition had was beginning to become available. The problem of the wagons and additional horses would have to be dealt with along the way. Braddock wanted his army on the march.

The rotating guard for the general was taken off, and a sergeant and twelve men from Dunbar's regiment were mounted as his baggage guard and ordered to march with it. The sick men of the two regiments were ordered left in the hospital at Alexandria with a small detachment of guards. Braddock appointed two officers and forty men from Halkett's regiment to assume responsibility for mounting the "Town Guard." However, even as the troops were preparing to move, drunkenness remained rife. Orders for Sunday, April 20, included the following admonition: "Any Soldrs that shall be found selling Liquors to any of the Rest of the men will be severely punished. Any Solders Wife that shall be detected in the same shall likewise be punished & Drummed out of the Camp."[20]

On April 19, the day before he left, Braddock penned a long letter to Sir Robert Napier in which he reported on his arrangements. In addition to complaining about the lack of support from the colonial governments, he explained his decision to divide his command: "I shall set out tomorrow for Frederick in my way to Fort Cumberland at Wills's Creek, where I shall join the two Columns which are now upon their March at about fifty Miles distance. This Disposition I was oblig'd to make for the Conveniency of Horses and Waggons, by which means I employ those of Maryland which would not be prevail'd upon to cross the Potomack."

Braddock continued thoughtfully in the vein of an inveterate micromanager:

> I am impatient to begin my March over the Mountains which in my last I told you were fifteen Miles over, tho' I now know them to be between sixty and seventy. . . . As I have and shall find it often necessary to oblige the Men to take with them seven or eight days provisions, it being frequently impossible to supply them by the great distance from one Magazine to another, in order to enable them to carry any Weight I have lighten'd them as much as possible, and have left in store their Swords and the greatest part of their heavy Accoutrements. I have also made a Regulation which I think will be of great Advantage in posting every Officer in time of Service to his own Company and ordering the oldest Battalion

> Company to act as Second Grenadier Company upon the left. . . . I was induc'd to make this Regulation on account of the additional Recruits that the Officers and Men might know one another, which by Companies they might easily do, but by Battalion scarcely possible; and in case of Alarm the Men and Officers will know their respective Post sooner than by the usual Method.[21]

Braddock quietly slipped out of town on April 20 with his military family accompanied by a guard of mounted troops of Virginia militia led by Major Adam Stephen. His stay at Alexandria had lasted almost a month. No doubt Major Carlyle and much of the local gentry were glad to see him go, even as they hoped desperately for the success of his mission.

Braddock departed without the fanfare that had greeted his arrival. However, tradition has it that before leaving he stopped at the door of Carlyle House to say good-bye to a female slave named Penny. The upbeat Braddock, much buoyed at being finally under way and his mind already on the victory ahead, teased her: "You are only a Penny now but I hope on my return you will be two pence."[22] And with that he entered his coach and rumbled off.

CHAPTER TEN

The Maryland March

BRADDOCK'S MARCH IN FACT BEGAN long before His Excellency and his band left Alexandria. It moved in stages, along two distinct routes. The first stage involved the securing of a storage depot at the mouth of Rock Creek, just south of Georgetown in Maryland, and the advance of Dunbar's 48th Regiment, and ultimately Braddock, from that place north to Frederick, Maryland. From there Dunbar's Regiment would make its way across Maryland to Fort Cumberland, which would be the final staging point before plunging into the wilderness. Braddock's entourage would leave Frederick separately, making a stop in Winchester for a planned meeting with Indian leaders. The other route through Virginia which Halkett's 44th and the artillery took, was from Alexandria westward toward Winchester and then north to Fort Cumberland.

In those days, before the narrowing of its mouth to accommodate the Chesapeake & Ohio Canal in the nineteenth century, Rock Creek was navigable for at least a short distance inland, and ships would enter it to dock and unload their wares. Captain John

Smith had explored it on his 1608 voyage up the Chesapeake. The land at the intersection of Rock Creek and the Potomac was home to tobacco warehouses owned by the Beall and Gordon families, prominent Georgetown merchants from Scotland. Not far from the intersection stood a large outcropping of rock which jutted into the river and was known as a local landmark to all who sailed upriver. The land between the mouth of Rock Creek and this rock, which later came to be known as Braddock's Rock, was the staging area for the northern column of Braddock's army.[1]

On Friday, April 11, while Braddock was awaiting the arrival of the colonial governors at Alexandria, Dunbar's 48th Regiment was put on notice to prepare to march but advised to await further orders. The next day Braddock ordered the regiment to march from Alexandria to Analostan Island (today's Theodore Roosevelt Island) in the Potomac from which a ferry ran to Georgetown. Boats from the two frigates *Seahorse* and *Nightingale*, as well as pressed civilian vessels, moved up from Alexandria under Spendelow's seamen to carry the men and supplies across the river, about three hundred yards wide, to Rock Creek. One soldier was drowned when a boat overturned. Otherwise the maneuver went smoothly, with all remaining men and supplies safely landed on the Maryland side.

Dunbar's 48th Regiment spent the weekend of April 12–13 at Rock Creek, a "pleasant situation," according to one of Spendelow's seamen. They loaded the regimental stores into wagons and paused for divine service on Sunday. One officer and thirty men of Dunbar's 48th were ordered to remain at Rock Creek to load and dispatch wagons "as fast as they came in." However, the bulk of Dunbar's regiment and the seamen commenced their march to Frederick at six the morning of Monday, April 14. With the sailors in the lead, the column headed up High Street, today's Wisconsin Avenue, in Georgetown to River Road and thence about fifteen miles to Owen's Ordinary in present-day Rockville, Maryland. Arriving at two in the afternoon, a seaman who kept a journal found it "very dirty."[2]

However, dirt was to prove to be the least of the troops' problems. Breaking camp at five the next morning, the column marched fifteen miles to Dowden's Ordinary, where they encamped upon "very bad ground" on the side of a hill. Pitching their tents as darkness fell, the wind shifted from south to north, and the weather changed from a "sultry hot day" to "excessively cold," with rain, thunder, and lightning until five in the morning and then, in the wee hours, snow–a foot and a half of snow in two hours. The men arose to beat the snow off their tents for fear it would break the tent poles.[3] Because of the snow and the standard practice of resting every third day while on the march, Dunbar ordered a halt for Wednesday, April 16. However, the situation was miserable. The seaman recorded it as "a terrible place, for we could neither get provisions for ourselves, nor fodder for our horses, and as it was wet in the Camp it was very disagreeable, and no house to go into."[4]

A plaque marks Braddock's Rock, near Rock Creek, Washington, DC, the staging area for the northern column of Braddock's army. (*NOAA*)

The next morning, Thursday the seventeenth, Dunbar resumed the march at six. After proceeding eleven miles the column came to the Monocacy River. Following the rain and snow, the river was swollen and fast-running. Spendelow's sailors rigged a float to ferry the army over. By three in the afternoon, the troops arrived on the outskirts of Frederick, a prosperous market town in a fertile valley populated by English and German settlers. The seaman noted that while their quarters were "very indifferent," the town of Frederick "had not been settled above 7 years, and there are about 200 houses and 2 churches, one English, one Dutch [German]; the inhabitants, chiefly Dutch, are industrious but imposing people: here we got plenty of provisions and forage." The batman judged it "a Pleasant fine Cuntry."[5]

On Friday April 18 the troops settled into an encampment on the north side of town, pitching their tents "upon good ground." The men rested over the weekend. The snow had melted, and the weather turned "very hot in the day," but the nights were "unwholesome, occasioned by heavy dews." The camp quickly settled into the normal pattern of regimental life: the men received two days' provisions and forage, and the officers whipped four men two hundred lashes apiece, one for desertion and three for drunkenness.[6]

Pursuant to Braddock's orders, Dunbar dispatched one company of Grenadiers to Conococheague to hold the crossing of the Potomac at that place and assist in forwarding stores from there to Fort Cumberland. Conococheague or present-day Williamsport, Maryland, is located at the intersection of Conococheague Creek and the Potomac River. It afforded a shallow crossing of the Potomac and had long been used as a crossing by the Great Philadelphia Wagon Road to the Shenandoah Valley of Virginia. (St. Clair's plan was to move the artillery stores to Conococheague and then transport them by floats on to Fort Cumberland.) Ten days later Braddock reinforced this detachment with a "covering party" under Captain Horatio Gates.[7]

Meanwhile, following in Dunbar's footsteps, Braddock had departed Alexandria on Sunday, April 20, for Georgetown, where the local merchants feted him with a banquet. His Excellency was apparently as glad to leave Alexandria as its residents were happy to have him go. Following his stop in Georgetown, Braddock wrote a letter to an unknown lady, probably George Anne Bellamy, which implicitly drew an invidious comparison between the two neighboring towns:

> We folks at home have been laboring under the very erroneous idea that our friends in America were little better than aborigines, whom they supplanted, but, my dear

> madam, we have all been in error, for never have I attended a more complete banquet, or met better dressed or better mannered people that I met on my arrival in George Town, which is named after our gracious majesty. The men are very large and gallant, while the ladies are the most beautiful that my eyes have never looked upon. Indeed, madam, I know of no English town that could produce so much beauty and gallantry as I have found in George Town. The habitations of these genial folk, dear madam, are stately buildings that have no superiors in England, and the interior decorations are things of beauty, while the gardens are laid out after our English gardens, and the shrubbery and flowers are well attended to. In fact, dear madam, I might sum up everything by declaring George Town is indescribably lovely. I am loath to leave it and its hospitable people.[8]

Braddock posted the letter with one of the naval ships that lay docked at Georgetown harbor, his last direct link with England.

Continuing his journey into Frederick the next day, Braddock and his entourage arrived about noon and proceeded to a stone tavern in town that had been reserved for his headquarters. The reports that awaited the general were not good. The troops were in "great want of provision, no cattle was laid in there."[9]

Governor Sharpe rejoined Braddock at Frederick and was obliged to report that the wagons and horses he had promised–the entire purpose of the diversion through Maryland–had not materialized. What is more, he acknowledged that he did not have the authority as governor to commandeer them. St. Clair came in from Fort Cumberland and brought similarly disappointing news about the state of provisioning there. Long-promised flour from Pennsylvania had failed to arrive at Conococheague. The land abounded in German settlers who wanted to avoid the English army. There were no more wagons to be had. As it was, St. Clair was shuttling wagons back and forth between Rock

Creek and Conococheague, making double and even triple duty of the few that he had. At that rate, it would take months to move the supplies. However, once in Frederick, Dunbar and Braddock discovered that there was no road across Maryland to Fort Cumberland. Therefore Dunbar and the 48th Regiment would have to march west to Conococheague and re-cross the Potomac River there and head back into Virginia.[10] Focusing on what he could influence, Braddock ordered his commissaries out into the countryside to buy cattle, which were relatively plentiful in the vicinity. Wagons were another matter. Braddock dispatched his staff officers into the countryside to show local authorities his orders from the king, which empowered him to impress wagons for transport. But there simply were no wagons to impress. An increasingly depressed and desperate Braddock sighed about "This drear and desolate country."[11]

Enter Benjamin Franklin. The dome-headed Deputy Postmaster General of the American colonies whose smiling lips dripped aphorisms had come to Frederick to arrange a series of postal relays for Braddock's reports back to Philadelphia, Williamsburg, and Annapolis and for the army's letters to England. The forty-nine-year-old Franklin was accompanied by his illegitimate son William (later to become a high Tory and last royal governor of New Jersey). Braddock was probably not fully aware of the elder Franklin's growing reputation as a scientist and colonial diplomat–only three years before, Franklin had flown his famous kite. He was almost certainly unaware of Franklin's secret mission as envoy from the Pennsylvania Assembly to smooth out relations with His Excellency. The Assembly had grown increasingly concerned about the criticism of Pennsylvania emanating from Braddock and his staff and had sent Franklin to meet with the general not just to arrange postal matters but also to defuse the disfavor in which it now found itself.

Franklin had access to Braddock and his staff while in Frederick, dining with the general, Dunbar, and others. In Franklin's own words, he "had full opportunity of removing all his prejudices, by the information of what the Assembly had before his arrival actually done and were still willing to do to facilitate his operations."[12]

Having, in his view, accomplished his mission, Franklin was about to depart for Philadelphia when Braddock's staff entered the headquarters to report on their failure to secure additional wagons. Franklin described the scene thus in his *Autobiography:*

Robert Feke's 1746 portrait of Benjamin Franklin. (*Harvard Art Museum*)

> The General and all the officers were surprised, declared the expedition was then at an end, being impossible, and exclaimed against the ministers for ignorantly landing them in a country destitute of the means of conveying their stores, baggage, etc., not less than one hundred and fifty wagons being necessary.
>
> I happened to say I thought it was a pity they had not landed rather in Pennsylvania, as in that country almost every farmer had his own wagon.
>
> "Then you, sir," Braddock replied, "who are a man of interest there, can probably procure them for us, and I beg you will undertake it." Franklin immediately agreed and asked Braddock what terms to offer the Pennsylvania farmers. Braddock said it was up to Franklin, and he gave him eight hundred pounds for advance payments.[13]

Franklin continued his dialogue with Braddock, discussing tactics after disposing of the issue of the wagons. Braddock outlined his plans for marching to Niagara after taking Fort Duquesne. Franklin had a more sober apprehension of the methods of Indian warfare. He told Braddock: "To be sure, sir, if you arrive well before Duquesne, with those fine troops, as well provided with artillery, that place not yet completely fortified, and as we hear with no very strong garrison, can probably make but a short resistance. The only danger I apprehend of obstruction to your march is from ambuscades of Indians, who by constant practice are dexterous in laying and executing them; and the slender line, near four miles long, which your army must make may expose it to be attacked by surprise in its flanks and to be cut like a thread into several pieces which from their distance cannot come up in time to support each other." Braddock "smiled at" Franklin's "ignorance" and smugly retorted that "These savages may, indeed, be a formidable enemy to your raw American militia, but upon the King's regular and disciplined troops, sir, it is impossible they should make any impression."[14]

After Franklin departed from Braddock's headquarters he engaged in a most remarkable ploy that demonstrated that guile and greed played more to the American character than either commands or appeals to patriotism. He composed an advertisement in the form of handbills he ordered printed at Lancaster, Pennsylvania, for distribution throughout the colony. The notice consisted of two parts: a statement of the terms for hiring the wagons and a letter from Franklin explaining why the wagons were needed. Pennsylvania newspapers dutifully picked up and printed the advertisements in both English and German with the date of April 26, 1755. The advertisements, signed in Franklin's name, promised the handsome sum of fifteen shillings a day for a wagon with four good horses and a driver and two shillings per day for each packhorse, starting at such time as they joined Braddock's expedition at Fort Cumberland, no later than May 10 and with seven days' pay promised in advance. It was a sweet deal. "The service will be light and easy, for the Army will scarce march above twelve miles per day," Franklin lied in the advertisements.

However, the notices also contained a thinly veiled threat: "If you do not this service to your King and country voluntarily, when such good pay and reasonable terms are offered you, your loyalty will be strongly suspected. The King's business must be

There are few surviving Conestoga-type wagons that may have been manufactured in the eighteenth century, and they differ from later versions of Conestoga, most notably in the nearly vertical front end panel and tail gate. This example, the only known complete one, carried a Lancaster, Pennsylvania, family to Ontario, Canada, in 1807. It may be similar to the kind of wagon used in the Braddock expedition. (*Ontario Pioneer Community Foundation*)

done; so many brave troops come so far for your defence must not stand idle, through your backwardness to do what may reasonably be expected from you; waggons and horses must be had; violent measures will probably be used; and you will be able to seek for a recompense where you can find it, and your case, perhaps, be little pitied or regarded."

And then came the corker: "I have no particular interest in this affair, as, except the satisfaction of endeavoring to do good, I shall have only my labor for my pains. If this method of obtaining the waggons and horses is not like to succeed, I am obliged to send word to the General in fourteen days; and I suppose Sir John St. Clair, the hussar, with a body of soldiers, will immediately enter the Province, for the purpose, of which I shall be sorry to hear."[15]

Franklin knew full well that St. Clair was not a "hussar." Indeed no such service existed in the British army at this period. However, word of St. Clair's rantings had preceded him, and the threat of a hussar ravishing the countryside resonated with the

German immigrants in Pennsylvania. "I cannot but honor Franklin for the last clause of his advertisement," laughed Shirley when he saw it.[16] So also had Braddock, who, according to Orme, "laughed for an hour together at it."[17] And "Sir John [St. Clair] himself looked on it as a kind of Compliment, till he heard, that the officers made themselves merry with it; and even now he seems rather to be angry with them than you [Franklin]."[18]

In the event, the wagons poured in from Pennsylvania, and the expedition's problem was solved.[19] The wagons were primarily Conestoga wagons, named after the Conestoga Valley near Lancaster. Unlike Virginia wagons which could be disassembled for carrying over mountains, the Pennsylvania wagons had to be emptied and then pushed or pulled up mountain grades by men and horses. On the descent the wagon was controlled by brakes and drag ropes. Apparently Braddock's expedition was the first time that wheeled vehicles had crossed the Appalachian Mountains.

But this particular piece of service was not the only good deed that Franklin performed at Frederick. While dining with Dunbar he heard of the wants of the young subalterns of the 48th Regiment. Many were not wealthy and had found America to be an expensive place to purchase tea, sugar, and other sundries that would soften the rigors of the field. Working with his son, Franklin concocted a list of parcels sure to warm the heart of the young officers so far from home and arranged for their delivery, courtesy of the Pennsylvania assembly. The package included such delicacies as "loaves of sugar, green tea, chocolate, Gloucester cheeses, Madeira wine, and well-cured hams."[20] It was little wonder that Franklin was one of the few colonials whom Braddock esteemed.

Washington was one of the others, and on April 23, while Braddock was at Frederick, the young Virginian set out from Mount Vernon for Fort Cumberland. He wrote his friend and neighbor William Fairfax that day that he expected to stay "too long" at Fort Cumberland because "the march must be regulated by the slow movements of the Train, which I am sorry to say will be tedious, very tedious indeed, as I have long predicted, tho' few believed."[21]

Embarrassed at his failure to deliver the promised Maryland wagons, at having uselessly diverted Braddock to Frederick, and at having been upstaged by the Pennsylvanian Franklin, Governor Sharpe sought to redeem himself by offering Braddock the use of his sleek chariot, drawn by six horses. Braddock insisted on paying for it and bought the vehicle outright from the governor, together with spare pole and axle tree. His Excellency could now travel in style.

With St. Clair's alternative road now cut, the Opequon Bear Garden bridge completed over the Opequon Creek, a tributary of the Potomac, and floats over the other rivers secured, there was no need to delay further in Frederick. Accordingly, after commissioning a court-martial which sentenced several more men to be whipped for drinking and ordering the 48th to draw Indian corn rations for six days, Braddock directed Dunbar to break camp and march on April 29 to Conococheague and back into Virginia, where they were to head south toward Winchester and then pick up the new road north to Fort Cumberland.[22]

The column struck out northwest from Frederick at six in the morning but not after first jettisoning some of its baggage, including, to their consternation, the seamen's hammocks. The men passed the South Ridge of the Shenandoah Mountains, "very easy in the ascent." That night they camped on "good ground" at one Walker's, eighteen miles from Frederick, in the wilderness near Boonsboro halfway between Frederick and Conococheague. The area is now known as Braddock Heights. The men noted that the area abounded in hares, deer, and partridges.[23] The next day the troops reached the shallow crossing of the Potomac at Conococheague and were ferried across early in the morning on the first of May.

Braddock tarried for several more days at Frederick and then, also on May 1, mounted his new chariot to ride to Winchester, Virginia, for a promised meeting with Indian chiefs that Dinwiddie had arranged.

The incursion of Maryland was over. During this phase of the march the entire expedition had come close to stalling for want of wagons. However, the intervention of one individual–Franklin–turned the situation around. The diversion into Maryland was not wasted motion after all. Luck had proven Braddock right in his decision to strike north because he secured, at long last, the necessary wagons for the march.

Chapter Eleven

The Virginia March

THE PROGRESS OF HALKETT'S COLUMN through Virginia unfolded simultaneously with the march of Braddock through Maryland. Even more than the Maryland march, it was an essay in confusion. Braddock's troops following the Virginia route were neither the first nor the last to experience the ancient military axiom of "hurry up and wait." In this particular case the delays were occasioned by the need for St. Clair to complete the cutting of the new Opequon Bear Garden road through Virginia to Fort Cumberland, erect a bridge over the Opequon, and position floats to ferry the troops over the remaining rivers.

The 44th Regiment thus proceeded north through Virginia to Fort Cumberland in a piecemeal fashion, leaving Alexandria on four separate days.

Six companies of Halkett's 44th first moved out from Alexandria at six in the morning Friday April 11, one day before Dunbar marched to Rock Creek, bound for Winchester, Virginia. They were to wait at Winchester until St. Clair finished cutting the new road. Braddock ordered the soldiers to leave their shoulder belts, waist belts, and hangers (or curved swords) behind and take with them only one spare shirt, one spare pair of stockings, one spare pair of shoes, and "one pair of Brown Gater's." Like the officers, the troops were to travel light. Each man received eight days' provisions. Eight of the precious wagons were allotted for the troops to carry tents and provisions. Lieutenant Colonel Gage stayed with the four remaining companies of the 44th to escort the artillery at a later date. At the same time, Braddock ordered most of the Virginia troops to Winchester. Braddock directed Captain Lewis and his rangers to proceed from there to the Greenbriar River, well into the mountains, to build two stockade forts in order to cover the western settlers from "inroads of the Indians."

Halkett's men broke camp at Alexandria and headed up the road known today as Braddock Road. They ascended a rise then known as Mash Pot Hill, at the base of which today rests a cannon from the expedition.[2] The smart-stepping troops, no doubt elated at finally being under way, quickly came to a fork in the road. The right-hand fork led to Leesburg–the Leesburg Pike–while the left-hand fork was an extension of Braddock Road. Halkett posted a guard at the intersection to direct the troops onto the correct, right-hand road.[3] Braddock ordered the march to follow the precise ninety-seven-mile route that St. Clair had earlier scouted and laid out.[4]

Halkett's first column passed through some of the most pleasant and scenic countryside in Piedmont Virginia, the best part of today's hunt country, but no known record of their adventures on the six-day march to Winchester has been handed down to us. However, the same British officer who had cast such a jaundiced eye on his dinner host and hostess in Alexandria left the following description of the Virginia countryside through which they marched:

> They make here a division between the Settlements and the Woods, though the Settlements are what we should call very woody in Europe. The Face of the Country is

> entirely different from any Thing I ever saw before; the Fields have not the Appearance of what bears the Name in Europe, instead of the ploughed Grounds or Meadows, they are all laid out in Hillocks, each of which bears Tobacco Plants, with Paths hoed between. . . . From the heart of the settlements we are now got into the Cow-Pens, the Keepers of these are a very extraordinary Kind of Fellows. . . . The Keepers live chiefly upon Milk. . . . They also have Flesh in Abundance such as it is, for they eat the old Cows and lean Calves that are like to die. The Cow-Pen Men are hardy People, are almost continually on Horseback, being obliged to know the Haunts of their Cattle. You see, sir, what a wild set of Creatures our English Men grow into when they lose Society.[5]

Such was the land through which Halkett's men marched on their way to Winchester. The ensuing columns would have taken in similar scenes.

At the same time that Dunbar's 48th Regiment was crossing the Potomac from Alexandria to Rock Creek on the Maryland route on Saturday April 12, one of the remaining Halkett companies and part of the artillery moved out toward Winchester in Virginia following the same route as the bulk of the 44th Regiment the day before. By April 13, St. Clair had the satisfaction of reporting that he had almost completed cutting the new road to Opequon Bridge en route to Fort Cumberland and that the artillery and powder wagons should march by that route and not have to detour to Winchester as the companies of foot soldiers.[1] A further company of the 44th accompanying seven wagons of powder left Alexandria on Wednesday April 16. A final detachment of the 44th, led by Lieutenant Colonel Gage and escorting the heavy 12-pounders, 6-pounders, and howitzers, followed suit on April 26.

Meanwhile, Washington had arrived at Winchester from Alexandria by April 30, to judge from his letter of that date to

Sally Fairfax.[6] Washington then turned east and rode toward Frederick, Maryland, to meet up with Braddock. They encountered each other just as Braddock was departing Frederick. Braddock and Washington crossed from Maryland into Virginia at Swearingen's Ferry (now Shepherdstown, West Virginia), somewhat south on the Potomac River from Conococheague. From there they proceeded to the Widow Barringer's and ultimately Winchester. Washington noted on May 4: "In company with Braddock arrived at Winchester," where the latter had come to meet with Dinwiddie's Indian chiefs.[7]

The Indians did not show, and Braddock spent four increasingly hot days fruitlessly waiting for them and fulminating against Dinwiddie. Winchester was a rude Scots-Irish frontier town of at most fifty log houses. It was decidedly not to His Excellency's taste. However, Washington was in heaven. He wrote from Winchester to his mother: "I am very happy in the General's family, and I am treated with a complaisant freedom which is quite agreeable."[8]

The movements of the various columns of the army across the Virginia frontier are clouded in mystery and confusion. As best as can be reconstructed, the first six companies of Halkett's regiment encamped near Winchester but did not linger long. The remaining companies, plus the artillery, marched toward Winchester but apparently avoided the town at St. Clair's direction.

Dunbar and the 48th Regiment crossed from Maryland at Conococheague, marched some sixteen miles along "very indifferent" roads, to quote the seaman,[9] to John Evans's (at Big Springs, just south of present-day Martinsburg, West Virginia) and then eighteen miles to the Widow Barringer's where the Great Philadelphia Wagon Road entered Virginia just north of Winchester.[10] At the Widow Barringer's the men received two days' provisions and the commanders drummed a woman out of the camp, probably for selling liquor. The weather had now turned so "excessively hot" that some officers and men were not able to get under way until the evening.[11]

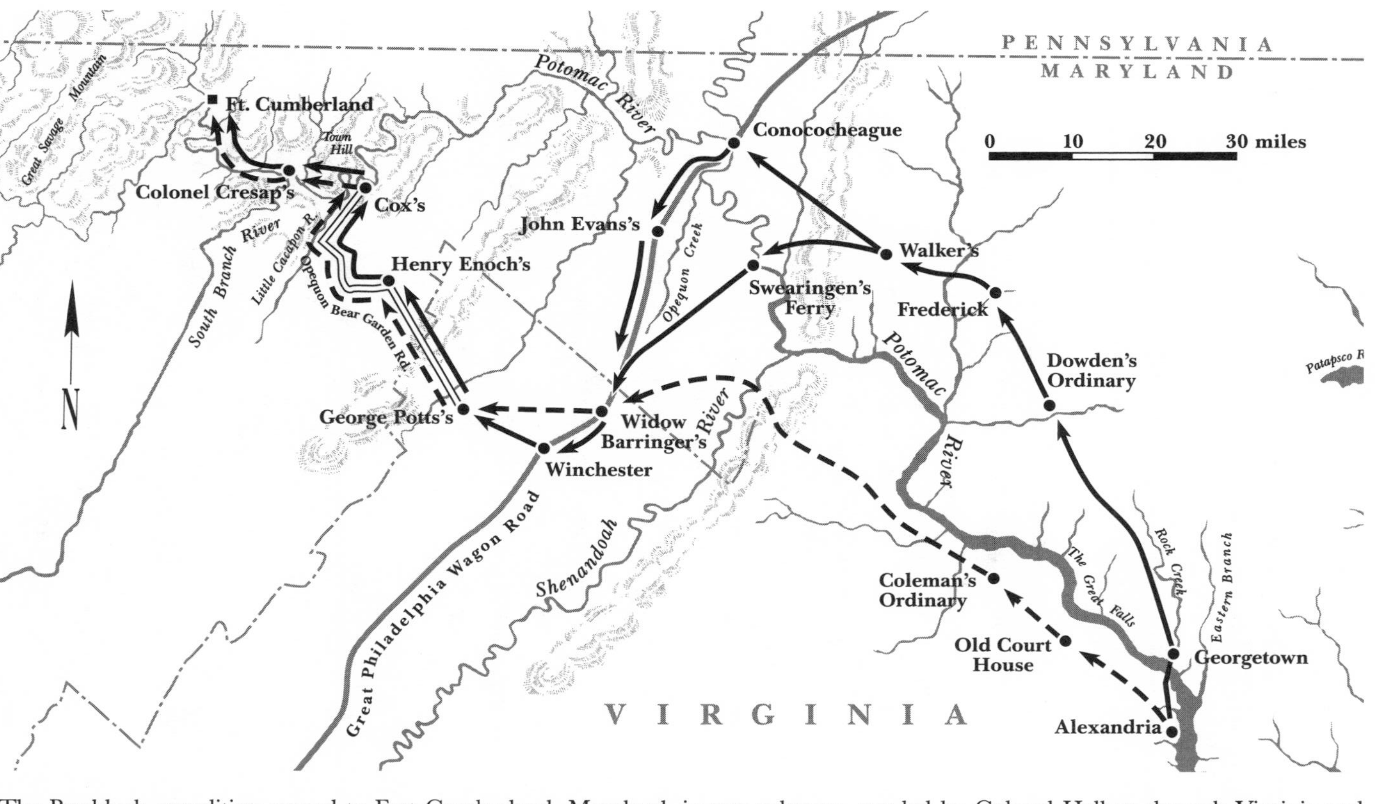

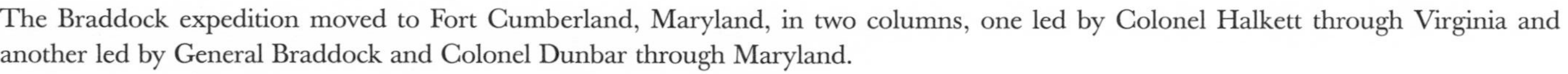
The Braddock expedition moved to Fort Cumberland, Maryland, in two columns, one led by Colonel Halkett through Virginia and another led by General Braddock and Colonel Dunbar through Maryland.

Dunbar would next have turned due west nine more miles to George Potts's and at that point taken off on the new Opequon Bear Garden road cut by St. Clair on which Halkett and the artillery would have by then preceded him. The Opequon Bear Garden road that St. Clair cut linked a series of clear way stations as it moved west and north from Winchester: from George Potts's to Henry Enoch's fifteen miles; to Cox's at the mouth of the Little Cacapon twelve miles; to Colonel Cresap's eight miles; to Fort Cumberland sixteen miles.

The names and distances do little to convey the roughness of the terrain or the uncertainty of proceeding through a country that was thinly settled and wild. It was to be the soldiers' first foretaste of the wilderness and was to leave a lasting impression on the men. St. Clair had arranged for provisions at some of the stops and oats or Indian corn for the horses. The seaman described the road to Potts's Camp as "very bad" but noted with interest the presence of wild turkeys along the way. At night the wind shifted and blew hard out of the northwest. No fires were allowed "within a Considerable distance of the Artillery on any Acct."[12] The road the next day to Enoch's led over "prodigious mountains" and across the same stream (Bloomery Run) twenty times within a distance of three miles. It rained all night and morning, and the wet tents made the baggage heavy. At a ford of the Cacapon, Dunbar's men found a company of Halkett's 44th encamped and waiting to escort the artillery train to Fort Cumberland.[13]

On May 6 Dunbar's troops halted at Enoch's for a day of rest, it being a third marching day. The officers passed the time with horse races, agreeing that no horse should run that was over eleven hands or carry a rider over fourteen stone.[14] Orme was later to reminisce in a letter to George Washington about their shared rough accommodations at Enoch's.

May 7 was more of the same as they marched to Cox's from Enoch's. The morning was very cold, but by ten o'clock, recorded the seaman, it was "prodigiously hot." They crossed another run of water nineteen times in two miles.[15] Braddock in his chariot, with his entourage and Washington leading a Virginia troop of light horse as escort, departed Winchester along the same road this day, well behind Halkett and Dunbar. Others ultimately followed, including the nurse Charlotte Browne. As Major Carlyle had aptly observed, the army marched with "the greatest Parade & Negligence" to Fort Cumberland.

Several men died from bites by poisonous snakes which abounded in the rivers and swamps along the line of march. In addition, a "Kind of tick or Forest Bug, which gets into the Legs and occasions Inflammations and Ulcers," began to play havoc with the soldiers, who itched so that they were "ready to tear off the Flesh." One unfortunate had to have his leg amputated because of a resulting infection. For lack of ovens, the men had to bake their bread in holes in the ground, which left it filled with dirt and grit. "We have nothing round us but Trees, Swamps, and Thickets," complained the unidentified British officer with the jaundiced eye. "I cannot conceive how War can be made in such a Country, there has not been Ground to form a Battalion since we left the Inhabitants."[16]

But snakes, chiggers, bad bread, and thickets were not the only problems. The men were on the verge of mutiny. A British officer wrote in confidence on May 8 to a friend in England:

> The mutinous Spirit of the men encreases but we will get the better of that, we will see which will be tried first, they of deserving punishments, or we of inflicting them, I cannot but say the very Face of the Country is enough to strike a Damp in the most resolute Mind; that Fatigues and Wants we suffer . . . are enough to dispirit common Men; for should I blame them for being low spirited, but they are mutinous, and this came from a higher Spring than the Hardships here, for they were tainted in Ireland . . . who, tho' they are Englishmen, yet are not the less stubborn and mutinous for that. They have the

> Impudence to pretend to judge of and blame every Step, not only on the Officers, but of the Ministry. They, every now and then, in their defence say they are free Englishmen, and Protestants, and are not obliged to obey Orders if they are not fed with Bread, and paid with Money; now there is often only Bills to pay them with, and no Bread but Indian Corn. In fine, in Europe they were better fed than taught; now they must be better taught than fed. Indeed the Officers are as ill off about food as they, the General himself, who understands good eating as well as any Man, cannot find wherewithal to make a tolerable Dinner of, tho' he hath got two good Cooks who could make an excellent Ragout out of a pair of boots, had they but Material to toss them up with.[17]
>
> In fact, in their own way, the officers themselves were beginning to slip into a fractious, if not mutinous spirit. However, for now, their only option was to get their men through this difficult phase of the march.

The topography through which the men marched on the new road crossed several mountains, including Bear Garden Mountain at one thousand feet and Cooper Mountain at fifteen hundred feet. The latter afforded a sweeping vista to the west that must have awed the men with their first glimpse of the American wilderness. Despite the definite tincture of wilderness and the roughness of the new road,[18] the scenes were not without beauty. Redbud would have been in bloom, softening the mountainsides with their sweet flower. The locusts, sycamores, willows, and occasional oak that blanketed the area would also have been sprouting. The purplish rocks of the Little Cacapon would have been visible in the hot, dry weather and not hidden by the spring freshets that normally coursed through the mountains at this time of year. Turning north toward the Potomac, the men entered a long narrow valley, today's South Branch Valley, remarkable for its fertile land and guarded at its northern exit by a barefaced rock mountain. The road led on to a further pleasant valley, known today as Corduroy Hollow in distant memory of St. Clair's corduroy road that ran from Cox's to Colonel Cresap's.

Colonel Thomas Cresap was a singular character of the frontier. He and his son Michael maintained a trading post with the Indians on the Maryland side of the Potomac at a crossing of the river known as Old Town or Shawnee Old Town. The crossing had been used since time immemorial by Indian war parties heading south and east. Cresap's establishment at the strategic junction was a log building fortified with a stockade.[19] The Indians called Cresap "Big Spoon" because of his largesse. The English called him a "rattlesnake colonel" and a "rascal."[20]

There was little question that Cresap was indeed a frontier rascal. He was a member of the Ohio Company, had helped provision Washington's 1754 expedition, and had been appointed an agent to help supply the commissary for Braddock's expedition. However, he provided spoiled meat which had to be destroyed when the barrels were opened, and his son, who had charge of a storehouse at Conococheague, had failed to fill wagons with promised provisions when they loaded at that location. These derelictions caused a serious shortage of food and required Braddock on May 27 to send two special expeditions of thirty precious wagons and three hundred horses back from Fort Cumberland to Winchester and Conococheague, respectively, over the rough roads, to obtain beef and flour. He also fired the elder Cresap and tried to arrest him, but he fled. However, these developments had not yet unfolded when the various elements of Braddock's army passed his way. The advancing columns were ferried north across the Potomac at Old Town and camped at Cresap's stockade as their final stop on a rainy May 8 before reaching Fort Cumberland. Braddock himself spent the night there May 9.

The march to Fort Cumberland was almost over. The march from Cresap's to Fort Cumberland was a mere fifteen miles along the bank of the river. To the west, on the approach to the fort a series of humped mountains undulated like a serpent. The Blue Valley led to the confluence of the Potomac River and Wills Creek. The fort perched atop a hill placed in the nips and folds of the mountains, whose tops were wreathed in haze even on a clear day. The men may not have realized it, but this–not the Opequon Bear Garden road–was the beginning of the true wilderness.

The columns straggled in along the river on the morning of May 10. Dunbar's men paused to rest. Braddock, who had made a late start, caught up with the troops at high noon as they lounged by the roadside. The men of the 48th snapped to attention, and their drummers beat the Grenadiers' March as the General approached. In an instant the mounted escort led by Adam Stephen and George Washington trotted by, followed by the great chariot with His Excellency moving at a roaring pace. In a cloud of dirt and dust they disappeared down the road. One hour later Dunbar's men heard the boom of a seventeen-gun salute as the general entered the fort.[21] Tradition has it that Braddock, much an admirer of John Churchill the Duke of Marlborough, wore an armored breastplate like his hero as he rode in his chariot.[22]

CHAPTER TWELVE

The Noble Savages of Fort Cumberland

EXACTLY ONE HOUR AFTER BRADDOCK roared through Dunbar's troops in his chariot on the road to Fort Cumberland, Dunbar ordered his troops to stop and form a circle. In less than one hour, he told his men, they would be at the fort. There they would see Indians for the first time. However, these were friendly Indians. Nonetheless, the men must have no conversations, directly or indirectly, with the Indians, for fear of affronting them. That was all. The troops regrouped and continued their march into the fort.

True to Dunbar's word, they reached the fort by two in the afternoon and found Halkett's troops encamped on a stump-pimpled hillside between the fort and the verge of the dark forest. No sooner had they pitched their tents next to Halkett's troops on the west side of the fort than Braddock ordered them to relieve the guard at the fort. There would be no rest for these troops after their arduous march of over 120 miles from Alexandria.

The fort itself was not impressive: a rectangular stockade planted on a hilltop, perhaps two hundred by fifty yards in dimension and consisting of raw green logs stripped of their bark.[1] At its highest, the palisade stood no more than twelve feet high. A Union Jack hung limply from a pole in the center of the fort. The stockade was fitted out for twelve guns, but only ten modest 4-pounders, sent up earlier by Dinwiddie, were actually mounted. The stockade also boasted mounts for swivels and loopholes for musket fire. It stood some four hundred yards from the Potomac River and two hundred from Wills Creek. Along the bank of the Potomac were a jumble of log cabins and shanties, tumbled like a handful of dice, that served the Ohio Company. Across the river, on the Virginia side, stood the main log warehouse of the company. The stockade had no well, so the men were compelled to fetch their fresh water in buckets from Wills Creek.

Notwithstanding Dunbar's admonition and their new guard duty, the men wasted no time in checking out the Indians. One of the seamen straightaway slipped into the Indian camp and recorded his wide-eyed observations:

> We found here Indian men, women and children, to the number of about 100, who were greatly surprised at the regular way of our soldiers marching, and the numbers. I would willingly say something of the customs and manner of the Indians, but they are hardly to be described. The men are tall, well made and active, but not strong, but very dexterous with a rifle barreled gun, and their tomahawk, which they will throw with great certainty at any mark and at a great distance. The women are not so tall as the men, but well made and have many children, but had many more before spirits were introduced to them. They paint themselves in an odd manner, red, yellow, and black intermixed. And the men have the outer rim of their ears cut, which only hangs by a bit top and bottom, and have a tuft of hair left at the top of their heads, which is dressed with feathers. Their watch coat is their chief clothing, which is a thick blanket thrown all

"Fort Cumberland in 1755," from the *History of Cumberland, Maryland*, by William Lowdermilk, 1878.

> round them, and wear moccasins instead of shoes. . . . These people have no notion of religion, or any sort of Superior being, as I take them to be the most ignorant people as to the knowledge of the world and other things. In the day they were in our Camp, and in the night they go into their own, where they dance and make a most horrible noise.[2]

The seaman also learned that it was a custom of the Indians for the women to dance, once or twice a year, while the men sat by. Each woman would take the man that she fancied, dance with him, and then sleep with him for a week, at the end of which time she returned to her erstwhile spouse and resumed normal life.[3]

This lesson was not lost on the English soldiers, many of whom began to invite Indian women into their tents and draw extra rations to feed them. Even the officers were not immune. One Bright Lightning, daughter of Chief White Thunder, was well on her way to having serviced the officer corps when Braddock issued an order that prohibited any Indian women from entering the army camp.[4]

Despite his reputation as a womanizer, Braddock's approach to the Indians was strictly professional. One of Braddock's first orders at the fort was to forbid the giving of rum or money to any Indian.[5] Indeed, one of the general's top priorities on reaching the fort was to try to line up Indian support for the expedition. Awaiting him at the fort were some fifty Pennsylvania Indians brought there by the trader George Croghan, the same man before whom St. Clair had declaimed like a "lion rampant." However, Dinwiddie had promised Braddock that there would be four hundred Southern Indians awaiting his arrival, ready to sign on. As with so many of Dinwiddie's promises, this one had come to naught. Braddock called Croghan to his tent.

"Where are the rest of the Indians?" Braddock asked.

"I don't know," Croghan responded.

"But," Braddock protested, "Governor Dinwiddie told me at Alexandria that he had sent four hundred who would be here before me."

"I know nothing of that," replied Croghan.

Croghan then summoned his translator, Captain Andrew Montour of Virginia, to try to answer the general's question. Montour was an Indian who had had a French Canadian grandfather. He dressed in a curious cross of the two cultures. His ears sported brass pendants, and he wore his shirt untucked, blouse fashion, over his pants under a scarlet silk waistcoat. His French-Indian mother had grown up believing that Christ was a Frenchman crucified by the English. Notwithstanding his provenance, Montour favored the English. He spoke French, English, and a variety of Indian dialects. The Indians much admired him.[6]

Montour explained that Christopher Gist's son had traveled south some time ago to enlist the help of the Southern Cherokees but there was no telling when he would return.[7] "What about the Delawares and Shawnees?" Braddock asked. Croghan explained that he had sent out a messenger to them. "Send another," ordered the anxious Braddock.

Indeed, ensuring Indian support for the expedition was such a high priority for Braddock that he summoned an assembly of those who were at the fort on Monday May 12, just two days after his arrival. Meeting in the general's tent at 11 in the morning, the Indians were greeted by the assembled officer corps and the general's guard, with their firelocks rested to signal friendship. Braddock ordered Montour to tell them that their brothers the English were their old friends and, speaking as he gestured toward a nearby mountain peak, that they had come to assure them that every misunderstanding of former times should now be buried under "that great mountain." Braddock then presented the Indians with a string of wampum to warm them up. He next produced a full belt of wampum and held it up. He declared that this wampum was to assure them of the friendship of the English, that everybody who was the Indians' enemy was also the enemy of the English. Moreover, the small force present was not the only one the English had, that numbers to the northward under the great war captains Shirley, Pepperel, and Johnson, plus others, were going to war. The English would settle the Indians happily in their country and make the French ashamed and hungry. However, Braddock had a warning as well. Any Indians after this declaration who did not come in and ally with the English would be treated as enemies. Braddock then promised them that he would have presents for them in a few days, at which time he would make another speech to them. He ordered his servant Bishop to pass drams of rum all round.[8]

Braddock scheduled a second congress of the Indians for Saturday May 17 but postponed it, presumably to allow time for more Indians to arrive and perhaps for tactical political reasons. The second promised conclave occurred the next day, Sunday, at noon in his tent. Braddock announced to the Indians his desire that they immediately send their families back into Pennsylvania and take up the hatchet against the French. He stated that the great King of England, their Father, had sent them the presents now spread before them (rings, beads, linen, knives, wire, and paint) and that he had ordered arms to be given to their warriors. He also expressed condolences over the loss of the Half King, who had died the year before. To cap his presentation Braddock handed them a string and three belts of wampum. The Indians promised their answer the next day. To show that they were pleased they made "a most horrible noise, dancing all night."[9]

As promised, the Indians returned the next evening. They met the general in his tent to give their answer. With great formality they announced that they were deeply obliged to the Great King their Father who had sent the English to fight for them and that they would all give their attendance and reconnoiter the country and bring intelligence. Braddock told them that he was their friend and would never deceive them. The Indians then sang a war song and for the first time, formally and with great gravity, declared the French as their "perpetual enemies." To help secure their trust, Braddock escorted them to the artillery and ordered three howitzers, three half-pounders, and three cohorns fired, with all the army's drums pounding and fifes squealing what was called a "point of war." This pleased the Indians greatly. They then retired to their own camp, ate a bullock, and danced a war dance that extolled their prior exploits and demonstrated how they fought and scalped.[10] On-looking British officers marveled at the performance. As described by one British officer,

> the Indians being dressed some in Furs, some with their Hair Ornamented with Feathers, others with the Heads of Beasts; their Bodies naked, appearing in many places, painted with various Colours, and their skins so rubbed with Oyl as to glitter against the Light [of the fire] . . . and artificial Tails fixed to many of them that hung down near unto the Ground. After they had danced some Time in a Ring, the Music ceased and the Dancers divided into two Parties, and set up the most horrid Song or Cry that ever I heard, the Sound would strike terror into the stoutest Heart . . . the Dancers all at once rushed out again, leav-

> ing one only behind them, who was supposed to have mastered his Enemy; he struck the Ground with his Tomahawk or Club, as if he was killing one lying there, then acting the motions of scalping, and when holding up a real dried Scalp, which before hung upon him amongst his Ornaments; he then sung out the great Achievements which some of the Nation had performed against the French, told the names of the Indian Warriors, and how many of French each had scalped.[11]

The next day eight warriors remained in the camp, while all the rest escorted their wives and children back to Pennsylvania. Braddock never saw the Indians again.

The Indian version of Braddock's speech, not surprisingly, differed from that recorded by Braddock's officers. Scaroyady, also known as Monacatoocha, was an Oneida who had fought with Washington in the Fort Necessity campaign. He claimed to have participated in thirty-one battles, and on his chest was tattooed a tomahawk and on each cheek a bow and arrow. He was present at the meetings with Braddock and later claimed that Braddock had said that "no savage should inherit the land" to be freed from the French and that only the English would "inhabit and inherit the land." Other reports had it that Braddock forbade the Indians to take scalps. Although Scaroyady remained loyal to the British and accompanied the expedition, he later called Braddock "a bad man." In the Indian's view, "he looked upon us as dogs, and would never hear anything what was said to him." He was full of "pride and ignorance."[12] It must be noted that the Indians made similar complaints against Washington after the Fort Necessity disaster.

Subsequent historians have tended to accept Scaroyady's ex post facto criticism at face value and to hold Braddock to task for not having handled the Indians properly. This is not supported by the facts. Cultivation of Indian allies ranked high on the king's instructions to Braddock and was the number two agenda item raised by Braddock at the Carlyle House congress. Certainly his speeches at Fort Cumberland to the Indians, as well as his personal deportment toward them, were impeccable. In truth, once again Americans with their own agenda played havoc with His Excellency's plans. Why did the Pennsylvania Indians melt away and the Southern Cherokees never materialize? Writing a letter on July 21, 1755, while still believing Braddock to be alive, Sir William Johnson, the British superintendent of Indian Affairs, who knew the Indians probably better than any other prominent person in America, described a "private conference" he had with some Indians who described their "chief reasons" for not going to Braddock's assistance. The Indians did not doubt Dinwiddie's influence over the Southern Cherokees but feared that if they were to meet the Southern tribes "some Broils might arise" because a "good understanding does not at present subsist between them" and that friction could prove "fatal to themselves and very disserviceable to our Cause."[13] In short, intertribal rivalry, not His Excellency's disposition, kept the Indians away.

In addition to trying to encourage Indian support for the expedition, Braddock's other top priority while at Fort Cumberland was the ordering and organization of his troops. Braddock was aware of the disorder which attended the army's advance to the fort. He was determined to remedy this shortcoming before the troops went into battle.

Braddock's first official act on reaching the fort was to confirm his long-promised appointment of Washington as aide-de-camp. Washington, for his part, was elated with the arrangement. He wrote to his brother: "The Gen'l had appointed me one of his Aide de Camps, in which Character I shall serve this Campaigne, agreeably enough, as I am thereby freed from all commands but his, and give Orders to all, which must be implicitly obey'd." Not only was his immediate position enviable, but Washington had not lost sight of the long-term political prospects capable of being nurtured from the association: "I have now a good opportunity, and shall not neglect it, of forming an acquaintance [with

Braddock], which may be serviceable hereafter, if I can find it worth while pushing my fortune in the Military way."[14]

Grand Chef de Guerriers Iroquois. Both the British and French learned to identify Indian leaders by their dress. (*New-York Historical Society*)

Having rounded out his "military family," Braddock next ordered that the Articles of War be read to all soldiers, "servants, women and followers of the army"[15] and undertook an inventory of his forces, both as shown on paper and in terms of effectives.[16]

The two British regiments had reached their hoped-for strength of seven hundred men each only by a sustained effort to fill out the ranks with American recruits. However, Americans had not been lining up to enlist. Indeed, the pool of American recruits was so suspect that a number of indentured servants and criminals had to be returned to their masters and jails after being recruited at Rock Creek.

Desertions and drunkenness began to leach through the encampment just as they had in Alexandria. On Monday May 12 a general court-martial was empaneled to sit. The court sentenced one Luke Woodward of the 48th Regiment for desertion, but Braddock pardoned him (probably because he needed to keep troop levels up rather than out of considerations of mercy). Three men who stole a keg of beer came off worse. Thomas Conelly received one thousand lashes and James Fitzgerald and James Hughes eight hundred each. Braddock confirmed the punishments but remitted one hundred lashes from the punishment of Conelly and two hundred from those of the other men. The men were whipped by the regimental drummers "at the head of the line," that is, at the morning formation of the troops over the course of three days.

Braddock also had to contend with inebriation of the Indians and an emerging secondary market in the trade goods presented to the Indians. On May 16 he issued an order: "Any Indian Trader, Soldier or follower of the army who shall dare to give any liquor to any of the Indians or shall receive or purchase from them any of their presents made to them by His Majesty thro' His Excellency Genl Braddock, shall suffer the severest punishment a court martial can inflict."[17]

Horse theft also was a problem. There was little forage so early in the season and in the mountainous location. Therefore, the soldiers let the horses loose in the nearby woods to graze on what they could find, mainly fresh shoots and leaves. The men tried hobbles and fences to no avail. The horses roamed, and many disappeared with the deserters and shifting population of wagoneers coming into and out of the camp.

Nonetheless, Braddock made do with what he had. He sought out men who "understand the springing of rocks" (meaning demolition experts), with a view to the blasting that would be necessary to clear the road through the wilderness. Braddock established a policy of holding a regular briefing at his tent every day from 10 to 11 in the morning to go over the state of his army. The men's arms were surveyed to determine if they were serviceable.[18] Each unit was allowed thirty-six rounds with ball to a pound of powder, but forty-six for "Field days and Exercise." Six women were allocated to each regiment and independent company, with fewer for other units, such as the seamen.[19] Any beyond the prescribed number could not draw provisions. The men were ordered to account with the director of the hospital. Under standard procedure the pay of the men in each unit was docked five pence per day for each man from the unit admitted to hospital, a practice bound to discourage slackers.[20]

Braddock also used this time to whip into line the American troops, for whom he had low regard. He earlier had dedicated one of his junior officers, Lieutenant James Allen, to take charge of the instruction and drill of the American recruits, the "bobtails." At Fort Cumberland they began to learn the lessons of British infantry practice in earnest as they drilled in formation and learned the art of firing from Major General Humphrey Bland's *Treatise on Discipline*, the eighteenth-century soldier's bible.[21]

The British infantryman was armed with flintlock smoothbore musket and bayonet, two innovative weapons which influenced the deployment of troops in battle. The flintlock and bayonet replaced the seventeenth-century matchlock and pike, respectively. In the prior century, foot soldiers had been more or less evenly divided between specialized musketeers and pikemen. Now, firepower and shock combined in the same soldier by providing suppressive fire delivered in preparation for maneuver. With the flintlock's superior rate of fire over the matchlock and the bayonet's elimination of pikemen, the new combination of enhanced firepower and individual protection fostered "linear tactics." "Linear tactics" governed infantry warfare throughout the eighteenth century. Troops marched to the area of combat in columns of two or more files of men. Once on the field of battle, the troops regrouped into ranks, each of the men facing forward and shoulder-to-shoulder to form the line of battle. This formation contrasted with earlier massed troop tactics which relied primarily on the element of shock for success. Linear tactics deployed the soldiers into several ranks for purposes of volley firing, with a further reserve rank in the rear to step forward and staunch any losses. The soldiers loaded and fired their muskets through a series of precise, step-by-step commands. The long lines of infantry used concentrated and continuous firepower in order to demoralize the enemy more than to inflict high rates of casualties, not unlike strategic bombing preparatory to invasion today. The flintlock's complementary component, the bayonet, was an instrument of shock designed to carry the assault at the critical moment. Ultimately, the attacking army would advance to the beat of a drum with their bayonets fixed.[22]

The limited range of the flintlock smoothbore musket generally meant that casualties were not taken until the army had advanced to within eighty or so yards of its enemy. The advancing soldiers would be ordered to hold their fire until they were even closer, perhaps fifty yards, and then the order to fire would ring out, with the attackers and defenders blasting at one another. At this moment, the synchronization of the drill paid off, with the advancing troops reloading and firing two, or with luck three, times without breaking stride. Once on top of the enemy the soldiers would attack with the bayonet. In such a tactic, rate of fire was more valued than accuracy. "Speed and precision," as one authority has written, "had to be combined with iron discipline."[23] And the only way to achieve them, as if by second nature, was through constant drill. Bland's methodology reached its apogee at the Battle of Fontenoy in the Low Countries in 1745, where the Coldstream Foot Guards, under the personal command of the Duke of Cumberland, mowed their elite French adversaries down with withering musketry, behaving throughout the conflict with exact discipline.[24]

The Virginia troops were a far cry from the Coldstream Regiment of Foot Guards under the Duke of Cumberland. The results of the training of the Americans were, in the British view, merely adequate. Orme, whose views reflected those of Braddock, wrote in his journal: "Mr. Allen had taken the greatest pains with them, and they performed their evolutions and firings as well as could be expected, but their languid, spiritless, and unsoldierlike appearance considered with the lowness and ignorance of most of their Officers gave little hopes of their future good behavior."[25]

Preparing the men for the wilderness march and battle, disciplining the American recruits, fostering relations with the Indians, all this and more kept the British busy at Fort Cumberland. However, Braddock tarried for other reasons as well. He still awaited the rendezvous of additional units at the fort. Captain Dobbs's North Carolina Rangers came in late because of the distance of their journey. Among their number was an obscure wagon driver named Daniel Boone. Also, Captain Horatio Gates, the young officer who was Walpole's godson and who had served with Cornwallis in Nova Scotia, joined Braddock at the fort with his New York Independents. But most important, Braddock waited for Lieutenant Colonel Thomas Gage to come up with the artillery and forty-two wagons with stores, as well as two attendant companies of Halkett's regiment. On May 16, they finally straggled into the camp after an exhausting haul of the heavy equipment through Virginia. As Orme put it, they had struggled over a "prodigious chain of mountains, and through deep and rocky roads."[26] They also had made the march only by pressing horses and wagons from the local farmers, a step that the army had hitherto been reluctant to order and which did not endear them to the local populace.

Just a few days earlier Braddock had run short of cash. On May 15 he ordered Washington to undertake a post-haste ride back to Hampton, Virginia, to fetch £4,000 from the army's agent. His orders were to stay no longer than two days in Hampton and return "as speedily as may be." One day out, Washington passed Gage and his column of artillery struggling up the Winchester road to Fort Cumberland. However, Washington pushed hard and made the four-hundred-mile round trip back to Winchester, with the money in his saddle bags, in twelve days. Washington acknowledged that he was "fatigued and a good deal disordered by constant riding in a drought which has almost destroyed this part of the country." He waited at Winchester for a guard to protect his cargo along the remaining dangerous stretch of road northward to the fort.

But even in the wilderness and on campaign, Washington was hedging his bets. Notwithstanding the urgency of his mission and the physical rigors he had just undergone, he took time to write his brother to ask him to "fish out Colonel Fairfax's intentions" about running for the House of Burgesses, with the notion that he would run himself if his mentor did not. He also instructed his brother to approach a list of the most influential people in Fairfax County to "discover their real sentiments without disclosing much of mine." In all his approaches, his brother was to affect "an air of indifference."[27] At the end of the day, Fairfax ran, and Washington stood aside.

On Saturday, May 17, a somber note was sounded as Captain Bromley from Halkett's regiment died of a fever. His funeral was held at ten o'clock the next morning. "The ceremony," the seaman wrote, "was a Captain's guard marched before the corpse, with the Captain of it in the rear, and the fire locks reversed, the drums beating the dead march. When we[28] came near the grave, the guard formed 2 lines facing each other; rested on their arms, muzzles downward; and leaned their faces on the butts; the Corpse was carried between them, the sword and sash on the coffin, and the officers following two by two."[29]

Braddock was also increasingly concerned about provisioning the men on the long march that was to come. He fully appreciated that once the army left Fort Cumberland it could not live "off the land" as it might have while campaigning in Europe. With the arrival of Cresap's spoiled supplies, he had issued an order to set up a market at the fort to encourage local farmers to bring their produce for sale. The only problems were that there were few local farmers on the edge of the frontier and, this early in the season, even fewer crops for them to sell. Speculation became rife, as picket patrols intercepted farmers approaching the fort and bought up their produce for resale in the camp. This abuse led Braddock to issue an order punishing that particular practice by death.

Braddock blamed Dinwiddie. The governor had promised five hundred head of cattle and other supplies which failed to arrive. This, together with other broken promises, almost delivered a coup de grace to the expedition. On May 18 a frustrated and increasingly despondent Braddock announced that he was ready to turn back and cancel the expedition in its entirety within forty-eight hours. He began to make preparations to do just that. Having assembled and equipped an army, having traveled thousands of miles, having marched to the edge of the wilderness, the hard-driving general had essentially decided that he had no choice but to call the whole thing off. The campaign was now at its nadir.

As one officer recorded at the time:

> Just as I wrote this we hear the best news I ever heard in my life. The General hath declared to the Virginians that if they do not furnish us with wagons and provisions in two days he will march back; he has just upbraided them for exposing the King's troops, by their bragging and false promises . . . but now it is impossible to go any farther without they comply with the promises; . . . these circumstances has brought the General into the present difficulties, and he has very justly told them, that if they marched any farther without a supply, he should be justly charged with destroying His Majesty's troops in the deserts, and thereby encourage the destruction of Virginia by encouraging the French; that if he was not supplied in two days he would march back and lay their breach of faith before His Majesty."[30]

With the two-day deadline passed, and Braddock beginning to make good on his threat, a group of Quakers bearing gifts made an unexpected visit on May 20.

A British officer wrote home describing what transpired: "In my last I acquainted you with the joyful News that our General resolved not to be any longer put upon by the Virginians. Orders were given for our March back, but the Day before that was appointed there arrived five Quakers decently dressed, they were pure plump Men, on brave fat Horses. . . . They acquainted him [Braddock] further that they had been cutting Roads to meet him with a Number of Waggons loaded with Flour, Cheese, Bacon, and other provisions, tho' this was good News I did but half liked it, I fear's it would occasion our Stay, and prevent our marching back; besides, it was ominous, your Cheese and your Bacon being the Baits that draw Rats to Destruction."

And then the officer added a note of judgment on Virginians that was becoming all too familiar: "The Fellows who drove the Waggons . . . looked like Angels compared with the long, lank, yellow-faced Virginians, who at best are a half-starved, ragged, dirty Set. . . . Some of the Braggadocio Virginians, who last Year ran away so stoutly, began to clamor against the Quakers and the General; so we marched."[31] The allusion to "Braggadocio Virginians" who "last Year ran away so stoutly" may have been a specific reference to Washington's troops at Fort Necessity.

With the Quakers came eighty wagons to join the expedition, courtesy of Benjamin Franklin, and eleven wagons full of the promised delicacies for the subalterns, nominally courtesy of the Pennsylvania Assembly but in fact arranged by Franklin. More wagons followed in the ensuing days. Halkett and Dunbar both wasted no time in writing personal notes of thanks to their benefactor.

As noted by the British officer, prospects of continuing the campaign began to look up rather quickly. The same day Braddock issued an order allowing six women to march into the wilderness with each company and, in a curious prerequisite for campaigning, directed the expedition's doctors to "search and see who was clean to" join the men on the march.[32]

Soon the fort hummed with a newfound activity and seriousness.[33] Soldiers were assigned to assist the commissary, Mr. Lake, in baking biscuits and were excused from any further duties. One hundred carpenters, under the direction of the carpenter of the *Seahorse*, set to building a magazine and constructing a bridge over Wills Creek and blacksmiths to making tools.[34] The army was getting ready to march. Braddock realized that his grand chariot would be "impractical" once the army struck out into the wilderness. He wrote Sharpe, offering it back, together with the harness for six horses. "I shall be much obliged to you and you will make use of it till I want it. . . . Let your servants take care of the harness and have it oiled if you don't use it," Braddock advised.[35]

Nor was military discipline, that ever-sure bellwether of serious intent, ignored. The provost was ordered to round up any soldiers and women beyond the picket lines, "tye them up and give them fifty lashes and to march them thro' the camp to expose them." Braddock ordered any noncommissioned officer or soldier caught gaming to "immediately receive three hundred lashes without being brought to court martial," with any onlookers or bystanders to receive the same.[36] This was hard discipline indeed. The grog ration was set at one gill of spirits mixed with three of water for each man per day, to be delivered every day at eleven o'clock. Any settler caught selling more without an officer present was to be sent to the provost.[37]

Yet another court-martial was convened May 23 under the practiced hand of Gage. The next day two men were discharged from Halkett's regiment for theft and desertion, after receiving one thousand lashes apiece and, according to the eyewitness batman, being drummed through the line with halters about their necks.[38] Another man, in a rare exercise of fairness, was acquitted of murder and released for the accidental shooting of a fellow soldier while hunting deer.[39] A separate "General Court Martial of the Line," presided over by Halkett and consisting, in addition to Halkett, of two field officers (Major Russell Chapman and Lieutenant Colonel Burton) and ten captains, was empaneled May 26 to try for the first time an officer. The officer was one Lieutenant McLeod of the Royal Regiment of Artillery, whom Braddock had confined on unspecified charges but possibly relating to desertion. The records are silent on both the charges and outcome. However, Orme noted cryptically in his journal that part of the sentence was remitted, suggesting a conviction.[40] Apparently the need for public example was less urgent among the officer corps.

As he prepared to move his campaign forward, Braddock felt increasingly betrayed by the Americans, especially the Virginians and Pennsylvanians. Still, he was prepared to try to set relations right, while dealing candidly with what he saw as a problem.

Governor Morris of Pennsylvania had gotten wind of St. Clair's "storming" before Croghan and had written Braddock a letter of complaint. The General responded by reprimanding St. Clair but leaving no doubt at to his views of American help. Braddock's secretary Shirley wrote privately to a correspondent: "Governor Morris has taken a very sensible and proper notice of Sir John St. Clair's behavior in his letter to the General. Sir John begins to find that he has mistaken himself and to draw in his horns."[41] To Governor Morris he separately wrote: "Sir John . . . has received what is called in the language of the camp a *set down*."[42]

Nonetheless, Braddock's frustration was palpable. He wrote to Morris:

> You will . . . be informed of the situation I am in by the folly of Mr. Dinwiddie and the roguery of the assembly, and unless the road of communication from your province is opened and some contracts made in consequence of the power I have given, I must inevitably be starved. Sir John St. Clair (who by the way is ashamed of having talked of you in the manner he did) has employed, by the advice of Governor Sharpe, a fellow at Conococheague, one Cresap, who behaved in such a manner in relation to the Pennsylvania flower [flour] that had he been a French commissary he could not have acted more to their interest. In short, in every instance but my contract for the Pennsylvania wagons, I have been deceived and met with nothing but lies and villainy. I hope, however, in spite of this that we shall pass a merry Christmas together.[43]

On Sunday, May 25, Braddock called his first council of war. He summoned all the field officers–Colonels St. Clair, Halkett, and Dunbar, Lieutenant Colonels Burton and Gage, and Majors William Sparkes and Chapman–but not Orme, Washington (who was en route back from Hampton), or Morris, his aides-de-camp. Meeting in his tent, Braddock presented his assembled senior officers with a plan of march he had devised. The general offered the plan to them for their opinions and expressly invited their objections and amendments as they thought proper. Underlying Braddock's plan was the paramount need for security as the army marched and camped through hostile wilderness. He was fearful of being encumbered by the "vast number" of carriages and horses of the train, which he believed it "absolutely necessary" to protect from anticipated attacks along the way by Indians. To cover as much the baggage as possible he therefore proposed to divide the troops into small parties, which would march in a single line through a road about twelve feet wide. It would also be necessary to extend small parties on the flanks, and in the front and rear, to prevent ambush.

The plan that Braddock devised, as related by Orme, was an essay in tight control and critical to the safe passage of the army. It was as meticulously prescriptive as it was lengthy:

> Each regiment was to find one Captain and three subalterns for the picket of each flank; and the independent companies, Virginia, Maryland, and Carolina rangers, One Captain and two Subalterns for each of the flanks of their division; and the field Officer of the day was to command the whole. The officers of the pickets were to march on their respective flanks. The waggons, Artillery, and carrying horses were formed into three divisions, and the provisions disposed of in such manner as that each division was to be victualled from that part of the line it covered, and a commissary appointed to each. The waggon master was to attend to their respective divisions . . . and to assist at every steep ascent by adding any number of horses from other waggons, till their respective divisions had passed.
>
> The waggons were subdivided again into smaller divisions, every company having a certain number which they were to endeavor to keep together, however the line

> might be broke: The Companies were to march two deep that they might extend the more, be more at liberty to act, and less liable to confusion.
>
> A field officer was to march in the van, and another with a rear guard. Sr Peter Halkett was to lead the column, and Colonel Dunbar to bring up the Rear. The field officer of the Picket had no fixed posts. There was also an advanced party of three hundred men to precede the line to cut and make the roads, commanded by a field officer or the quarter master general. This detachment was to be either a day's march before the line or to move earlier every morning, according to the country we were to pass through, or the intelligence we could get of the enemy.

Nor did Braddock neglect the order of the army at rest. As related by Orme:

> The form of encampment differed very little from that of the march. Upon coming to the ground, the waggons were to draw up in close order in one line, the road not admitting more, care being taken to leave an interval in front of every company. When this was done the whole was to halt and face outward. The serjeants' flank parties were to divide, facing to the right and left, and to open a free communication by cutting down saplings and underwood, till they met the divisions of the other serjeants' parties: they were then to open a communication with the corporal in front, who was to keep his men under arms. The serjeant was then to advance half his party, which was to remain under arms whilst the corporal opened his communications to the right and left. . . . Whilst this was executing, half of each company remained under arms, whilst the other half opened communication to the right and left and to the serjeants in front, and also cleared ground for the tents, which were pitched by them, and placed in a single row along the line of baggage, facing

> outwards. These parties were then to be relieved, and the corporal's party was all posted in centinels, which made a chain of centinels round the camp. The grenadiers were to encamp across the road.[44]

Although the council of war unanimously approved Braddock's plan, the general himself had second thoughts. Two days later he called a second council of war. He was concerned that the one hundred and ninety wagons (one hundred and fifty of which Franklin had arranged from Pennsylvania) and six hundred pack horses he had could not carry seventy days' worth of flour and fifty of meat, which were the minimums he calculated to be necessary for the march without resupply.

The general therefore proposed "the sending forward of a party of six hundred men, workers, and coverers, with a field officer and the Quarter-master-Generall; that they should take with them two six pounders, with a full proportion of ammunition; . . . that they should make the road as good as possible, and march five days towards the first crossing of the Yoxhio Geni [Youghiogheny], which was about thirty miles from the camp, at which place they were to make a deposit of the provisions, building proper sheds for its security, and also a place for arms for its defence and the security of the men."[45] Halkett was to lead, as before, with Burton taking up the middle with the Americans and the artillery, munitions, and part of the supplies, and Dunbar the rear, together with the returned wagons from Winchester and the advance party and the pack horses. As noted by Orme, "The whole of the General's plan was universally approved of, and agreed to; and the Resolutions of the first, and of this Council of War were signed by the members."[46]

However, the unanimity of the council of war masked growing discontent within the officer corps. The Coldstream Lieutenant Orme complained at being excluded from the first council of war and demanded that Braddock include him in the second, a request to which fellow officer Braddock acceded. The arrogance of this demand, coming on top of Orme's increasingly assertive role in shaping Braddock's thinking about the campaign, displeased Halkett, who was far more experienced than Orme, even if he commanded only a humble regiment of the line. Halkett declared that if he ever came to command he would dismiss the upstart Orme the next day from the army and that he "regretted much that the General had such a man about him who's advice would both be the ruin of the General & the expedition."[47] Halkett, an honest man, was prophetic. However, others, closer to His Excellency's inner circle, had a more favorable view of Orme, even while acknowledging his tendency to take over.

Thus, despite the decision to march and the flurry of activity aimed at getting the army moving, a dispiritedness had begun to corrode the very heart of the mission. At the same time that Braddock wrote to Governor Morris on May 29 of his disgust with Dinwiddie, Sharpe, and the Pennsylvania Assembly, his young secretary Shirley wrote Morris a confidential letter that hinted ominously of an expedition about to collapse:

> We have a G_____ [eneral] most judiciously chosen for being disqualified for the service he is employed in, in almost every respect. He may be brave for ought I know and he is honest in pecuniary matters. But as the King said of a neighboring governor of yours when proposed for the command of the American forces about a twelfth month ago, and recommended as a very honest man though not remarkably able, "a little more ability and a little less honesty upon the present occasion might serve our turn better."
>
> It is a joke to suppose that secondary officers can make amends for the defects of the first. The main spring must be the mover. The others in many cases can do no more than follow and correct a little its motions. As to them, I don't think we have much to boast. Some are insolent and ignorant; others capable but rather aiming at showing

> their own abilities than making a proper use of them. I have a very great love for my friend Orme, and I think it uncommonly fortunate for our leader that he is under the influence of so honest and capable a man, but I wish, for the sake of the public, he had some more experience of business, particularly in America.
>
> As to myself, I came out of England expecting that I might be taught the business of a military secretary, but I am already convinced of my mistake. . . . You will think me out of humour. I own I am so. I am greatly disgusted at seeing an expedition (as it is called) so ill-concerted originally in England and so ill-appointed, so improperly conducted since in America; and so much fatigue and expense incurred for a purpose which, if attended by success, might better have been left alone. . . .
>
> I should be glad you would burn it [this letter] as soon as you have read it.[48]

If such was the mood in the general's tent, it was no better in the officers' mess. Intrigue, the other sure handmaiden of failure, had infected the general's military family to the point it had become public knowledge among the officer corps. The intrigue went beyond the antipathy between Orme and Halkett. Relationships between the senior officers had begun to harden. Burton, Orme, and Morris were the favorites of the General; Halkett and Dunbar, the second and third in command, respectively, were on the outs, as was St. Clair.

In a letter home an unidentified British officer confirmed the conniving that Dr. Hamilton had first noticed at Alexandria. He pointed the finger especially at Orme:

> Add to all this the pride, Insolence and overbearing Spirit of the first aid du camp C. Orme–despensing all former military orders ordinances and Customs of an Army in flanders or any where else either in old, or latter times,

> Commandeing and dictating to every Branch from the lowest to the highest and no Bounds of Resentment against those who would not bow to Dagon and who had resolution enough to tell him the bad Consequences attending such measures which (to our misfortune) he had always influence enough to obtain the Generals sanction to.
>
> The heads of both military and Civil Branches with us were despised as ignorant &c and if ever their opinions were ask'd (which was rarely) after a Sneer at them–the Contrary was sure to be follow'd. Poor Sr Peter Halkett . . . was publickly told "he was a fool, he wanted leading strings" . . . he was in Disgrace–and the reasons he gave himself for it was, for his advising to train some people to the Great Guns as we had so few who understood that branch, likewise disapproving of the Line of March and proposeing to build block houses or stockades at proper passes for Magazines both for places of security as well as to encumber our March less with Carridges[49] . . . after which he neither was consulted nor did he ever go near the Genl. but once when he was sent for about some story that had been Carried to the Genl. that he and some others were living well when their officers wanted, at which time Sr Peter had only the King's salt provisions and could get no other–notwithstanding he was threatened with his Regt . . . to which he answer'd he did not depend on it for a livelyhood–and had not his honour been Concern'd he never would have Come on the Expedition.[50]

The same officer noted that Braddock only once had direct contact with his army and that at a review of the troops. He termed Orme "his favourite–who really Directed every thing and may Justly be said to've Commanded the Expedition and the Army."[51]

Braddock's army–drunk, flogged, and barely supplied, managed by an aloof general seemingly under the influence of an arrogant young aide, and riven by conflicts among the senior officers–prepared to quit Fort Cumberland and continue its march into the wilderness. However, it had little choice. The New England and New York prongs of the British strategy laid out at the Carlyle House congress were scheduled to deploy. The calendar had already advanced well into the spring campaigning season. Even though the general had come within a day of canceling the expedition, enough wagons and supplies had arrived to foreclose any excuse to retreat.

About this time, a sole Delaware had appeared at the fort. He claimed to have come from Fort Duquesne and said that the French fort was manned by only fifty soldiers but with reinforcements of nine hundred on the way. He said the French intended to blow up Fort Duquesne if attacked and to melt into the woods, carrying on *petite guerre* (or what would later be known as guerrilla warfare) against the English inhabitants of the frontier.[52] Although the British officers thought him a spy because no Delawares had answered the English call for assistance, the message was incontrovertible: the French were on the move and the consequences would be disastrous for the colonies if Braddock did not meet and defeat them. Besides, in his heart Braddock wanted to do battle.

But another factor was also at work. On May 23, two days before the first council of war, the English soldiers fired at their own Indian allies, thinking that they were under attack from the French.[53] The camp was getting nervous. It was time to move.

On Tuesday May 27, following the second council of war, every man was issued ten flints and twenty-four rounds of ammunition and put on notice to march within twenty-four hours.

The march that was about to be undertaken was unprecedented in North America: a 116-mile trek through barely charted wilderness with no forage, across seven ridges of mountains and countless rivers and streams, while hauling cannon and expecting attack by Indians at any moment. The journey was to be made in stages by an advance party to clear the road, followed by the main army. The main army was subsequently split into a so-called "flying column" and a baggage train to speed its progress. In all, the march was to take forty-two days (May 29–July 9, 1755). Moving like a giant dismembered miles-long centipede, the army was to make between two and eight miles a day, stopping at some twenty-one encampments in western Maryland and Pennsylvania before reaching its destiny just seven miles short of the Forks of the Ohio, the site of modern-day downtown Pittsburgh.

Chapter Thirteen

Advance Across the Allegheny Mountains

On his first trip to Wills Creek in January, Sir John St. Clair had poked his nose across the river and into the mountains that loomed to the west. He reported by letter to Braddock: "When I had got about two Miles on the other Side of the South Branch, I had a full view of the Mountains on each side of the Patomack above Will's Creek, and from what I cou'd see, there is a Road easily to be made across the Country to the Mouth of the Savage River. . . . The Mouth of the Savage River is the place where we ought to cross the Alleghany Mountains." But St. Clair added: "I have only been able to find one Woodsman who can give me any distinct Account of that Ground."[1]

Thus, from the very first days, even before the expedition landed in America, St. Clair's reconnaissance had foreordained the road through the wilderness. That road was to follow, in large part, a trail blazed in 1752 by the Delaware Indian Nemacolin with Gist and Cresap, the same trail Washington followed in 1754 to Jumonville. However, the trail was familiar only to the Indian guides, Washington, and the few white traders who had penetrated that far into the wilderness, and was unknown to Braddock and his army except through native accounts. The trail led over innumerable runs and rivers and five steep mountain ridges in Maryland before reaching Great Meadows: Haystack Mountain, Dans Mountain, Big Savage Mountain, Meadow Mountain, and Negro Mountain. Once beyond Great Meadows, Pennsylvania promised two more formidable mountains: Laurel Hill and Chestnut Ridge. Moreover, the narrow Indian trail would have to be widened and cleared in order to accommodate the cannon and supply wagons.

Braddock gave the order to march Thursday, May 29. True to the revised plan of march endorsed by the second council of war, a detachment of six hundred men under the command of Major Chapman, with two field pieces and fifty wagons, broke camp and plunged into the wilderness to open the road to Little Meadows. They were accompanied by St. Clair, two engineers, Lieutenant Spendelow of the Royal Navy, six sailors, and several Indian guides. St. Clair's predisposition on cutting roads was to site them wherever possible over high ridges rather than in valleys, both to avoid washouts from rain and to minimize the risk of ambush. However, this approach had its burdens. They marched eight hours but achieved only six miles because of "very Bad roads that we Were Oblig'd to halt Every hundred yards and mend them."[2] Crossing Haystack Mountain, looming over 1,200 feet high just two miles from the fort, the "ascent and descent were almost a perpendicular rock." Three wagons broke loose from their tackles and, with teams and all, careened off the rocks and were smashed to pieces, while "many more were extremely shattered,"[3] according to Orme. Braddock himself rode out and reconnoitered the mountain. He was so concerned that it would be impassable for the howitzers that he ordered the engineers and three hundred more men to work on improving the road over it. While they started their toil, Spendelow, who had returned to the fort with his contingent of sailors, informed the general that he had discovered a route around the foot of the mountain in contravention of St. Clair's maxim of marching over the ridges. Braddock ordered one hundred men to cut a road according to Spendelow's suggestion for the benefit of the main body of the army that was to pass. The road followed a valley between Haystack Mountain and Wills Mountain. Captain Harry Gordon, the chief engineer of the expedition, judged the road to be "impassable in wet weather, all through a Defile, but pretty level. . . . The hill rough, its rise quick, its fall quick and narrow, the rest tolerable."[4] (This highly visible gap to the west of Fort Cumberland is often mistaken today for the Cumberland Gap through which westward migration later passed. In fact, the Cumberland Gap is at the intersection of Virginia, Kentucky, and Tennessee, far to the south.)

Once over Haystack Mountain, the troops sensed that they were well into the mountains. Indeed, the vista and entire horizon were now defined by mountains, with their green mantles as thick as horse blankets. This was a virgin forest of deciduous hardwoods for as far as the eye could see, unlike any mountains the soldiers would have remembered from Britain. Buzzards soared high overhead.

After the advance detachment spent the night at its first encampment at a location some six miles west of Fort Cumberland that they dubbed Grove Camp, St. Clair led a working party forth to cut the road at four the next morning. Their route followed a stream, now known as Braddock's Run, westward. The remainder of the advance detachment moved out at six but, because of the slow progress in cutting the road ahead of them, were able to march only three miles by the time darkness fell at eight o'clock that evening. Two hundred strong, swinging hatchets and tools, St. Clair's road cutters labored under the watchful eyes and guns of a "covering party" of one hundred men–a ratio of one guard for every two road cutters. Before they left, Braddock had offered an incentive for the soldiers to work at road building (according to army regulations, he could not simply order them to do it but had to pay them): three shillings per subaltern, one shilling per sergeant, nine pence gold to every drummer, and sixpence sterling to each private. However, because there was no place for them to spend the money in the wilderness, payment was to be withheld until they were in winter quarters at the end of the campaign.[5] Deferred compensation did not settle well with the men.

Meanwhile back at Fort Cumberland, the rest of the troops remained on twenty-four hours' notice to march. Washington rode into camp on Friday, May 30 with the payroll after waiting "a day and piece" at Winchester–"this vile post," he termed it–for a guard to accompany him.[6]

On the same day, the tail end of the Braddock expedition prepared to leave Alexandria. The commissary Browne, his sister Charlotte the head nurse, her nursing staff, and a variety of recuperated soldiers were preparing to join the campaign at Fort Cumberland. While St. Clair was cutting the road into the wilderness and Washington was arriving with the payroll, Charlotte Browne wrote: "Extreem hot. Very busy making Bread and Ginger Bread and boiling Hams for our March. Had Company to dine with us in our Anti Chamber which is as hot as a Bagnio. We are to march on Sunday for Will's Creek if Mr. [Lieutenant] Faulkner our commanding Officer does not get lit [drunk] in his upper Rooms and forget it."[7]

For Braddock there was no end to worrying. The next day, Saturday, May 31, he wrote St. Clair expressing concern that the road might be proceeding too fast. He advised that "It was very far from my intention that our detachment should be seven day march from me." Orme rode out with the message. However, Orme was no mere messenger. He was there to inspect the progress at first hand and report back to the general. St. Clair responded that the general need not worry, the cutting of the road was proceeding much more slowly than expected.[8]

However, there was a delicate game of relay being played between St. Clair and Braddock. "Your Excellency need not be apprehensive of us getting too far ahead, I wish with all my heart that the ground would permit it. I believe with much difficulty we shall be able to get to the little Meadows the 7th day but should be sorry to stop at that place for fear of destroying your forage more than one night."[9]

Indeed the progress was slow. The batman recorded that on May 31, the day Braddock wrote to St. Clair, the advance detachment had been able to march a scant three miles. After stopping to cook their dinner, the road cutters, together with their obligatory covering party, were ordered to "Cut the Roads up a large mountain."[10] This mountain was the second ridge in the Allegheny chain over which they were crossing: Dans Mountain. The road blazed by the working party followed a long, creeping ascent deeper into the enveloping folds of the mountains. Dans Mountain, higher even than the "perpendicular" Haystack Mountain, was thick with undergrowth tangled about gray rocks, making the going laborious. It is difficult to imagine how strenuous the work must have been. Standing at angles on a slope that rose forty degrees or more, the men swung their hatchets and cleared away the vines, bushes, and saplings. They felled larger trees with axes and hauled them away from the road. The "miners" pried boulders loose and rolled them out of the way. They planted more recalcitrant rocks with gunpowder and blew them to pieces so that the army might pass. As recorded by the batman on June 2 while still clearing the road over Dans Mountain, "We marched about 6 Miles, the Rocks being so large that we were obliged to blast them several times before we Came to our [camp] ground."[11] The result was a rough roadbed twelve feet wide strewn with rocks, potholes, and stumps but which might, in a pinch, serve the purpose of allowing the teams and wagons and big guns to climb the mountain.

The same day, June 2, St. Clair was able to report to the general that he had accomplished his immediate mission: his pioneers had cleared the road across Dans Mountain all the way to the far side of Georges Creek (just south of present-day Frostburg,

Maryland). "We have taken a great deal of paine upon the road over it," St. Clair informed his commander,[12] while proposing a rendezvous of the whole army at Georges Creek rather than Little Meadows in order to avoid getting too far ahead of Braddock, who remained back at the fort.

Orme responded to St. Clair for His Excellency: "The General received your letter and has ordered me to inform you that he does not choose to have you advance more than the seven days and he is very desirous of getting from this place as soon as possible and that his Excellency intends a junction of the whole convoy at Georges Creek instead of the Little Meadows."[13] In short, Braddock agreed with St. Clair's suggestion. Moreover, the response provides further evidence that Braddock was not dallying wantonly at Fort Cumberland but was anxious, as he had been ever since arriving in America, to get his army into the field.

What was preoccupying His Excellency while he waited for the road to be cut? First, and always foremost, there was the matter of military discipline. Yet another court-martial was convened on June 3, this one sitting under Major Sparkes, with Shirley as the judge advocate. The court did its work handily, finding Richard Shelton and Calbib Curry of Captain Dobbs's North Carolina company guilty of desertion and sentencing them to one thousand lashes each. The court also tried John Igo, a "convict servant," of theft and receiving and concealing stolen goods. His sentence: five hundred lashes with a cat-o'-nine-tails. Finally, John McDonell of Halkett's regiment was tried as an accomplice of Igo but acquitted for lack of evidence.[14] The sentences were promptly carried out. Despite the frequency of these courts-martial, no man yet had been, or ever was, executed for desertion, as threatened by the general at the start of the expedition.[15]

Second, there was the ongoing loading of supplies and organization for the main body of troops to march. Various detachments were directed to parade each morning at reveille and receive orders from Engineer Gordon for work details on the road. The 44th and 48th remained on twenty-four-hours' notice to march. The camp buzzed with anxiety and anticipation.

View from Chimney Rock in Catoctin Mountain Park. Portions of western Maryland still provide a sense of the vast, rugged, and thick wilderness encountered by Braddock's troops. (*National Park Service*)

The situation out on the road was also one of ratcheting intensity. Following their strenuous efforts to clear the road over Dans Mountain the men had had little rest. On the night of June 2–3, shots in the distance awakened them at ten o'clock. They stood to arms immediately and remained in that state until two in the morning. They then bedded down, laying on top of their muskets all night, sleeping with Brown Bess. The next day they marched six miles and sent out a working party to cut the road as if nothing had happened.[16]

Their mission was formidable. Rising immediately to the west of Georges Creek loomed Big Savage Mountain, at 2,800 feet the highest mountain in the Alleghenies that the road cutters would have to cross and clear. Taller than five Washington Monuments stacked one on another, it was wreathed in clouds and mist at the top even on late spring days. The trees also changed on Big Savage Mountain: no longer the blanket of green but only the stubble of naked, spindly trees that survive at such an altitude. Like Dans Mountain, it was blemished with eruptions of brownish gray rock. Just on the far side lay the mouth of the Savage River, a narrow mountain run nestled in a gap between Big Savage Mountain and Little Savage Mountain, and then Meadow Mountain, at 2,780 feet, followed by a high rolling plateau, the site of Little Meadows, all as chosen by St. Clair for the line of march. Out on the road, the advance party halted at a stream and sent the working and covering parties forth to do further cutting. The detachment's designated hunter bagged a bear and a wolf for the men and tracked a panther for six miles before giving up.[17] Any sane man would have missed home.

On Wednesday, June 4, while the advance detachment toiled over Big Savage Mountain, the 44th Regiment and Captain Mercer's Company of Virginia Carpenters received word to hold themselves ready to march on an hour's notice.

That same day, Charlotte Browne, bringing up the very rear of Braddock's far-flung expedition, encamped at Hillsboro, Virginia, at the home of the same Quaker Thompson who had hosted Halkett's Regiment two months earlier. "An old sage Quaker with silver Locks," Browne called him. Thompson's wife of forty-four years advised Browne that she and her husband had been married so long that "we have lived to see the Days that we have no Pleasure therein." When the soldiers accompanying Browne fell into a supply of peach brandy, the part-time preacher Thompson lectured them on the virtue of temperance. They, in turn, "stared at him like Pigs."[18] Browne acknowledged that she preferred the company of "My Friend Thompson," whom she viewed with a certain sympathetic amusement, over that of the soldiers.

The following day brought violent thunderstorms to both Fort Cumberland and the road slowly inching westward, with rain, wind, thunder, and lightning so severe that the storms ripped several tents and frightened the soldiers. Still, the men labored on, clearing Meadow Mountain and marching for ten hours the remaining four miles to Little Meadows over "very Bad Roads

Over Rocks and Mountains almost unpassable," thus advancing farther than the rendezvous point at Georges Creek ordered by Braddock. At Little Meadows they stopped. They were a mere twenty-four miles beyond Fort Cumberland, still in Maryland, just past the Eastern Continental Divide (near today's Grantsville). And in utter wilderness, where ambush could come at any time. That day, their hunter, who supplied the advance party with meat, shot two elks, a bear, and a deer.[19]

The working party cleared the grounds around Little Meadows the next day. At their encampment, the advance detachment unloaded all their wagons and sent them back to the fort, as planned by the council of war. They also began to construct a storehouse for the unloaded provisions. The men celebrated reaching Little Meadows, their first objective on the march, by feasting on rattlesnake, bear, and deer.[20]

They were a long way from home. In London, the King was celebrating his official birthday. Braddock's old neighbor Horace Walpole was busy chronicling the start of the social season with his accustomed acerbic wit. George Anne Bellamy had just landed a starring role as one of the "rival queens" in a revival of Lee's tragedy *Alexander* at Covent Garden. She delighted in playing Roxanne, the daughter of the King of Persia, opposite her archrival Mrs. Woffington in the role of the Queen of Babylon. Billed as the "Battle Royal between the Queen of Babylon and the Daughter of Darius," the play was the sensation of London.[21]

Braddock's house in Arlington Street was locked, and the furniture in his drawing room draped in linen dust covers against his return.

Chapter Fourteen

To Little Meadows

With the advance party safely at Little Meadows, St. Clair sent a rider back to announce the news of their arrival to Braddock at Fort Cumberland. This was the signal Braddock had been awaiting. The army was ready to march.

Rain, thunder, and lightning heralded the departure of the main body of Braddock's army from Fort Cumberland on the morning of Saturday, June 7. Sir Peter Halkett and his 44th Regiment led the van, marching with two field pieces and wagons groaning with provisions. They moved out at daybreak and marched in the tight formation dictated by the council of war the six miles to Grove Camp, following Spendelow's newly cut road around the foot of Haystack Mountain. After seeing them off, Braddock reduced his personal guard to one sergeant, one corporal, and twelve men because there were no longer two regiments at the fort to alternate guard duty.

Realizing it might be his last opportunity for a long time, Braddock wrote a report to Napier in London. The bitterness of betrayal seeped from his pen:

> . . . the whole of the Forces are now assembled, making about two thousand Effectives, the greatest part Virginians, very indifferent Men, this Country affording no better; it has cost infinite pains and labour to bring them to any sort of Regularity and Discipline. Their Officers very little better, and all complaining of the ill usage of the Country, who employ'd them last Year without pay or provisions. . . . This part of the Country is absolutely unknown to the inhabitants of the lower parts of Virginia and Maryland, their Account of the Roads and provisions utterly false. From Winchester to this place which is Seventy Miles is almost uninhabited, but by a parcel of Banditti who call themselves Indian traders, and no Road passable but what we were oblig'd to make ourselves with infinate Labour. It would take up too much of your time were I to tell you particularly the Difficulties and Disappointments I have met with from the want of Honesty and Inclination to forward the Service in all Orders of people in these Colonies, which have occasion'd the great Delays in getting hither, as well as my being detain'd here a Month longer than I intended. . . . Nothing can well be worse than the Road I have already pass'd and I have a Hundred and Ten Miles to march thro' an uninhabited Wilderness over steep rocky Mountains and almost impassable Morasses. From this Description which is not exaggerated you conceive the difficulty of getting good Intelligence, all I have is from the Indians, whose veracity is no more to be depended upon [than] that of the Borderers here.[1]

Still, Braddock tried to look on the bright, if somewhat fatalistic, side: "Inclos'd I send you the Return of Forces I propose to proceed with, had I more it would be out of my power to subsist them. With these I flatter myself to be able to drive the French from the Ohio, and to open a Communication with the rest of His majesty's Forces in the other provinces."[2]

In addition to writing to his superiors, Braddock took advantage of his remaining days at Fort Cumberland to tidy up loose ends. In light of his prospective departure, he appointed Colonel James Innes of Virginia as governor of Fort Cumberland. Braddock ordered the fort guard to join their regiments as soon as Innes had taken command and posted his sentries. In addition, he ordered twenty-four wives of soldiers back to Philadelphia, writing out passes for their safe conduct and ordering dockage of one third of their husbands' pay for their support. Their surnames–McFarland, Campbell, Duncan, Fergason, and others[3]–bears witness to the heavily Celtic origin of the regular troops.[4] Other women, perhaps not wives, remained with the soldiers for the march. However, after one day's march, Braddock thought better of having more than two women on the march with each company. He ordered all in excess of two per company back, on pain of death.

On June 9, Braddock directed all men who were sick and unable to march confined to the general hospital at the fort and placed a subaltern in command of them. Because of the steady diet of bad salted beef, a rage of the "flux" had swept the camp. The list of sick and disabled was swollen beyond what it might normally have been.

The next day, June 10, was set for their departure. All the remaining troops marched from Fort Cumberland under the command of Braddock, "a brace old experienced Officer, in whom we had a great deal of Confidence," to quote one of his privates.[5] Having retired his chariot and heavy coach, Braddock rode a large British-bred charger. The entire main column, including the previously departed van, was just over two thousand five hundred strong, including wagoneers. It boasted provision wagons loaded to the weight of eighteen hundred to two thousand pounds–almost a ton–apiece and groaning on their axles. It also included thousands of pack horses carrying three months' provisions for two thousand men and the main artillery train: four 12-pounders (it is not clear whether these were the brass, iron, or a combination of the two types), six 6-pounders, four howitzers, and fifteen cohorns with three hundred rounds for each. The going was not easy on the newly cut road. "The March was attended with many difficulties owing to ye road and carriages being bad, & though ye line of March was intended to be only two Mile & an half in Extent, Yet they were frequently twice that distance," wrote one officer. "This was a circumstance impossible to be helped, accidents occasioning many halts in different parts of the line."[6]

Braddock was immediately dissatisfied with the pace of the march. Arriving at the end of the second day at a camp ground called Spendelow Camp in honor of the young naval lieutenant who had discovered the road around the mountain, Braddock called together all his officers and "recommended to them" that they return to Fort Cumberland all their baggage which was not "absolutely necessary." He also urged them to hand over their "able horses" to the "publick cause." He and his military family, including Washington, set the example by contributing twenty horses. Eventually, the officers gave up one hundred of their personal mounts to pull the guns and wagons. It was a major sacrifice for British officers on campaign not to travel in style with baggage and marquees and to have to sleep in regular soldiers' tents. But that was not all. Braddock called his third council of war, attended by Halkett, Gage, Chapman, Dunbar, Burton, and Sparkes (but not Orme, Morris, or Washington, as aides-de-camp were never voting members of a council of war). It was agreed to send back two 6-pounders, four cohorns, and their allotted ammunition and stores, thereby freeing up some twenty wagons. The council also agreed to send back all the king's wagons, which had come all the way from Ireland, because they were too heavy and required larger draft horses than the expedition had been able to procure. Thus, June 11 was spent shifting the powder, fitting the wagons, and rearranging the stores. The wagons were reloaded to a lighter carriage of twelve to fourteen hundred pounds. The difference was shifted to horseback. Seven of the most able horses were assigned to each of the heavy howitzers and five to each 12-pounder. Four horses pulled each wagon. The other horses carried flour and bacon. Although the contracts for the pack horses required them to carry two hundred pounds each, these horses were jades, the rejects of the Indian traders, and they sagged under only one hundred pounds' weight.[7]

The army encamped according to the plan approved by the council of war. With the wagons and gun carriages closed up, the camp, from front to rear guard, extended a half mile. Sentinels stood with their bayonets fixed, under orders not to allow anyone to approach within ten paces without giving the countersign of the day. Likewise, orders prohibited anyone from firing a musket within one mile of the camp. The sentinels had started to build shelters of boughs of trees. The general's orders now forbade these "hutts or bowers."

It took two days to reload all the wagons. On Friday the 13th the entire convoy started up again at four in the morning. The army marched to Martin's Plantation, only five miles from Spendelow Camp. There, Braddock continued to adjust his orders for the line of march: "Upon the beating of the General,[8] which is to be taken from the 44th Regiment, all the troops are to turn out, accoutre and form two deep at the head of their encampments upon all halts, tho' ever so small; the picket and companies are to face outwards. The officers of the pickets are to take care that their pickets keep at a proper distance upon their flanks. Upon the firing of a cannon, either in front, centre or rear, the whole line is to form, face outwards, and to wait for orders."[9] Braddock took care to warn the batmen, wagoneers, and horse drivers not to let the horses eat the poisonous leaves of the laurel bush that abounded in that part of the country, which would be "certain death to them."[10]

The same day punishment was meted out to four men of the North Carolina company who intended to desert but who were informed upon by a fifth man, one of their co-conspirators. Without apparent resort to a court-martial (and without having actually deserted), one man received one thousand lashes, another man nine hundred, and two others five hundred apiece. The delivery of such a harsh punishment under dubious circumstances was apparently impelled by the belief that the men intended to desert to the French and betray the English position.

Saturday, June 14, saw the column again on the move, rumbling a further six miles over Dans Mountain to the camp at Georges Creek, now abandoned as the rendezvous point in favor of the original meeting point at Little Meadows.

Immediately to the west of Georges Creek loomed Big Savage Mountain, the highest mountain in the series of ridges and the most difficult that either the advance detachment or the main army was to cross. The road cleared by the cutters followed a steep, rocky ascent of more than two miles, virtually to the highest point of the mountain from which the troops enjoyed a commanding view of the wilderness to the west. The descent of half a mile was also steep and rugged. Orme describes the passage of the mountain:

> The line began to move from this place [Georges Creek] at five of the clock; it was twelve before all the carriages had got upon a hill which is about a quarter of a mile from the front of the Camp, and it was found necessary to make one-half of the men ground their arms and assist the carriages while the others remained advantageously posted for their security.
>
> We this day passed Aligany [Big Savage] Mountain, which is a rocky ascent of more than two miles, in many places extremely steep; its descent is very rugged and almost perpendicular; in passing which we intirely demolished three waggons and shattered several. At the bottom of the mountain runs Savage river, which when we passed was an insignificant stream; but the Indians assured us that in the winter it is very deep, broad and rapid. This is the last water that empties itself into the Potomack.

> The first Brigade encamped about three miles to the westward of the river. Near this place was another steep ascent, which the waggons were six hours in passing.
>
> In this day's march, though all possible care was taken, the line was sometimes extended to a length of four or five miles.[11]

But the army's ordeal was only beginning. No sooner had it cleared the mountains and forded Two-mile Run than it entered the eerie Shades of Death. This was a vast virgin white pine forest the passage of which visibly spooked the men. Sargent, the centennial historian of the Braddock expedition, paints the picture: "The loneliness and perfect monotony of such a scene are not readily to be described; it more resembled the utter stillness of the desert than anything beside. No bird chirps among the foliage, or finds its food in these inhospitable boughs; no wild creature has its lair beneath its leafy gloom. Like the dark nave of some endless, dream-born cathedral, the tall columns rise before, behind, on every side, in uncounted and bewildering multiplicity, and are lost in the thick mantle that shuts out the light of heaven. The senses wear of the confusing prospect, and imagination paints a thousand horrid forms to people its recesses. At every step the traveler half looks to find a bloody corpse, or the blanched skeleton of some long murdered man, lying across his pathway through these woods, so aptly named the *Shades of Death!*"[12]

Once clear of the Shades of Death, the army took another two days to cross Meadow Mountain, requiring a "great deal of cutting, digging and Bridging and a great deal of Blowing" over a ridge "very rough and steep" and a descent "very rough, a hard pinch,"[13] according to chief engineer Gordon. Braddock finally reached the camp at Little Meadows on Monday, June 16—"inclosed with an Abbatis, dry, fine feeding, good water source"—but Dunbar's rear units did not make it until the next day. One would imagine that it was with a sense of relief that the army made its rendezvous.

Meanwhile at Little Meadows, the advance detachment more than a week earlier had already made its first contact with the enemy. This encounter occurred on June 8, two days before Braddock marched forth from Fort Cumberland. Several of the Indian guides crept about five miles westward from the camp and came upon "many French Indians" roasting a deer. On seeing the advancing "English Indians," the enemy had run away, leaving their dinner. The scouts were outnumbered, however, and therefore returned to camp to get reinforcements with which to pursue them. Although the reinforced unit went in immediate pursuit, the French Indians eluded them.[14]

Separately from this probe, a force of volunteers and Indians had struck out on June 9 from Little Meadows toward the Great Meadows to see if the French were there, as intelligence reports indicated.[15] They returned two days later reporting that they had seen no French.[16]

However, mixed intelligence began to pour in. On June 10, the day Braddock finally marched from Fort Cumberland, Scaroyady's son (or son-in-law under some accounts, Indian relationships being perplexing to white observers) arrived from Fort Duquesne bringing a report to St. Clair that he had seen some seventy Indians and one hundred French there. He reported that the fort was daily expecting reinforcements of two hundred more who had been delayed by low water because of the drought. He added that the fort mounted six recently arrived 4-pound cannon. Ominously, he also advised that the French knew the British army was on the march, thanks to a deserter from the Independent Company in the advance detachment. On the brighter side, he reported that the Delawares had been lobbying the Shawnees and Mohawks to stop supporting the French. St. Clair immediately relayed all this intelligence by letter to the general.[17]

At the same time, life was beginning to look up for Charlotte Browne as she made her bone-jarring trip by wagon toward Fort Cumberland. Lieutenant Falkner entertained her at their stop on June 7 with several fine tunes on his flute, and they chatted until ten at night. The next day Falkner "said he would do himself the pleasure of staying with me. We spent the day very agreeably: had for Dinner some Veal and greens, to drink french Wine, and for Supper Milk Punch."[18] The subsequent day Falkner "went a shooting" and brought Browne some squirrels, which she dressed for dinner. Their next stop had no food, but Falkner came to the rescue by shooting pigeons of which Browne "made us a fine Regale" for supper. At ten, she went to her wagon to bed but lay "extremely cold." The attentive Falkner ordered a sentinel posted at Browne's wagon all night "so that no one should molest me."[19] However, the going was increasingly rough. Browne was traversing the same Bear Garden Mountain road leading to Cresap's crossing of the Potomac River at Old Town that the main army had marched and cursed one month earlier. By June 11, the wagons began to break down. Browne walked until her feet were blistered. That night she "drank Tea and supt on the Stump of an old tree." Dinner was salt pork and "humble Grog."[20] On Friday the 13th, Browne finally reached Fort Cumberland, "the most desolate place I ever saw."[21]

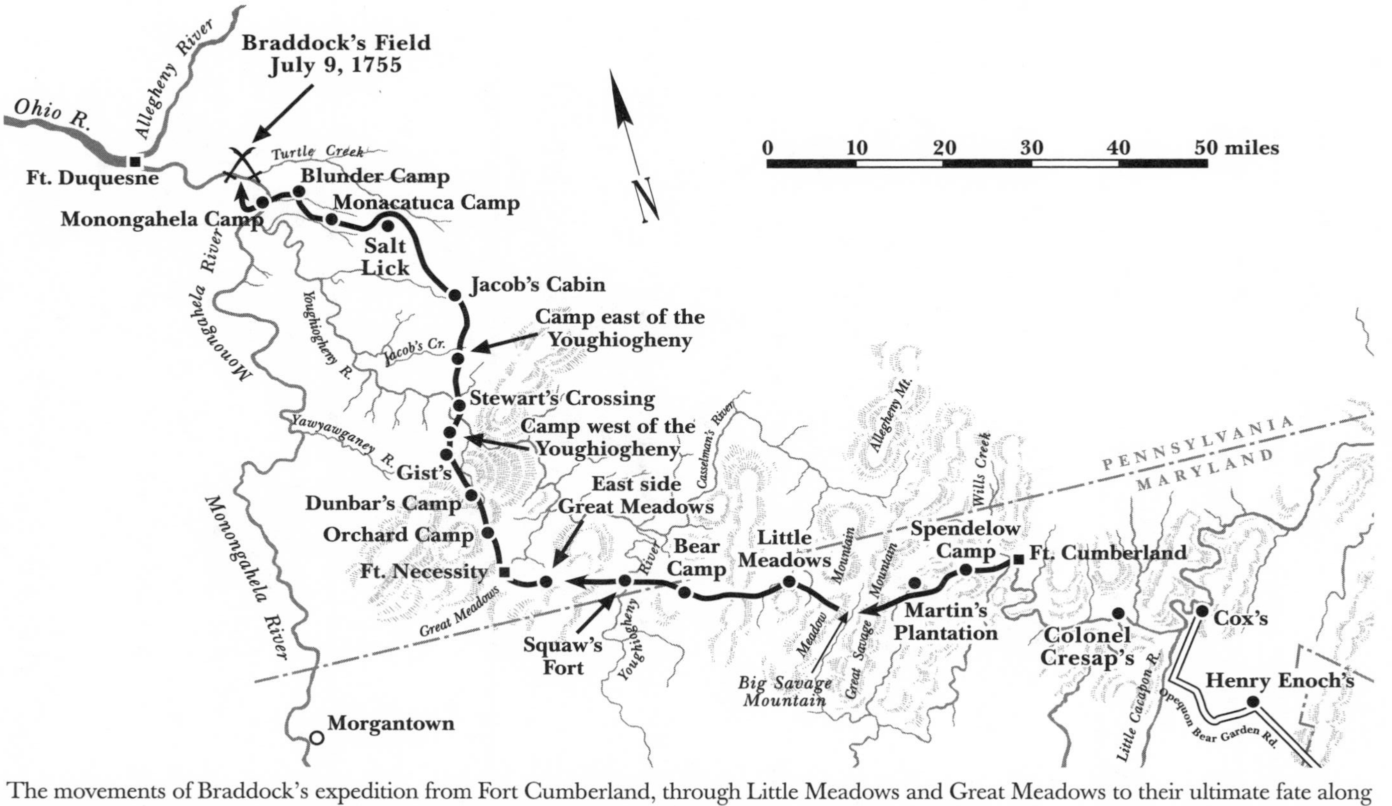

The movements of Braddock's expedition from Fort Cumberland, through Little Meadows and Great Meadows to their ultimate fate along the Monongahela River just east of their objective, Fort Duquesne.

Chapter Fifteen

The Flying Column

THE CANDLES FLICKERED IN THE THICK night heat of the general's tent at Little Meadows. So did tempers, fueled by wine at His Excellency's dinner table (apparently Braddock continued to carry his cellar with him, despite the shortage of wagons and horses). Colonel Dunbar had been asked his opinion of great generals under whom he had served. The avuncular colonel was expounding with reason and examples of what distinguished his former commanding officers. Braddock smiled indulgently from the head of the table. The asp-tongued Orme retorted that Dunbar's discourse was so much "stuff."

"You might as well be talking of your grandmother," Captain Orme sniffed.

"Sir, if she was alive," the older and more experienced Dunbar replied, "she would have more sense, more good manners, and know as much of military matters as you do."

Braddock coughed and intervened. "Gentlemen, you are both warm."

"General," Dunbar protested, "you see the provocation I got."

The matter ended there, but Braddock never again sought Dunbar's opinion on any matter. He relegated him to a supporting role. Orme had succeeded in splitting the general from both of his deputy commanders.

The three days spent at Little Meadows shaped the course of the remainder of the expedition, with devastating consequences.

Braddock fought the fear that his convoy was not operating as effectively as it should. In many ways a perfectionist, he continued to tinker with methods to increase its speed and compactness. His concern grew as the likelihood of fresh reinforcements arriving at Fort Duquesne or of an Indian ambush along the line of march increased with each passing day. The general solicited the views of his officers. He conferred with Washington, knowing that he had marched the route the year before. Because he was familiar with the mobility of the Indian traders, Washington advocated fewer wagons and more packhorses. Washington then made a fateful recommendation. Perhaps it had already been at the back of Braddock's mind. Washington "urged it in the warmest terms I was master of, to push on; if we even did it with a chosen detachment for that purpose, with the artillery and such other things as were absolutely necessary."[1]

On Tuesday, June 17, without calling a council of war, Braddock made the decision to split his troops. He would establish a "flying column" of hand-picked troops to sprint to Fort Duquesne and lead the assault. To cut the road, St. Clair would depart the next day with four hundred men, two companies of Virginia rangers, and the Indian scouts. Braddock would follow the day after with his military family, the two senior Grenadier companies, five hundred and fifty of the best soldiers from the two line regiments, all brought from Ireland, as well as the sailors under Spendelow and eighteen of the Virginia light horse troop that had acted as his bodyguard earlier on the march. The remainder of the troops were to follow under Dunbar with most of the baggage as best they could. No women were to accompany the flying column, an order which was in practice disobeyed. At least two women, and maybe more, continued to march with each company, even in the flying column.

Braddock designated Halkett, Gage, Burton, and Sparkes as the senior field officers in command under him. Below Major Sparkes he named eight captains, twenty lieutenants, and nine ensigns as chosen for the flying column.[2] St. Clair was to have his standard armament of two 6-pounders, plus three wagons of clearing tools. The main party of the detachment, under Braddock, would carry four howitzers with fifty rounds for each, the four 12-pounders with eighty rounds each, three cohorn mortars, and thirteen wagons, one of which bore presents for the Indians and the others ammunition. The column's packhorses would carry thirty-five days' food and provisions. Braddock increased the horsepower of the wagons and gun carriages to elevate speed. He now assigned six, rather than four, horses to each wagon. And he increased the complements of horses for the cannon to seven for the 12-pounders and nine for the howitzers. An extra one hundred replacement horses joined the four hundred specially chosen for the column. Each soldier's cartridge box was loaded with twenty-four rounds. The aims were speed, compactness, firepower, and self-sufficiency.

It was a potent force by eighteenth-century standards. There were a total of thirteen cannon for approximately 1,200 combatants in the flying column or a ratio of artillery to infantry of 1:92. By comparison, the Americans and Hessians at the Battle of Trenton just over twenty years later boasted artillery to infantry rations of 1:135 and 1:250, respectively. Similarly, the Battle of Princeton was fought with American and British artillery to infantry ratios of 1:129 and 1:150 to 200, respectively.[3] Both of these battles were fought on the Eastern seaboard, not in a mountain wilderness, which makes the projection of force all the more remarkable.

However, Dunbar disliked the arrangement. Braddock tried to appease him by telling him he would never be a day's march ahead of him and that in case of necessity the two columns might rejoin on two or three hours' notice. Braddock ordered Dunbar to fire a 6-pounder if he wanted his assistance. Two or more cannon shots from Braddock meant for Dunbar to join him with all the force he had and leave the baggage.[4] Dunbar grumbled, but he had no choice in the matter.

The flying column moved out as planned, with St. Clair leading the advance at four in the morning of June 18, and Braddock following the next morning. Fluttering above Braddock's column were the colors of the king and the regimental flag of the 44th, followed by that of the 48th, whose combined elite now marched under Braddock's command. His Excellency had now taken personal command.

Washington rode with Orme and the others in Braddock's military family. But Washington was a sick man, stricken with the same bloody flux that had laid low scores of soldiers. Still, a man of iron constitution, he rode on.

Before he left, Braddock ordered the entrenchment and fortification of Little Meadows as a supply depot to receive provisions coming from the settled areas of Pennsylvania. He also stated that he hardened the position because, as one British officer observed, it was on the west side of the Appalachian Mountains. It thus preserved the king's rights against the French, who "pretended that those Mountains bounded his Majesty's Dominions."[5] While they labored at Little Meadows the men enjoyed salt pork supplemented by deer, wild turkey, and other game.

But all was not happy at Little Meadows once the flying column moved out. Dunbar was already on the outs with the Braddock–Orme axis and smarting from being ordered to bring up the rear. However, as a professional soldier, he knew he had a job to do. The problem was that it would not be easy. Dunbar's wagon masters had informed him that he had been left with only one hundred teams for one hundred and fifty wagons, and those at only four horses each. He was equally short of packhorses. The only solution would be to operate a relay team, moving up as many wagons and packhorses as possible in the wake of

Braddock's advance, unhitching or unloading them, and returning them back for another haul. It was, in short, an impossible situation. The fretting colonel dashed Braddock a note explaining the problem. The general replied, in effect, that Dunbar should do his best and stop pestering him.

The advantages of the flying column became immediately apparent. Even though it was traversing rough, mountainous country, the distance covered in a day increased markedly. Moreover, the line of march shrank from four or five miles to less than a mile. The encampments were comparably compacted.

On the first day the flying column crossed Casselman River, about eighty yards across and knee deep. Some four miles from Little Meadows Braddock's column caught up with St. Clair's advance party and was obliged to stop and encamp while it waited for St. Clair to cut a traverse road over what Orme called an "immense mountain."[6] This was Negro Mountain, the fifth ridge that the expedition had to surmount. At 2,740 feet, it stood almost as high as Big Savage Mountain. Deformed, stunted trees covered its top.

Immediately after the soldiers had made the camp, the expedition's Indian guides came running back, "extremely frightened." They claimed that a great body of the enemy was marching to attack the advance guard. Braddock sent forward an aide-de-camp to try to verify the report. He found that Gage had already moved to take possession of the top of the mountain, with his men "very advantageously posted." It seems that the Indians had discovered the tracks of several men near the advance party, causing the alarm. Gage remained on the crest of the mountain, under arms, for several hours. He scoured the neighboring woods but saw no enemy. Eventually he descended but left pickets to secure the heights for the night.

A closer call visited Scaroyady. The same day a war party of seventy French and Indians not far from the advance party surrounded him and took him prisoner. The French wanted to kill him. Their Indian allies refused. The latter agreed, however, to tie him to a tree, where they interrogated him. They asked questions about the English artillery and strength. They were greatly surprised by his (apparently truthful) account. The French scoffed that it was impossible to march artillery through such a wilderness and therefore concluded that Scaroyady must be lying. The French and Indians then departed, leaving Scaroyady tied to the tree. However, his son, who had accompanied him, escaped and ran back to the English lines. Several of the Indian scouts went out and found and freed him. As a result of these incidents, Braddock tightened even further the system of pickets.

At the same time, the colonial newspapers provided decidedly upbeat assessments of the advancement of the army. They heralded the arrival of wagons and supplies from Pennsylvania and the good conditions prevailing at Fort Cumberland. "The Army in general are very healthy, impatient to enter on Action, and wait chiefly for the Arrival of the Forage. . . . We are told that His Excellency Major General Braddock, and all the Forces under his Command, are gone from Will's Creek towards the Ohio. May the Great God of Hosts Crown their Enterprize with Success."[7]

On Friday, June 20, the army marched for twelve hours, from seven in the morning until seven at night, covering a good eight miles along a stony road. The troops pitched their tents just south of the Pennsylvania line at a spot on a high rolling plateau that they dubbed Bear Camp. There they halted for two days while they waited for St. Clair's advance party to cut more road in the side of a mountain and to corduroy some swamp. There they passed the summer solstice, so far west that the sunlight lingered until late at night. Braddock gave orders for the pickets to "load afresh" when they went on duty and to "take particular care to save the ball, which the commanding officers of companies are to see returned to the train."[8] He also ordered the Articles of War to be read again to the men and that the article relating to the alarming of camps be "particularly explained" to them. Despite the general's palpable concern about attack, the weekend passed quietly.

To judge from the diagram of the line of march made by Orme after the fact, the flying column on the march followed the directions of the council of war to the letter. At its head rode the Virginia light horse, one center and two flanking units under Captain Robert Stewart, a Scotsman transplanted to Virginia. Next came a detachment of thirty sailors, surrounded back and sides by three detachments of Grenadiers. Then rolled three 12-pounders, surrounded by more Grenadiers. The vanguard followed, with the train of wagons running behind them like a spine. In the exact middle rode Halkett (and presumably Braddock), followed by more train and the rear guard. The end of the line of march consisted of one 12-pounder guarded by Grenadiers and a mirror image of the light horse units from the head of the van. Not shown on the diagram but also present were at least a handful of women camp followers and a drove of beef cattle. In all, the line on the march stretched to perhaps a little over one thousand yards, or two-thirds of a mile. John Rutherford, an officer in Halkett's regiment, left a more vivid picture: "The Knight [Sir John St. Clair] swearing in the van, the Genl cursing & bullying in the center & their whores bringing up the rear."[9]

When the line stopped to camp it attenuated somewhat and resembled nothing so much as a human body, with the light horse units the head, flanking units of sergeants and subalterns with ten and twenty men, respectively, the shoulders, the guns and the wagons the spine, Braddock's guard and tent the heart, and the rear guard the legs. Pickets surrounded the whole, the fingers and toes of the column, the first to sense any intrusion. Formed into this living organism, Braddock's army crabbed its way cautiously through the unknown perils of the wilderness. Each unit, each man, knew his place and adhered to it strictly both on the march and in the encampment. The only departure from the military choreography would come when the sailors dropped back to help pull the heavy cannon up the side of a mountain. Then the entire column must have stopped while the tars chanted and heaved on the ropes. The same would have happened on the steep descents,

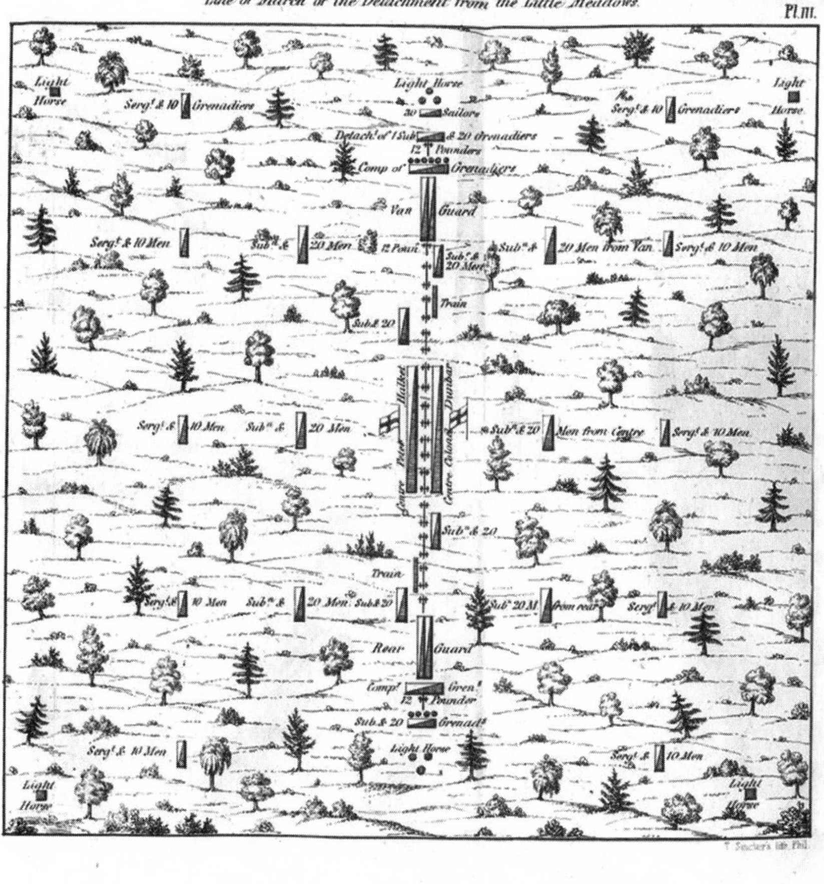

Captain Robert Orme's diagram of the "Line of March of the Detachment from the Little Meadows," from Winthrop Sargent's 1855 *History*. Orme inexplicably places Colonel Dunbar on the right-hand side in the center of the flying column. Since Dunbar did not accompany the detachment, this was more likely General Braddock's position in the flying column.

when the sailors deployed their tackles and dug in their feet to keep the cannon from racing out of control. By such laborious, controlled movement the army advanced, sweating over every inch of the rising and falling rock-strewn and bog-laden terrain in the blistering midsummer heat. By the time they reached Bear

Camp at the Pennsylvania line, two months after leaving Alexandria, they had traveled less than one hundred and fifty miles from what is now downtown Washington, D.C.

The army moved out on Monday the 23rd at five in the morning. Washington did not move with them. Now desperately ill with the flux, he lay prostrate in his tent. He later recorded that "my illness was too violent to suffer me to ride, therefore I was indebted to a covered wagon for some part of my transportation; but even this I could not continue, for the jolting was so great that I was left upon the road with a guard and necessaries, to await the arrival of Colonel Dunbar's detachment, which was two days march behind. The general giving me his word and honor that I should be brought up before he reached the French fort; this promise and the doctor's threats that if I persevered it would endanger my life, determined my halting."[10]

The army crept six miles northwestward from Bear Camp on "very bad road" to within a mile of the Youghiogheny. Engineer Gordon recorded "a great deal of cutting and digging, and a few bridges" and the quality of the road as "3 miles tolerable with a few hard pinches, the ridge 1/2 up in zigzags, 2 miles stoney, 2 1/2 miles in a defile."[11] They named their camp that night Squaw's Fort.

However, any doubt that they were in hostile territory was dispelled by a visit that evening by three Mohawks pretending friendship. They claimed to have come from Fort Duquesne. They warned that reinforcements had just arrived at the fort from Montreal, with many more on the way. "The General caressed them, and gave them presents, but they nevertheless went off that night, and with them one of our Indians, whom we had very long suspected. This fellow had frequently endeavored to conceal himself upon the flanks on the March, but was always discovered by the flank parties. Notwithstanding this, we could not punish him, as the Indians are so extremely jealous that we feared it would produce a general disaffection."[12] This Indian, Jerry by name, fought for the French thereafter. He later scalped several British

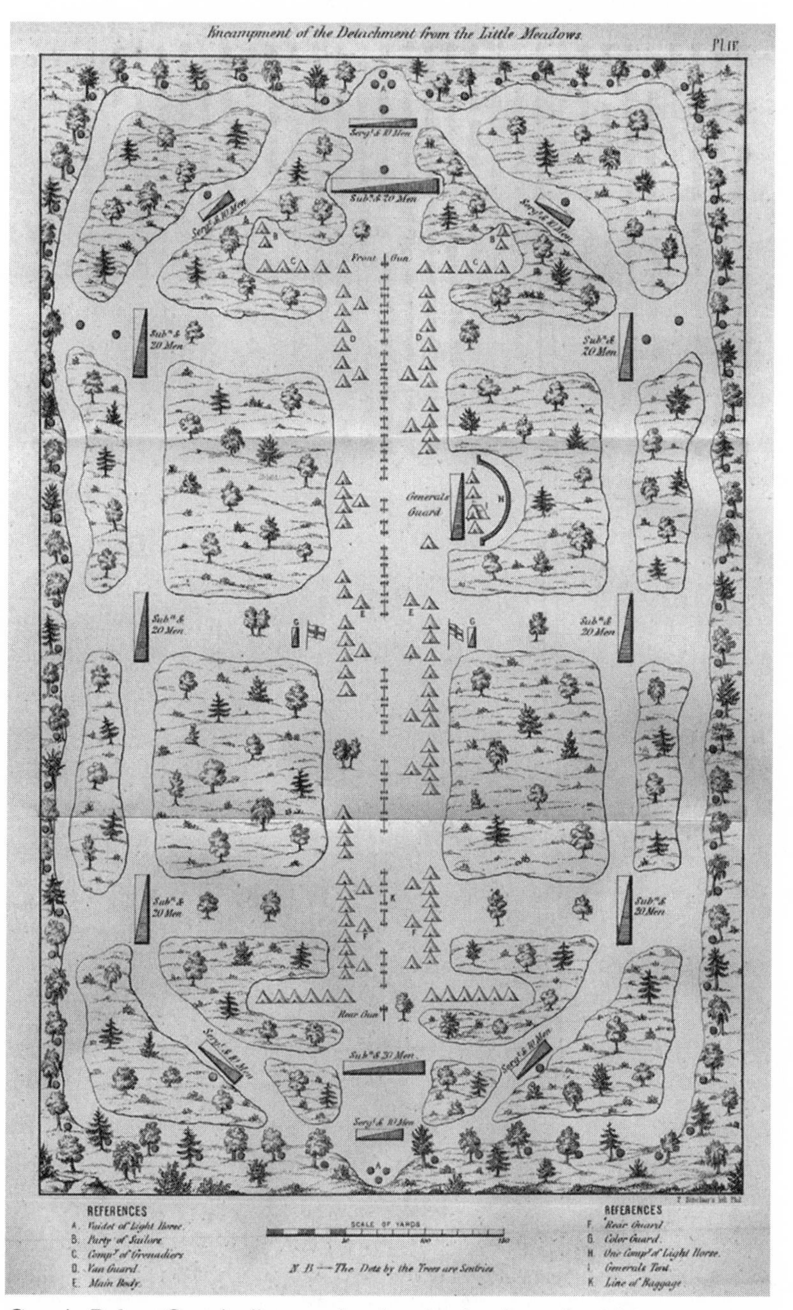

Captain Robert Orme's diagram showing the detachment's night encampment and the meticulous security measures employed. (from Sargent's *History*)

soldiers. Dunbar captured but, somewhat inexplicably, pardoned him. A year later he was murdered in upstate New York by some soldiers of the 44th who remembered him from the Braddock expedition. They decapitated him and placed his head on a post at the head of the regiment.[13]

Braddock ordered the men to light no fires within one hundred yards of the gun carriages so as not to give away their position at night. He also admonished the pickets to examine the firing pans of their muskets each morning and replenish them with fresh powder if deficient.[14]

Next day, following their encampment at Squaw's Fort, the flying column traversed the so-called "Great Crossing" of the Youghiogheny. The river there was about one hundred yards wide, three feet deep, and with a strong current. (Today the crossing has been inundated by a dam and is the site of Lake St. Clair, a recreational facility.) The fording of the Youghiogheny was a significant landmark in the advance of the column. So too was what happened next.

During the march on the 24th the men discovered a recently abandoned Indian camp. The guides advised that it had held up to one hundred and seventy braves. The departed Indians had stripped and painted some trees, upon which both they and the French had written "many threats and bravados with all kinds of scurrilous language."[15] As the column continued, the Indian guides thought they saw many hostile Indians lurking in the woods. As stated by the batman, "This day we marched 10 miles and drove many of the French Indiens before us."[16] That night the column camped just east of the Great Meadows, the site of Fort Necessity. Early the next morning a wagoneer went out to bring in his horses and was surprised by a party of Indians, who shot him four times in the stomach. He made it back to the camp but died afterward. Later that morning four more people ventured out to collect their horses and were killed and scalped.[17] The flying column named the place of their encampment "Scalping Camp."

A brass 12-pounder cannon and carriage. The Braddock expedition towed four of these cannons along with four iron naval 12-pounders. It is unclear from existing inventories taken after the battle which cannon accompanied the flying column, but it is likely that the longer and heavier naval cannon were left at Fort Cumberland in favor of the brass 12-pounders. (*Fort Ligonier, Ligonier, Pennsylvania*)

The same day, back at Fort Cumberland, a wave of Indian attacks descended on the backcountry settlers. Two families, of fourteen or fifteen people, were massacred. Among them was a boy found in a creek, sobbing. He had been scalped and was drenched in blood. The soldiers carried him back to Fort Cumberland, where the doctors dressed his wounds. However, they found two holes driven into his skull by the blows of a tomahawk. He died within a week.[18]

CHAPTER SIXTEEN

Terra Incognita

FORT NECESSITY DID NOT IMPRESS the British officers. Its demolished remnants sat squarely at the bottom of the Great Meadows, open to sweeping fire from any direction, and defended only by a rudimentary trench. The Americans' swivel guns from the year before lay disabled by the French and abandoned in the trench. "There are many human bones all round ye spott," recorded one British officer.[1] Fearing ambush, the flying column marched right by it and encamped at a more defensible location some two miles to the west of the Great Meadows. Washington, who had lingered for four days at Bear Camp imbibing Dr. James's Powder ("one of the most excellent medicines in the world," he swore to his brother), had now joined Dunbar's elephantine advance and was spared the embarrassment of revisiting the scene of his defeat.

Orme noted that both French and Indians "endeavored to reconnoitre the camp, but wherever they advanced, they were discovered and fired upon by the advance Centinels."[2] One Indian allied with the French was killed. Braddock ordered the subalterns and officers who marched with the outer detachments always to keep one of their men within sight of the line of march. He stipulated that these parties were to be no closer to the line of march than one hundred yards, with the detachments of sergeants and corporals to be no closer to their officers than fifty yards. He threatened to arrest any officer who failed to obey.[3] To lift the spirits of the men, Braddock offered a bounty of £5 for any Indian scalp taken.

Notwithstanding their exhaustion and the ever-closer threat from the Indians, Orme found the men's spirits to be rejuvenated on reaching the Great Meadows. "The soldiers were now so accustomed to open the communications, and understood so well the reason and method of our encampment, that they performed this work with great alacrity and dispatch; and the marching through the woods, which they at first looked upon as unnecessary fatigue, they are convinced to be their only security, and went through it with the greatest cheerfulness."[4]

However, the flying column did not linger long at the Great Meadows. Mindful of the potential for ambush and the threat posed by imminent reinforcements at Fort Duquesne, the column moved out at five in the morning on Thursday, June 26. The column began to climb Chestnut Ridge, the last mountain it would have to surmount. On the ascent the soldiers passed open meadows that afforded breathtaking views of the western country laid out like a blanket. They also passed within a quarter mile of the gray rock ledge at Jumonville Glen where, almost exactly a year earlier, Washington and the Half King had started what was to become the French and Indian War.

Cutting old and standing timber, with "a little bridging and digging,"[5] the men made only four miles before having to stop to wait for the advance party to clear more road. At the site of their bivouac they discovered another Indian camp. Like the one before, this one was recently abandoned but with its fires still ablaze. The trees were stripped and painted in red with depictions of the scalps taken the day before. The names of three French soldiers appeared–Rochefort, Chauraudray, and Picauday[6]–together with "many insolent expressions." The soldiers also found a lost commission which mentioned that the party was under the command of the Sieur Normanville. The camp stood high on a rocky promontory with a steep ascent. A spring bubbled at the center of the camp, which was located at the end of an Indian path to the Monongahela at the confluence of Redstone Creek. The party which had engaged Washington the year before had traveled through the same pass.[7] Known as the Half King's Rocks, the site had been the secret campground of Washington's old ally.[8]

That night the flying column encamped a further three miles on the side of Chestnut Ridge at a location they dubbed Orchard Camp or Steep Bank Camp because of the sharp descent a quarter mile behind the camp. At midnight the alarm sounded as Indians fired at the sentries. One hundred men were ordered out to protect the flanks of the camp.

Despite the interrupted sleep, the drummers beat the general early the next morning, and the flying column pressed forward, now turning almost due north (toward present-day Connellsville, Pennsylvania). The column followed the narrow crest of the mountain in keeping with St. Clair's predilection for the high ground. It was still rocky and steep, but by the afternoon, the column had cleared the mountain and entered into fine rolling land. Halkett celebrated the passage of the mountains by ordering rum delivered to all his troops at five o'clock the next morning. With the worst terrain past, Halkett also ordered St. Clair's advance party to return and reintegrate with their regiments. If any further road cutting needed to be done, it could be handled by one integrated column. That night the troops encamped at the ruins of the plantation of Christopher Gist (the fur trader and guide to Washington the previous year), which the French had recently burned.

On Saturday, June 28, the column marched five miles to a camp on the west side of the Youghiogheny near what was later known as Stewart's Crossing (after Captain Robert Stewart of the Virginia light horse which served as the general's bodyguard). They found the country they crossed to be so lushly overgrown with weeds that a man on horseback could not see the men twenty yards in front of him.[9] They were to cross the river once again. Because the river flows from Pennsylvania in a southeasterly direction and because the column had veered almost due north, the line of march intersected the stream twice. The drought of the previous weeks broke, however, and heavy rain drenched the men as they trudged into camp. A party ventured out to scout for Indians in the downpour, but they saw only a bear sitting in a mulberry tree.[10]

The actual crossing of the Youghiogheny was reserved for the next day. Here the river ran about two hundred yards wide and three feet deep. The advance guard passed first, taking up a post on the far side to cover the crossing by the artillery and baggage. Once they were safely over, the remainder of the men forded the river.[11] After the crossing, the column encamped about a mile on the eastern side of the river and halted for a day to allow the further cutting of the road and the baking of bread to feed the men on the next leg of the journey.

There had been some nervousness about an ambush at the time of the crossing, but the fears were never realized. Some men began to see Indians where there were none and started firing their muskets "in a very irregular manner." Braddock ordered Halkett to chastise them and threaten arrest if it were ever to happen again. Even a jammed gun could not be fired, but had to be taken to the appropriate commanding officer and specific permission obtained from one of the general's aides-de-camp to fire the piece. Braddock wanted no false alarms.[12]

On July 1, aware that they were entering increasingly hostile country, Halkett gave orders to strengthen the advance party by one hundred men and forbade the pickets to use tents or blankets (at this juncture, Halkett assumed more of a command role than Braddock for reasons that are not entirely clear). On the march, the men amused themselves by picking up lumps of coal which abounded on the surface of the ground. The march took them through about nine miles of pleasant country, and at least some officers began to wonder if they had already passed Fort Duquesne.[13] That night they camped at a place called Terrapin Camp, the exact location of which is uncertain.[14]

The following day they marched some six miles to an encampment near a large swamp at Jacob's Cabin on the east side of Jacob's Creek. The engineers had to bridge the swamp in order to get the men over. By now provisions had begun to run low so that each man received only three-quarters of a pound of flour and a half-pound of bacon per day.[15] Braddock had earlier sent back to Dunbar for more food, but it had not yet arrived. The horses were dying fast of exhaustion and lack of adequate forage.

Perimeter security remained a constant preoccupation among the senior officers. On July 3, before the four-mile march to Salt Lick Camp (so named because it was the site of a salt lick frequented by deer, buffalo, and bear), Halkett ordered a doubling of the pickets, with two men at each post. The officers were to have half their pickets constantly under arms, with bayonets fixed, and relieve them every two hours. The relieved pickets could lay down their arms but not leave their post. All arms were to be inspected each evening to ensure that they were clean and operational for the next morning.[16] Action could happen at any time.

Dunbar, meanwhile, struggled to keep up. He had only now reached the Squaw's Fort camp at the Pennsylvania border, some eleven days' march behind the flying column at the rate they were proceeding. Washington, recovered from his fevers but still too weak to ride a horse, planned to leave that day with the food relief wagons to rejoin Braddock at the front. At Salt Lick Camp St. Clair now raised the sensible question: should they bring up Dunbar's troops to rejoin the flying column? Braddock called his fourth council of war to consider the question. Attending were Halkett, Gage, Sparkes, Burton, and St. Clair. Orme recorded the event, but neither he nor Morris attended as voting members.

The debate was open and free-ranging. At the end of the meeting, the unanimous consensus was not to wait for Dunbar. A variety of considerations led to this decision:

> The state of the roads and the number of carriages Dunbar had with him would mean that Dunbar could cover the distance no faster than they had done, and they therefore would have to halt and wait at least eleven days for him to come up.
>
> The flying column would exhaust its provisions while waiting the eleven days.
>
> Even if they sent horses back post haste to assist Dunbar, their return passage would require an additional two days.
>
> The horses were already so weak they probably could not accomplish the mission.
>
> No advantage would accrue from reuniting the forces, as Dunbar still could not keep up with the flying column.
>
> Dunbar was in any event unable to spare many men.
>
> In moving up, he was more likely to be attacked than at his present rearward position.
>
> The intervening time would allow the French to receive their reinforcements and entrench themselves and strengthen Fort Duquesne or to position themselves at the strongest passes to attack the column. The fact that they had not done so already was viewed as proof that the long-rumored reinforcements had not yet arrived.

Taking all of these considerations into account, the council of war voted to march on in two separate columns.

Braddock called in Croghan and ordered him to try to persuade the Indian guides to reconnoiter Fort Duquesne for intelligence, a request that he had made before. However, the Indians refused, despite presents and promises from the general.[17] Braddock tried again the next day, which was the first anniversary of Washington's defeat at Fort Necessity. This time the major general succeeded in getting two of the Indians to scout for intelligence toward the French fort. As a precaution, Braddock also engaged Christopher Gist, who had joined the expedition, to reconnoiter the fort. That night, after a march of only three miles through rocky open country and woods of white oak, they encamped at their sixteenth stopping point, Thicketty Run.

The following day, July 5, the army rested and received much-needed supplies from Dunbar–one hundred oxen and flour, plus a hundred men under Virginia Captain Adam Stephen–all very welcome. Resupplied and refreshed, the army broke camp the next morning, July 6, and marched six miles through thickets to Monacatuca Camp. The expedition was now less than twenty miles from Fort Duquesne. This camp received its name because of an unfortunate accident. About eleven o'clock in the morning French Indians attacked the baggage at the rear of the flying column. They scalped a soldier and a woman attached to the general's cattle. They also wounded a man in the shoulder and were in the process of scalping another when the rear guard rescued him. For the first time, marchers in the flying column itself–not just stragglers–were liable to be picked off at any time by Indians darting from the woods. The resulting nervousness of the soldiers erupted two hours later when the soldiers found the same group of French Indians lurking in the woods at the head of the column. They began firing at them, and the Indian guides came up to assist them. In a "friendly fire" accident, the English soldiers mistakenly shot and killed the son of Scaroyady (also known as Monacatuca). Braddock sent for Scaroyady and offered his condolences, as well as presents. In a gesture much appreciated by the Indians, Braddock ordered a full military funeral that evening, with all officers attending. As the soldiers lowered the corpse into the ground an honor guard fired their muskets over the grave. Scaroyady was disconsolate. He said it would have been a trifling for his son to have been killed in battle with the French, but he regretted most having to lose him to his own allies. The soldiers never apprehended the attackers who had caused the accident. They had chased them for some miles and found two spears and other items that identified them as Ottawas, possibly under the personal command of the Ottawa chieftain Pontiac.[18]

Earlier that day, the two Indians sent out to reconnoiter Fort Duquesne returned about ten o'clock in the morning. They reported that they had seen few soldiers at the fort and no new fortifications. They also advised that the enemy held no passes between the camp and the fort and that very few French or Indians were out on observation duty against the column. They saw some boats under the fort and one with a white flag going down the Ohio. They brought with them the fresh scalp of a French "officer" they had encountered hunting about a mile from the fort.[19] The scalp, which they presented to the general for the bounty, in fact belonged to Pierre Simard, age twenty-three, a Canadian militiaman.[20] Gist came in later that day with a report similar to that of the Indian scouts. However, he had almost been captured by two French Indians near the fort.

On Monday, July 7, the army picked up again and resumed its march, going three miles to the east side of Turtle Creek. They encamped at a place dubbed Blunder Camp (in the vicinity of present-day Circleville and Stewartsville). The origin of this name came from the need of the men to retrace their steps. The column departed from the Indian path it was following in order to try to cross Turtle Creek, a tributary of the Monongahela River, some twelve miles from the mouth of the creek so as to avoid a dangerous gorge where it flowed into the Monongahela (Braddock feared attack from the overlooking bluffs). Meanwhile, St. Clair had moved ahead of the column to scout out the ridge that led down to Fort Duquesne.[21] However, Braddock rejected the ridge route because of the deep ravines cut by streams and almost perpendicular precipices along the route. He also wanted to avoid the dangerous gorge cut by Turtle Creek. Consequently, once started along the ridge route, the column moved back and retraced its steps to encamp at a point not far from the previous night's campsite. Along the way they flushed out two French Indians. When they fired at them, thirty more rose up and fled.

The column was now closing to within striking distance of Fort Duquesne. More than six months had passed since the troop ships left Cork, Ireland. Braddock's army had inched through the wilderness alone and out of touch with civilization, an isolated sealed community intent on its own preoccupations. Little did that column weaving its way over the mountains and through the forests know that the French philosopher Jean-Jacques Rousseau had just written of the "noble savage" in his *Discourse on the Origins of Inequality*. One speculates that the Enlightenment might have caused a cynical snicker had the isolated soldiers even known about its stirrings.

Tuesday, July 8, saw a further march of eight miles, three of which were through a narrow pass fifty yards wide, bounded by the Monongahela and steep hills on either side. On reaching their encampment, Monongahela Camp (near present-day McKeesport), St. Clair raised with his fellow senior officers, but not with Braddock (who by this point was all but invisible), whether a detachment should be sent forth that night to invest the fort. There was concern, replied the officers, that the distance from the fort was too great to allow rapid reinforcement in the event of resistance. Wouldn't it be better to cross the Monongahela first with the full force and then send the detachment out from the next night's camp, which would be only six or seven miles from the fort? St. Clair acknowledged the logic of the concerns and desisted.

The officers summoned the Indian guides to discuss the intervening territory. The guides described the two fords of the Monongahela as both being shallow and without steep banks. The officers therefore decided to pass the river the next morning. The maneuver was a complicated one, designed to avoid the narrow defiles and potential for ambush from the bluffs on the east side of the Monongahela. (Along this stretch, the river flows from

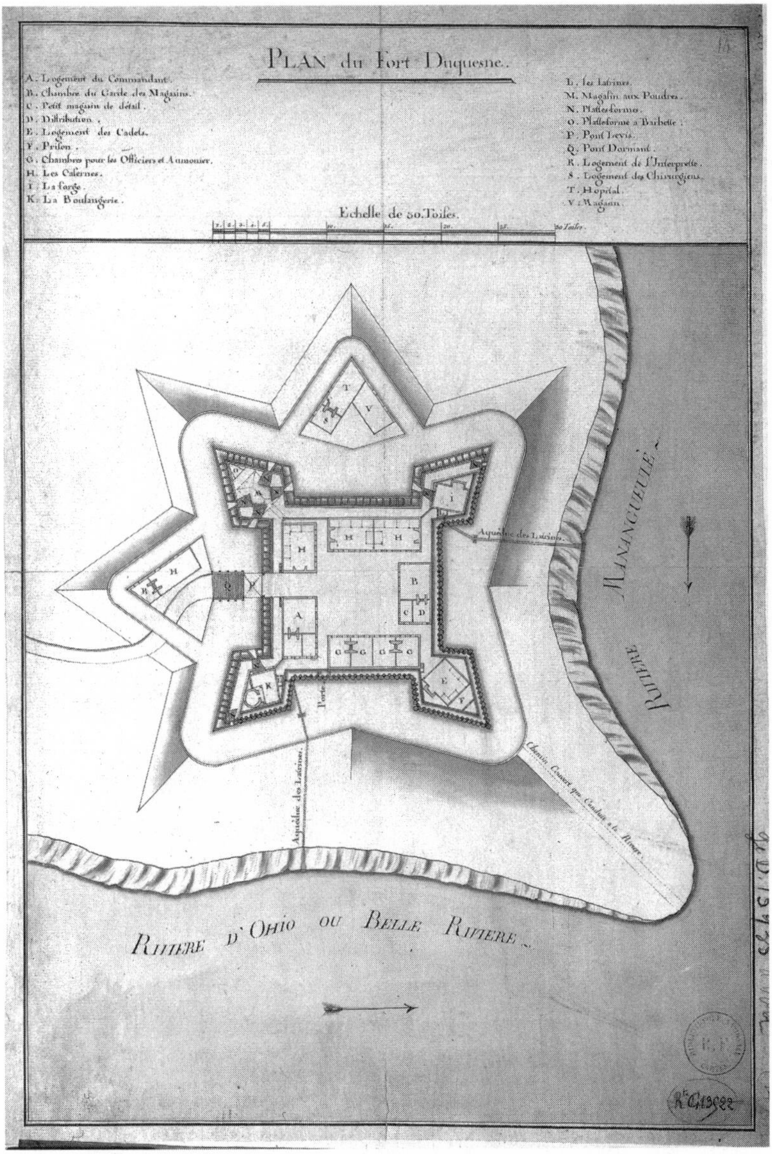

First built in 1754 at the confluence of the Allegheny, Monongahela, and Ohio Rivers, Fort Duquesne, the first objective of the Braddock Expedition, as shown in an original French diagram, c. 1754–1758. The British planned to capture this fort and then move north in a coordinated effort to drive France from North America. It would end up taking three more years before the fort was finally captured and destroyed. (*Bibliothèque nationale de France*)

southeast to northwest, making the east side the direct approach to the Forks.) The troops would cross over from the east to the west side of the river, march past the mouth of Turtle Creek on the opposite bank, and then recross the river back to the east side for the final, short approach to the Forks of the Ohio and Fort Duquesne. Because the whole area was heavily forested and with little room to maneuver along the narrow river banks, the officers were concerned about leaving the columns exposed to an ambush.

Halkett ordered Gage to march at two o'clock in the morning with two companies of Grenadiers, one hundred and sixty rank and file of the 44th and 48th Regiments, Captain Horatio Gates's Independent Company, two 6-pounders, and the Indian guides. Halkett instructed Gage to pass the fords of the Monongahela and take the post after the second crossing to secure the passage of the river for the rest of the column. Halkett ordered St. Clair to march at four o'clock in the morning with a detachment of two hundred and fifty men to cut the roads for the artillery and baggage, which were to march with the remainder of the troops at five.[22] The soldiers were to travel light to speed the crossing. The troops in Gage's party were issued twenty-four rounds of powder and ball each and instructed to draw rations for two days and take their knapsacks and haversacks but leave their tents behind. All officers in Gage's unit left their baggage with the quartermasters of their respective regiments.[23] The commanding officers agreed that the army should "march over the river in the greatest order, with their bayonets fixed, Colors flying, and Drums and Fifes beating and playing, as they supposed the Enemy would take a view of them in the crossing."[24] The decision to march across the river in battle formation thus appeared to stem as much from psychological warfare as from apprehension of an attack by the enemy on the dangerous crossing.

That evening George Washington arrived in a covered wagon in the rear of Dunbar's relief column and rejoined the general. Dunbar by this time had reached a camp on Chestnut Ridge at the confluence of what would later be called Glade Run and

Dunbar Creek, not far from the glen at Jumonville. It was to be his final stop, Dunbar's Camp, some thirty-six miles to the east of the position of the flying column and fifty miles from Fort Duquesne.

Braddock secluded himself in his tent to prepare for battle. Halkett was uneasy, full of premonitions. He knew Braddock did not value his advice and had therefore remained apart from the general, busying himself with the day-to-day exigencies of command. Nonetheless, he approached the general that night in his tent. With a "melancholy earnestness" he pressed Braddock about the necessity of examining every foot of ground between the camp and the fort, lest through neglect he imperil the army. Halkett's recommendation was that the advance party beat the forests as the hunters of the Highlands would drive their game. However, Braddock would have none of it. The plan was "unsuitable to the exigencies" of their position.[25] Halkett glumly withdrew.

What was running through Braddock's mind that last night? Was it a lifetime of training now brought to the test? Was it the family honor felt by a major general in the Coldstream Guards, the son of a major general in the Coldstream Guards? Was it the absolute certainty of the superiority of British arms over all comers? Or was it the nagging fear that French reinforcements had arrived at Fort Duquesne? Perhaps his Indian guides had lied. At least Gist had seen nothing. But conditions might have changed in the previous several days. Or was it the concern that his untested American auxiliaries would cut and run at the first sight of battle? Perhaps it was other things. Was it a memory of his house in Arlington Street, of the good times gambling and drinking, and wenching? Did he think of Mary Yorke, the lover he requisitioned from one of his lieutenants? Or did Edward Braddock's thoughts, that hot July night in the wilderness, turn to the one woman whose life had truly been entwined with his own, George Anne Bellamy, his lovely "Pop"? We shall never know. But one safe bet is that he was not deep in prayer.

Chapter Seventeen

Captain Beaujeu's Prayer

Captain Daniel Hyacinth-Marie Lienard de Beaujeu knelt to make his confession and receive communion from the gray-robed chaplain, the Recollect Father Denys Baron, in the log-framed chapel of the Assumption of the Blessed Virgin at Fort Duquesne. Beaujeu was no ordinary soldier. He was the forty-four-year-old son of a former mayor of Quebec and the grandson of an officer in the king's royal guard at Versailles. The lion rampant on his family crest was as fierce as the greyhound courant on Braddock's was graceful. Beaujeu was a captain of the Troupes de la Marine,[1] a former commander of the French forts at Detroit and Niagara, and a holder of the Cross of St. Louis awarded by the king. He was the Marquis of Duquesne's personal choice to succeed Contrecoeur as commander of Fort Duquesne. He also was stripped to the waist like an Indian and wearing a silver gorget as he knelt in prayer.[2]

As early as June 8, before Braddock departed Fort Cumberland, Cadet Normanville and a large raiding party of French and Indians had left Fort Duquesne to scout and harass

Braddock's army. Another group of seven French and one hundred and thirty Indians under Cadet Niversville left on June 18. Two further, smaller raiding parties left on June 26 and 30. They had had Braddock's column within their sights as soon as it crossed the Casselman River. However because of the column's size they could do little more than pick off stragglers. A further party of thirty-three Hurons went out on July 5. They returned the next day with no scalps but with the intelligence that "the English were within 8 leagues[3] marching briskly with their Artillery."[4] Further reports quickly poured in from other scouting parties. The Chevalier de la Parade was sent with some French and Indians to confirm the discovery by the Hurons. However, his guide, an Iroquois settled on the Ohio, got cold feet and would go no more than three or four leagues. The Ottawas and others held a meeting with Contrecoeur and determined to foray all together the next day. They did so, along two different routes. On their return, they confirmed the report of the English being eight leagues away, with a force estimated at some three thousand men and a strong train of artillery.

Captain Daniel Hyacinth-Marie Lienard de Beaujeu. (*National Archives of Canada*)

Contrecoeur remained in command of the fort pending resolution of the crisis. He favored capitulation. The sheer size of the English force (exaggerated as it was in the Indians' reports), together with the big guns hauled over the mountains, would make resistance useless. Contrecoeur, like Washington before him at Fort Necessity, was prepared to surrender on honorable terms. He took steps to mount a single gun on a carriage to provide the pretense of eighteenth-century etiquette that the fort was surrendered with a loaded cannon and lighted match.[5]

However, Contrecoeur had not definitively decided to hand over the fort and continued to mull over his course of action on July 7. The next day, when news reached the fort that Braddock would not follow the ridge route to the Forks of the Ohio but, rather, cross and recross the Monongahela, Beaujeu approached Contrecoeur with a proposal to sally forth and dispute the second crossing. According to tradition, Contrecoeur was reluctant to endorse the plan and suggested that, if he went, Beaujeu should take only volunteers because of the hazard of the venture. However, the commander reconsidered and offered to assign regular detachments, provided Beaujeu could rally most of the thousand or so Indians gathered about the fort to participate.[6] The Indians at the fort were a diverse but fierce lot. They included Delawares from the Susquehannah in Pennsylvania, Shawanoes from Grave Creek and Muskingum, scattered members of the Six Nations, Ojibwas and Pottowattamies from Michigan, Abenakis and Caughnawagas from Canada, Ottawas from Lake Superior (tradition has it, led by Pontiac, who possibly participated in the earlier attack on Braddock's column), Hurons from Montreal, and various "praying Indians" from all about.[7]

Beaujeu immediately called all the Indians together and "invited" them to join the French in driving out the English. "Mr. Beaujeu began to Warsong & all the Indian Nations Immediately joined him" except the Pottowotamies from Detroit. Their reluctance caused a delay of one day while all the tribes tried to reach a consensus. "How, my father, are you so bent upon death that you would also sacrifice us?" they asked Beaujeu. "With our eight hundred men do you ask us to attack four thousand English? Truly, this is not the saying of a wise man. But we will lay up what we have heard, and tomorrow you shall know our thoughts."[8]

While they waited, the Shawanoes and Iroquois of the Six Nations who lived near Fort Duquesne came in and pledged their assistance to the French,[9] provided certain unrecorded demands were met. The French considered and agreed to their demands and promptly armed them. "It was resolv'd we should the next day march out to meet them with all the Indians, only reserving some french for the Defense of the Fort."[10]

But the alliance was not yet sealed. The Indians held a council the night of the 8th. As related by McCardell, the bulk of the Indians informed Beaujeu that they had decided not to go.

> "I am determined to meet the English," Beaujeu told the Indians.
>
> The Indians were adamant. They would not go with him.
>
> "What! Will you let your father go alone?" he cried. "I am certain of defeating them."
>
> Some of the more reckless braves, naked except for breach clouts, already had daubed themselves with red, blue, black and brown war paint. . . . A Huron chief, Anthanases, and . . . Pontiac wavered.
>
> As they hesitated, a party of Indian scouts who had been up the river watching the British came into the fort. They told Beaujeu they had left the troops near the upper ford of the Monongahela. Apparently the British were going to follow the trail along the river.
>
> "You see, my friends," said Beaujeu, turning back to the hesitant chiefs, "the English are going to throw themselves into the lion's mouth. They are weak sheep who pretend to be ravenous wolves. Those who love their father, follow me! You need only hide yourselves in the ravines which line the road, and when you hear us strike, strike yourselves. The victory is ours!" A flutter of excitement burst into a frenzy. Suddenly the braves crowded around the bullet and powder kegs at the gate, scooping in with their powder horns, filling their bullet pouches. The Indians had changed their minds.[11]

However, the French and Indians also were being observed. The day before the Indians had brought in a young American, eighteen-year-old James Smith, whom they had captured working on the Pennsylvania road under construction between Rays Town and the Youghiogheny. Held prisoner, he had been temporarily blinded with sand, beaten, and interrogated. The Indians intended to keep him and convert him into one of their own. Smith asked one of his Delaware captors what news there was of Braddock's army. The Indian, who spoke rudimentary English, said the Indians spied on them every day and showed him, by making marks on the ground with a stick, that the army was advancing in very close order and that the Indians would surround them, take to the trees and, as he put it, "Shoot um down all one pigeon."[12]

At eight o'clock on the morning of July 9 Smith saw Beaujeu, stripped for battle, run from the fort leading a frenzied mob of, according to one French count, 637 Indians, 146 Canadians, and 72 French regulars to intercept Braddock.[13] It was not to be the only sight that Smith would see that day which he would remember the rest of his life.

CHAPTER EIGHTEEN

The Trampling of the Vineyard

WEDNESDAY, JULY 9, 1755, dawned hot and clear, a splendid summer's day with the sunlight peeking over the mountains to the east. Gage and his advance party had marched much earlier, at two o'clock in the morning, in the pitch of the night. Consisting of two Grenadier companies and one hundred other troops, together with two 6-pounders, the advance party marched some five miles in the dark and even before the road had been cleared to the first crossing of the Monongahela, which they passed before dawn. They then continued a further two miles to the second crossing, arriving at eight in the morning. When they approached the river some of the troops thought they saw many French Indians on the other side. Others were unsure. To be on the safe side, Gage ordered the two cannon readied to cover the crossing. The men marched in strict line of battle across the three hundred yards of knee-deep water until they reached the opposite bank, which rose some eight yards from the river in a perpendicular wall. They immediately set to work chopping and sloping it to make a ramp before they could surmount it. Another two hundred yards inland from the bank stood the abandoned house and blacksmith shop of one John Frazer, a Philadelphia German who had set up there in 1742 before the troubles to farm and trade with the Indians. He was possibly the first white settler west of the Allegheny Mountains. Washington and Gist had spent the night there both going and returning on their Rivière aux Boeufs mission in 1753.

Once back on the east side of the Monongahela, Gage posted sentries to secure the camp while the men rested. Those who had any food took breakfast, it being then about nine-thirty. Most had nothing to eat, and some had had nothing the day before. The batman and his master breakfasted on "a little Ham that I had and a Bit of gloster Shire cheese and I milked the Cow and made him a little milk Punch (of) which he drank a little."[1] Gage dispatched a rider back to Braddock to inform him that he had secured both crossings of the Monongahela without incident and had posted his troops according to the general's orders.

Meanwhile, at daybreak the main army broke camp and began its march. The going was slow, as the troops waited for St. Clair and his pioneers to clear the road. About eight they reached the first crossing, which one British officer described as "extreamly fine having a view of at least 4 Miles up the river."[2] Braddock, who now assumed more of a personal role in the command, ordered 150 men over in the front, followed by half the guns and limbers, then a further 150 men. Next came the packhorses and cattle, followed by the baggage and remaining guns and limbers and, finally, the rear guard troops who had stood watch on the heights to cover the crossing.[3]

Once over, the general ordered a halt and reformed his units in the proper line of march. Gage's dispatch rider arrived with his reassuring note after they had advanced just one mile. On reaching the second crossing a further mile to the west at about eleven o'clock, the general saw that the men were still working to clear and widen the slope on the opposite bank to accommodate the heavy howitzers and 12-pounders. He ordered the artillery and baggage drawn up along the beach to wait. The work was completed within about an hour.

Now was the moment of decision. Sitting atop his great bay charger on his leopard skin saddle pad, His Excellency surveyed the scene and with the wave of his hand gave the signal to order the 44th Regiment over first, with the picket of the right. The wagons and packhorses and then the 48th Regiment, with the left pickets which had covered the crossing from the heights, would immediately follow.

The crossing at high noon was the culmination of General Braddock's career. It was a spectacle, a deliberate statement of the inexorability of British arms. The crossing impressed all who witnessed it, as many who did were later to remark.[4] This was, after all, its intended effect, for Braddock suspected that the enemy was watching. Once the redcoats had assembled, Braddock literally marched the men across the river in formation, with their forty regimental drums beating and their fifes playing the "Grenadiers' March." The ripping reverberations of the forty regimental drums, a sound unaccustomed to either Indian or modern American ears, would have resounded through the wilderness for miles and carried down the river valley a good way of the distance to the Forks of the Ohio. The soldiers' close-shouldered arms stood upright, and their bayonets glistened in the hot July noon sun. The oversized King's Colour (a Union Jack with the King's insignia) fluttered at the head of the column. The exhausted horses plunged and clattered across the pebble-strewn riverbed drawing the big naval cannon and shining brass howitzers. Each regiment proclaimed its presence and identity with its regimental flag snapping in the breeze.[5] As Braddock led atop his charger and surveyed the clockwork precision of the crossing, with its tight discipline, splash of color, and time-honored war march, he must have felt pride at the prowess of British military might. Never before had the American wilderness seen such a spectacle.

Once across and reformed on the east side of the river, Braddock and the men let slip a sigh of relief. They figured that if there were any place the enemy would challenge them, it would be on this second crossing of the river. Thinking that all the dangerous passes were behind them, Braddock reined in his advance party and ordered it to march within a few yards of the main body. The army was now within seven miles of Fort Duquesne. The soldiers thought that they might at any moment hear the explosion of the French blowing up the fort in retreat. If not, by that evening or tomorrow at the latest, the army would be encamped before Fort Duquesne and limbering up the cannon that it had so impossibly brought to bear across ocean, mountains, and rivers. For the first time in months there was an air of anticipation and a spring to the soldiers' step as they moved out.

The landscape through which they marched was sloping, intermittent woodland carpeted with grass and rising to outcroppings of rock at its crest. Water from a spring in the heart of the gentle slope tumbled down to the river. Ancient trees lay fallen along the edge of the forest line, while wild grapevines marked the demarcation line of the plain scoured by the spring floods and the thicket-tangled upper reaches of the slope. Three concealed ravines, four or five feet deep and eight to ten feet wide, creased the slope. Basking in the early afternoon sun, more than one soldier might have mistaken the hillside for a frontier Elysium.

The army marched only eight hundred yards.

Captain Beaujeu quickened his pace to a run as he heard the "Grenadiers' March" wafting from the distance. Catching the first far glimpse of the river through the forest, he knew that the English had forded the river and deprived him of the challenge that he planned for the crossing. Fortunately, the three hundred Indians who had split from his force and crossed to the west side of the Monongahela had thought better of their diversion and had rejoined him only minutes before. Spotting the English marching in tight order through the broken grassland before him and the pioneers beginning to attack the tree line with their axes, he took off his three-cornered hat and waved it to his troops, signaling them "Go left!" and "Go right!" The Indians and French instinctively fell into a half-moon formation as they fanned out and took cover behind the trees at hand. Others quickly found the ravines and jumped into their natural protection.

At one o'clock an engineer at the head of the British column thought he saw the fleeting figure of a French officer, stripped to the waist like an Indian but wearing a three-cornered hat and silver gorget, dart between the trees. Gordon, the chief engineer, soon saw what he estimated to be three hundred Indians running through the woods. At the same time the shrill scalping halloo rang out. The English froze in their tracks.

The crash of a volley of fire erupted from nowhere. However, the front lines of the vanguard were out of range, and it had no effect. Nonetheless, the flying column shuddered and came to a halt. Gage ordered the Grenadier companies at the van to fix their bayonets and form in line of battle, with the intention of gaining a hill to the right that was already partially in possession of a party of redcoat pickets scouring the right flank. The Grenadiers quickly followed the first order, but "visible terror and confusion appeared amongst the men," and they refused to move to the posts Gage assigned them or leave their line of march. However, Gage succeeded in forming them into position in the middle of the road.

"God save the King!" cried a British officer. "Huzzahs" resounded from the ranks as they moved a little further along the road to within musket range of the forest line. Every few steps they executed the classic British formation, kneeling, firing, reloading, kneeling, firing, in ranks according to Bland. The deafening volleys of Brown Bess fire delivered with speed and precision split the wilderness.

On the first volley from the Grenadiers the French Canadian auxiliaries, one half of the non-Indian French forces, turned tail and ran, shouting "Sauve qui peut!" ("Every man for himself!"). On the third volley a lucky shot struck Beaujeu, killing him just minutes into the battle. His second in command, Captain Jean Daniel Dumas, who had been an ardent advocate of the plan to intercept the British, assumed charge.

"Seeing no enemy, and themselves falling every moment from the fire," Howard Pyle's illustration of General Braddock's forces under attack that appeared in *Scribner's Magazine*.

But in fact there was little for the British to shoot at. The French and Indians crouched behind rocks and trees. The staccato firing from the fringe of the forest and war cries erupted at random. As soon as the Grenadiers heard a report or saw smoke, the assailant had ducked or melted back into the forest or skulked behind another tree. The Grenadiers fired wildly, hitting the ground or wasting their balls in the air. Meanwhile, bunched and exposed, they began to drop under the withering fire poured in on them.

Sir Peter Halkett rode up. A wounded Indian sitting disabled in the field observed him and slowly leveled his gun at him. Christopher Gist saw that the Indian was trying to draw a bead on Halkett but, having just fired his own weapon, he could not reload quickly enough to prevent the Indian from firing. The shot struck and killed Halkett. Gist thereupon stepped up, with his own musket now loaded, and blew the Indian's brains out. Halkett's younger son James, a lieutenant in the 44th, went to his father's aid and was also killed as he attended him.

The worst fire came from the left. However, on the right a group of Indians suddenly took possession of several immense fallen trees and also laid in an annoying fire. An officer and a party of Grenadiers moved up to dislodge them and "by a pretty brisk fire kept our right tollerably easy."

The Braddock Expedition has inspired numerous prints, paintings, and drawings ever since the disaster. Nearly all are inaccurate in details, but most convey the panic and ferocity of the battle. These two undated illustrations, probably from the early nineteenth century, show the opening ambuscade and the British and colonial militia attempting to return fire at an unseen enemy. Note that the soldiers' uniforms are those of the War of 1812 period. (*New York Public Library*)

At the same time, Gage deployed the two 6-pounders that were at his disposal in the van. Ramming them with round and grapeshot, the two guns did great execution. The blast of the artillery and rake of the grapeshot caused the Indians to falter and fall back. With Dumas egging them on, however, the Indians quickly regrouped and began to direct their fire on the soldiers manning the cannon. But even as the gunners were felled by bullets, more moved forward to replace them. The Indians ran from one place to another, requiring the Grenadiers "to wheel from right to left, to desert ye Guns and then hastily to return & cover them." Nonetheless, the British kept the two cannon firing for a total of some eighty rounds. Despite the initial shock of the cannon fire and the loss of their commander, the French and their Indian allies quickly rallied and began to push the British back along the road. Gage's Grenadiers fell back upon St. Clair's pioneers, some fifty paces to the rear. St. Clair came up to see what was happening. A bullet smashed into his chest and shoulder. St. Clair remained on his feet, though grievously wounded.

Meanwhile, Braddock, from his position toward the middle of the column, heard the heavy firing as soon as it started. He sent an aide forward to bring him an account of the attack, but the firing continued so he also galloped up to the front. Once there, he found his men bunched and panic-stricken, dropping right and left. The American troops ran up at the same time. Acting without orders, they inserted themselves into the ranks of the Grenadiers, causing great confusion. Other Americans ducked behind trees and began to take on the Indians in their own fashion, with some effect. One group of Virginians in particular, some eighty men under Captain Waggoner, took up a position behind a large log, five feet in diameter, atop the hill and opened a hot fire on the enemy. However, the wildly firing British regulars mistook them for the enemy and killed fifty of them. Even British officers began to fall from "friendly fire" from their own platoons. Other units in the flying column moved up to the scene of the fighting. The men bunched twenty or thirty deep, convinced that numbers provided safety. In fact, they provided a target, which the enemy continued to decimate with unerring fire.

One British officer noted that the enemy fire made a popping sound, "with little explosion" and "only a kind of Whiszing noise; (which is a proof the enemys Arms were rifle Barrels)."[6] This conclusion is not inconsistent with the earlier reports of Indian facility with rifles.[7] With their superior range, the enemy rifles would have prevented the British with their Brown Bess muskets, which were effective only up to about fifty yards, from approaching close enough to damage their ranks, even if the redcoats could have seen the hidden and moving enemy. Thus the Indians allied with the French, if armed with rifles, would have simply outgunned the English and Americans with superior longer-range weapons and with a particularly devastating effect on the British and American officer corps. If the British officer's eyewitness observation was accurate (and there is no reason to think it was not), the engagement was probably one of the first battles in history fought with rifles and one of the first in which they may have been a critical factor affecting the outcome.

A thickening cloud of smoke from the black powder of the guns, both muskets and rifles, wreathed the scene and occluded the elusive targets as the British regulars tried to find their marks. British officers were later to declare that they never saw more than five of the enemy at one time during the entire battle. The enemy ousted the British flanking party that had earlier partially seized the hill to the right. They now controlled the high ground.

Braddock quickly sized up the danger. Pulling a large white handkerchief from his pocket, he tied his three-cornered hat about his head and galloped about the front. Taking charge, he ordered the colors advanced in different places to try to separate the men of the two regiments. He ordered the soldiers to group and fire in platoons. However, on the narrow road, and with hostile fire coming in from all directions, the maneuvers were impossible. Braddock stormed back and forth on his charger, raging at the men, calling them cowards and striking them with the flat side of

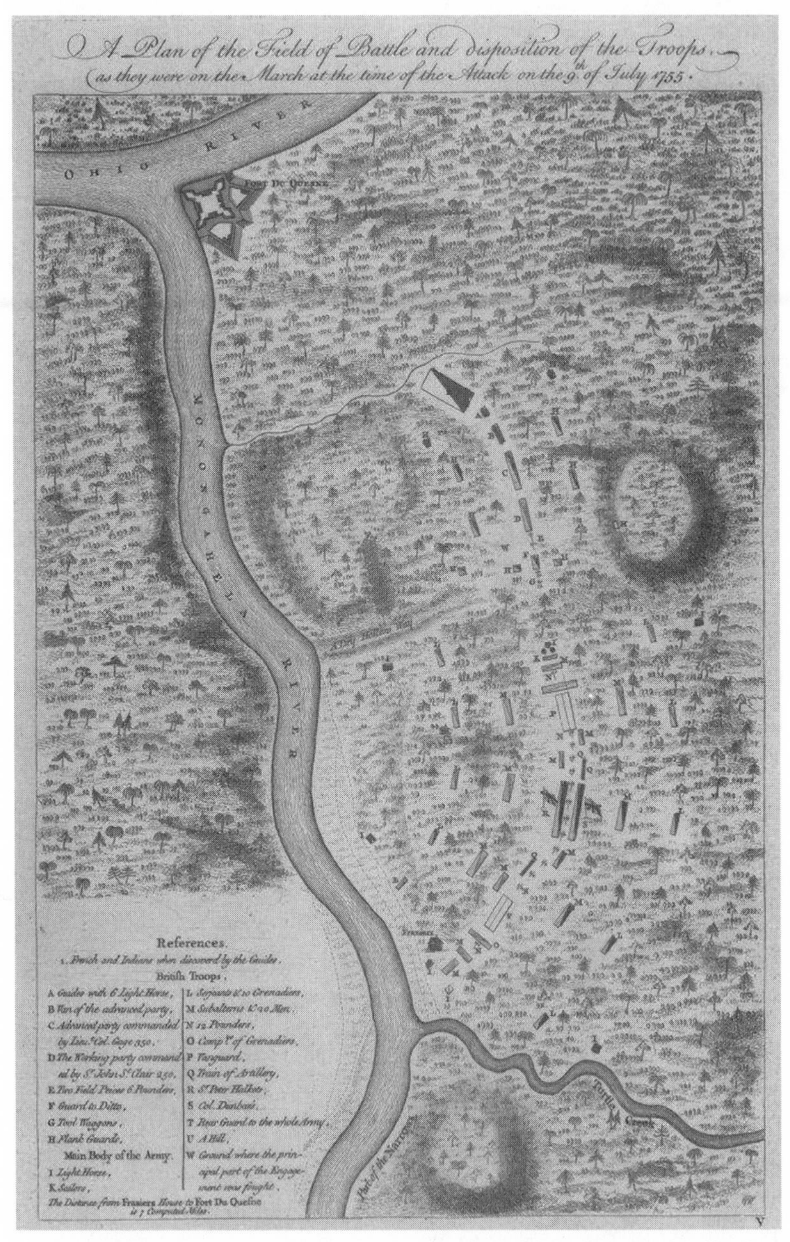

Captain Robert Orme's diagram of the plan of the field of battle and distribution of the troops as they were on the march at the time of the attack, from Sargent's 1855 *History*.

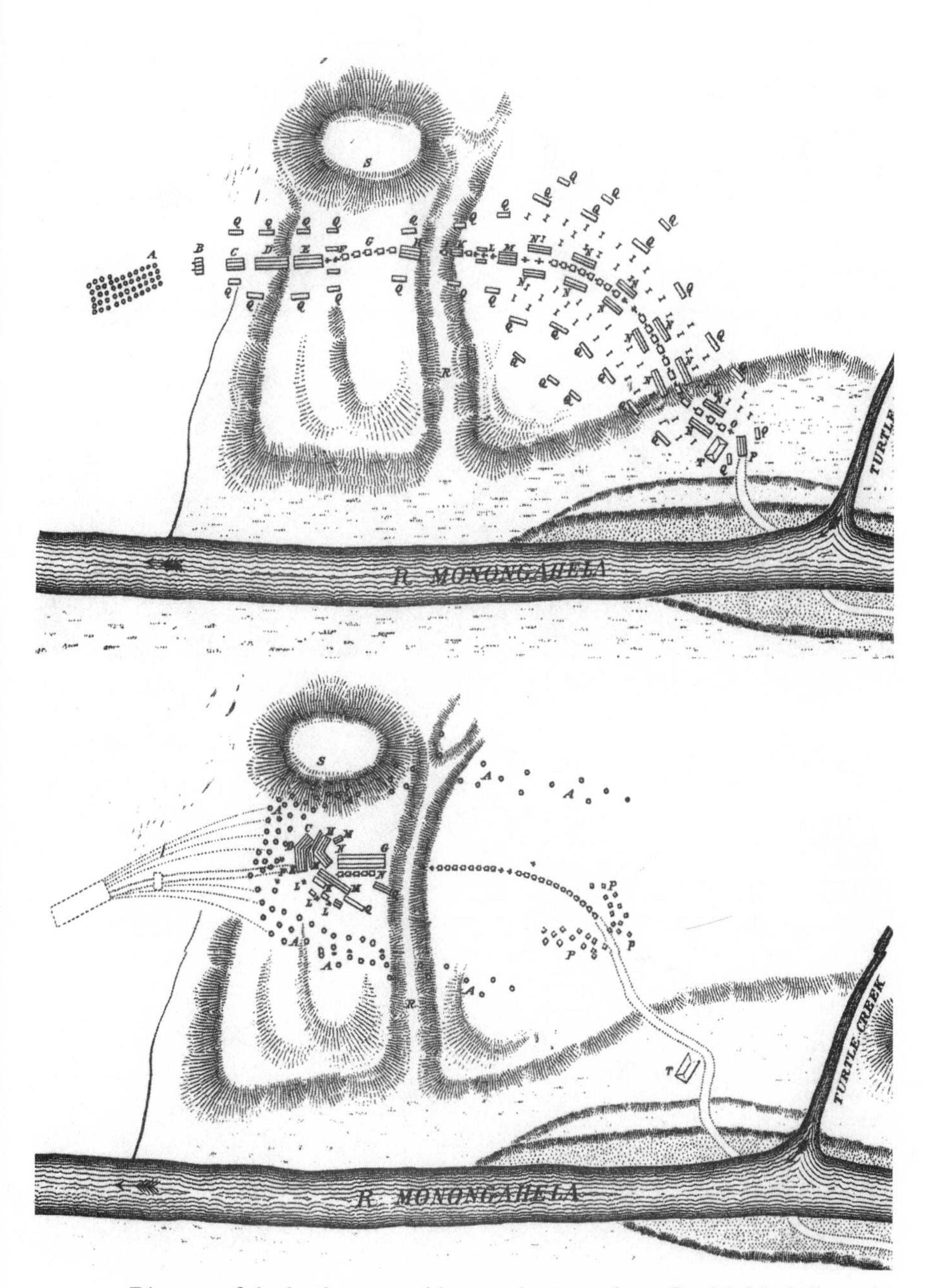

Diagram of the battle prepared by eyewitness engineer Patrick Mackellar published in Francis Parkman's *Montcalm and Wolfe*.

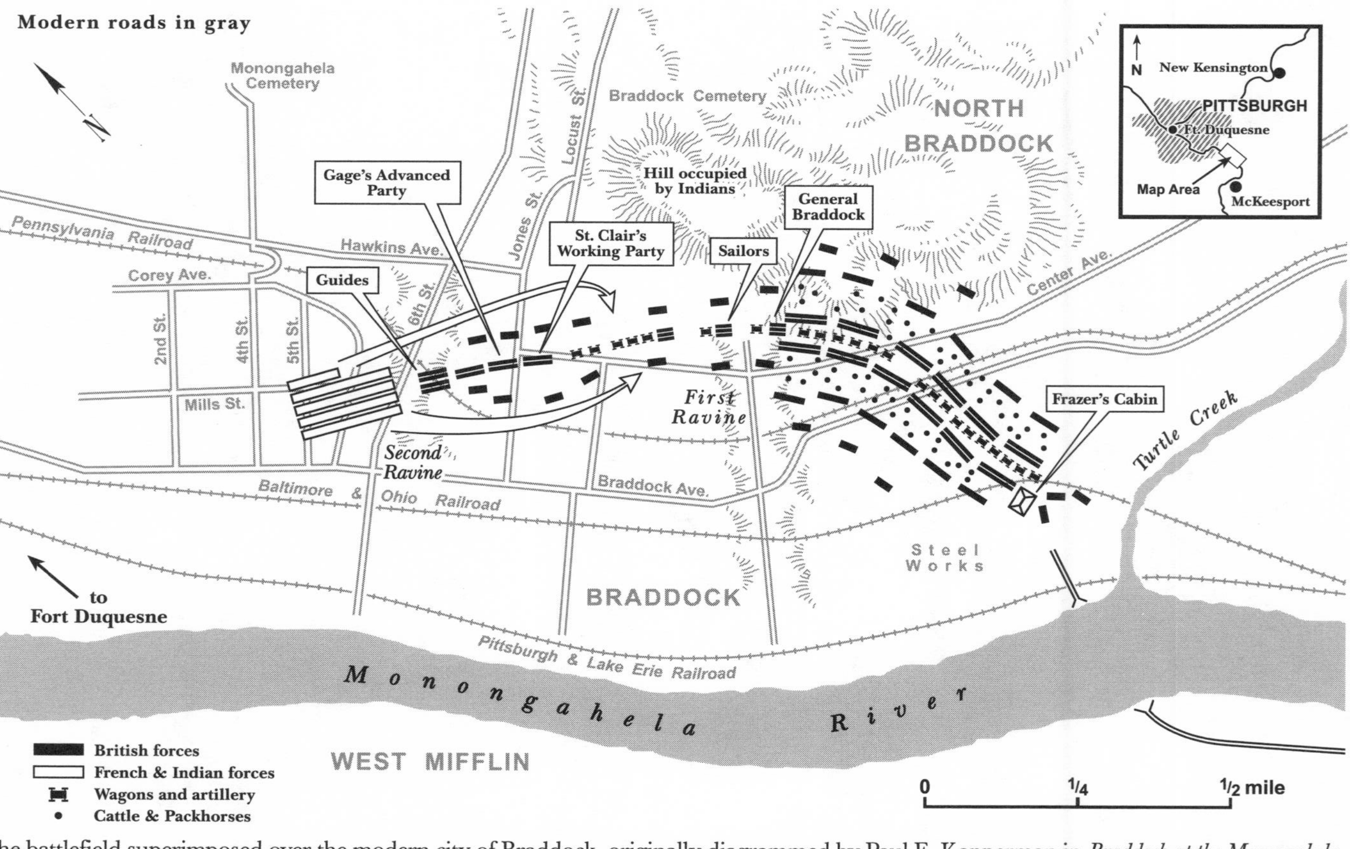

The battlefield superimposed over the modern city of Braddock, originally diagrammed by Paul E. Kopperman in *Braddock at the Monongahela.* The troop disposition is based on engineer Patrick Mackellar's eyewitness drawing. Local tradition places the action south of the his sword.[8] Within two and a half hours, the British retreated three or four times, but each time Braddock and his officers rallied them.

Braddock realized that he would never prevail unless he dislodged the enemy from the high ground. He ordered Burton up with eight hundred men and three big 12-pounders. The convoy closed up. However, before Burton's men could reinforce the front, they ran into Gage's retreating vanguard and St. Clair's crumbling pioneers. All was a mass of confusion. St. Clair, still conscious, stumbled toward the general. Babbling in Italian which he had apparently learned during his service with Count Browne, St. Clair declaimed to Braddock that he was defeated, all was ruined.[9] Braddock, who had vacationed in Italy and also may have spoken some Italian, cut him off scornfully. St. Clair then told him that "by the fresh bleeding of his wound he did not expect to Survive many minutes, and therefore could have no Interest in dissembling or saying what he really did not think."

"For God's sake, the rising on our right!" St. Clair cried in English as he pointed, and he passed out.

Braddock glanced up at the hill and agreed. He passed the order to Burton, who rallied some men of the 48th and led them and a force of Grenadiers against the crest of the rising slope. The charge began to attain traction. But then Burton and several Grenadiers dropped, and the remainder crumbled and retreated very fast, leaving their officers shouting at them and even begging, but to no avail.

More officers, acting with the utmost bravery, threw themselves into the breach, but their men would not follow. The officers "dropped like leaves in Autumn." Majors, captains, lieutenants, ensigns, subalterns, all down, wounded and dying, in the peppering fire from the forest and gullies. Orme and Morris fell, both wounded, *hors de combat.* So did Horatio Gates of New York, shot through the left breast and no longer able to use his left arm. Lieutenant Spendelow of the Royal Navy was shot and killed. Captain Tatton of the 48th lay dead from the "friendly fire" of his own men, as did Captain William Polson of Virginia and Captain Cholmondeley of the 48th.

More Americans, especially the Virginians, rushed to the scene of the hottest action to try to engage the enemy on their own terms. Fighting frontier fashion, the Americans took to the high ground, firing from behind trees and rocks, while the faltering British huddled in a wavering mass on the road and fired wildly. Washington, "on horse-back, tho' very weak and low," rode into the thick of the battle, accompanying Braddock and encouraging the Virginians. At one point Washington asked Braddock if he could post the men behind trees to continue the fight. Braddock's servant later recalled hearing the general curse and respond, "I've a mind to run you through the body! We'll sup today in Fort Duquesne or else in hell!" The Virginians fought from behind trees anyway, and Washington had to be content with the "charming" song of the bullets playing all around him while he attended Braddock as his only remaining unwounded aide. Though his clothing was pierced by bullets four times and two horses were shot out from under him, Washington was not hit.[10] Scaroyady and the Indian guides fought alongside the Americans with bravery that was noted by all.

The fighting only grew worse. Braddock galloped to and fro in the thick of the battle, trying in vain to rally his men in the face of a hail of bullets. Braddock had four horses shot out from under him, and bullets pierced his clothing several times. But with dwindling officers, the soldiers were helpless to obey. And, as they had been supplied with only twenty-four rounds, their ammunition began to run low. The soldiers stripped cartridges from the dead and wounded to use. A bullet slammed into the head of young Shirley, Braddock's secretary, riding at his side. He was killed instantly.

After Burton's failed attempt to take the hill, the cannon, including the rear pieces protecting the baggage, kept up a reasonable rate of fire, getting off between twenty and thirty rounds. They soon had to be abandoned, however, because their guard

Two mid-nineteenth-century prints featuring George Washington heroically rallying the remaining troops at the moment Braddock was struck down. This battle helped establish Washington as a national celebrity, due in part to a popular misunderstanding of his actual role in the engagement. (*Library of Congress*)

had all been killed. Gage next fell wounded. The enemy was now spread out on all sides of the column and attacking it from front to rear and firing on every part. The British and Americans fought to the death, terrified of the Indians and knowing that no quarter would be given. At one point the enemy seized the colors of one regiment. Chaplain Hughes retook them and lived to tell the tale. He later remarked that he was "the first Chaplain who ever saved a Pair of Colours, which I took within fifty yards of the Cannon, when the Enemy were Masters of them."[11]

Late in the fighting, while mounting one of his relief horses beneath a large tree and giving orders for yet another attempt to seize the ridge, Braddock took a bullet through his arm and into his lung. No longer able to ride, but conscious and in agony, he lay on the field of battle attended only by his servant Bishop and later by the head of his bodyguard Captain Robert Stewart of the Virginia light horse and the wounded Orme. After the battle, several of his own men took credit for having fired the shot that hit Braddock. There was particular persistence to the claim by an American enlisted man, Tom Fausett of Fayette County, Pennsylvania, that he had shot Braddock to avenge the death of his brother, whom Braddock caught cowering behind a tree and ran through with his sword. Fausett was a hot-blooded, rough-hewn character who swore by his story. Fausett's claim has never been proven or disproven, despite a thorough effort by Sargent to debunk it.[12] Fausett stuck by his story all his long life, and it was widely believed in western Pennsylvania, where he settled after the war.[13]

Not long after, in late afternoon, the British line began to break. It started with the wagon drivers to the rear of the column. Fearing a defeat, they unhitched their horses from the wagons and gun limbers and galloped away so quickly that even if by a miracle the English had turned the tide they would have had no horses left to draw the train forward. Among those who cut loose their horses and galloped away was a twenty-year-old sharpshooter-turned-wagoneer with Captain Dobbs's North Carolina Independents named Daniel Boone, a gentry-born frontiersman who was later to earn the epithet "Panther" for his exploits in the wild.[14] The battle may well have been nearing its end when Boone finally joined the fleeing throngs. In any event, having fled

The climax of the battle was the shooting of General Braddock. The fact that the commanding officer of such a large and formidable army was targeted and killed remains one of the most dramatic events in colonial American history. The painting at top was commissioned by the state of Wisconsin to show the French trapper Charles de Langlade leading Wisconsin Indians in the attack on Braddock's column. (Top: Edwin Willard Deming, *The Defeat of General Braddock*, 1903. *Wisconsin Historical Society*; bottom left: *Library of Congress*; bottom right: *New York Public Library*).

the battlefield, he continued on to eastern Pennsylvania, having to kill a fierce Indian who tried to block his path in the Juniata region. The story provided early grist for the self-invented legend of Daniel Boone. Another retreating wagoneer was Boone's friend Daniel Morgan, who was later to become an American general and master of irregular tactics in the Revolution.[15]

Then, at about five o'clock, "as if by beat of Drumm," the entire army "turned to ye right about & made a most precipitate retreat every one trying who should be first."

Orme, though badly wounded in the thigh, tried to arrange to have Braddock carried off the field. In the headlong rush to retreat, he could get no one to help. He even offered to bribe men with sixty gold guineas, but none came to his aid. Disgusted and wanting to die "like an old Roman," the general at last refused to be carried off the battlefield. However, Orme disobeyed him and, with the help of Washington and Stewart, removed Braddock's red officer's sash and used it as a sling to carry him to the rear of what was left of the column.[16] There, in the baggage train, they found a two-wheeled tumbrel to remove him from the field of battle. As he was being eased into the cart Croghan came up. Braddock eyed Croghan's pistols and asked for them so that he might put an end to it and die with honor. Croghan ignored the request.

The Indians swooped down from the forest in pursuit. Screaming war cries and with their tomahawks flailing, they attacked and butchered the fleeing British and Americans, who were dropping their arms and shedding their clothes in order to run faster. With the general now safely off the field, Washington galloped to the upper ford of the river to try to stem the continued flight of the men and found the wounded Gage already there employed in that effort. Washington returned to the general's side.

One British officer, wounded in one leg and the other heel, sat down at the base of a tree begging every soldier that ran by in

Braddock's blood-stained officer's sash, left, was used to carry the mortally wounded Braddock from the battlefield. Woven of scarlet silk, twelve feet long by thirty inches wide, it is embroidered with a row of standing figures and the date 1709 (old style), the year Braddock's father was commissioned a Major General. (*Mount Vernon Ladies Association*) Howard Pyle's 1893 illustration, right, in *Scribner's Magazine* shows George Washington and other officers lifting the mortally wounded Braddock onto a cart.

retreat to shoot him dead. A Virginian stopped and turned to him. "Yes, countryman, I will put you out of your misery. These dogs shall not burn you." He then put his piece to his head, but the British officer changed his mind at the last instant, cried out and dodged behind the tree. The gun fired and missed. The American ran on. Soon after, Lieutenant Grey, who was with a rear unit, ran by as the firing died down and had the officer carried off.

The Indians chased the fleeing soldiers down to the banks of the Monongahela. As the soldiers ran across the river, "they shot many in ye Water both Men and Women, & dyed ye stream with their blood, scalping and cutting them in a most barbarous manner." One officer recorded three weeks later: "I cannot describe the horrors of that scene, no pen could do it. The yell of the

Indians is fresh on my ear, and the terrific sound will haunt me till the hour of my dissolution."[17]

One foot soldier, Duncan Cameron, a private in the 44th and a battle-hardened veteran of campaigning in the Low Countries, was stunned in the initial action and left for dead. He awakened, to find that his own unit had retreated, the enemy was in hot pursuit, and the immediate area of the battlefield was for the moment deserted by friend or foe. He therefore sought refuge in a hollow tree and through a knothole watched the Indians wreaking terror on the survivors. At one point an Indian looked directly at the knothole, and Cameron shook with panic. But his foe did not see him and resumed his scalping of the fallen redcoats, many of them still alive and screaming in agony. Cameron saw the French commander Dumas try–without effect–to stop the Indians from scalping those who were not quite dead. Cameron later retreated under cover of darkness.

NOW, BOTH THE INDIANS AND THE FRENCH started plundering. One of their first prizes were two hogsheads of rum. The victorious force was soon drunk and in mayhem. They stopped pursuing the fleeing British and Americans. Looting the bodies and baggage was all that occupied them.

The British and Americans regrouped on a small rise a quarter mile on the far side of the river. The wounded Burton posted sentries. Braddock, still conscious but grievously wounded, ordered Washington, with an escort of what was left of two Grenadier companies, to ride the almost fifty miles to Dunbar's camp with a request for medical supplies, food, and wagons to transport the wounded. The relief supplies and retreating column were to rendezvous at Gist's plantation or nearer, if possible.

The general made a quick head count of his losses. It was possible that he had lost two-thirds of his army and more than sixty of his eighty officers killed or wounded. As the losses began to be confirmed, the situation was even worse than he feared. His Excellency Major General Edward Braddock, Generalissimo of All His Majesty's Forces in North America, had presided over one of the most disastrous British military defeats in history. According to a contemporary report in the *Maryland Gazette,* among the many officers killed were the two Halketts (the elder son, Brigade Major Francis Halkett, survived), Shirley, Hatton, Beckworth, Gethans, Allen, Townsend, Nartloe, Cholmondeley, Crimble, Widman, Handfort, Brereton, Hart, Smith, Spendelow, Talbott, Stone, Soumaien, Polson, Payronee, Hamilton, Wright, Splitdorff, Waggoner, and Dr. Swenton, the surgeon. The wounded included St. Clair, Lesby, Orme, Morris, Gage, Burton, Sparkes, Lettler, Dunbar, Treby, Simpson, Locke, Disney, Kennedy, Pennington, Power, Ross, Barbett, Galdwyn, Edmondton, Monthresure, McMullen, Craw, Sterling, Buchanan, McLeod, McLullen, McKeller, Gordon, Williamson, Floyer, Gates, Howard, Gray, Stevens, Stewart, and many others.[18] Almost all the medical staff were either dead or wounded, as were twenty-five of the thirty seamen.

Captain Jean Daniel Dumas. (*National Archives of Canada*)

The estimates of the overall English losses vary. According to Sargent, of a total of 1,466 English and Americans present, 456 were killed and 421 wounded, for a total of 877 out of 1,466 (however, the casualty rate was even higher if the noncombatants who took no part in the battle are factored out).[19] The losses were heaviest among the officers, a tribute both to their bravery and to their apparently deliberate targeting by the enemy, probably using rifles if first-hand accounts are to be believed. Of the eighty-nine commissioned officers, sixty-three were killed or wounded. Not a single field officer escaped unhurt. The figures for servants and women are unknown, but most were probably killed. Only three batmen survived.

The Virginians suffered heavily. Their three participating companies were virtually destroyed. Half of their company officers were killed outright. In Captain La Peyroney's company, the captain and all officers and noncommissioned officers down to a corporal were wiped out. Only one of Captain Polson's officers remained alive. Washington later estimated that in the three Virginia companies not more than thirty men survived.[20] In contrast, not a single Pennsylvania wagon driver was hurt. History would later record the losses, both in absolute numbers and percentages, as exceeding even those in the more famous British loss, the Charge of the Light Brigade, almost one hundred years later.[21]

As dusk fell, the drunken French and Indians left the battlefield strewn with the picked-over and scalped bodies of soldiers and debris of battle. A French Canadian described the scene two days later: "The French & Indians at the time of Battle have kill'd a Quantity of Horses, they have kill'd a great many more since, broke all the Carts & destroyed everything they possibly could. Powder & Flower are scatter'd over the Field of Battle the Indians have brought off a great deal of the last. The bodies of a great number of men kill'd & those of eight Women or Girls enitrely strip'd, lie promiscuously with dead horses for more than half a League."[22] The victors did not even post a guard over the field, much less pursue the retreating British and Americans. If they had crossed the river sober and in pursuit, there is little question that they could have wiped them out to a person.

As it was, their own total losses were eleven killed and twenty-nine wounded. Contrecoeur, the commander of Fort Duquesne, was later to write "Messieurs Dumas and de Ligneris had a great part in our recent success, since victory was very much in the balance when M. de Beaujeu was killed, but these 2 men encouraged our troops so well that all came out for the best and–or perhaps, I should say, God put himself on our side."[23]

In the revelry that attended the victory Dumas could find little help in providing succor to the wounded French officers and men. He was unable to find anyone to carry Captain Beaujeu's body back to the fort. He therefore hid the corpse in a ravine "a little removed from the road" in order to prevent his own Indians from scalping the dead French commander.[24]

In the lengthening shadows of the long summer evening the Indians and their sponsors joyfully made their way back to Fort Duquesne. The captured American James Smith watched as exultant Indians and French came in that evening with "a great many bloody scalps, grenadiers' caps, British canteens, bayonets, &c." After that another company of about one hundred Indians came in, every one of whom carried scalps dripping blood. Then a further company, with wagons and more scalps. "Those that were coming in, and those that had arrived, kept a constant firing of small arms, and also the great guns in the fort, which were accompanied with the most hideous shouts and yells from all quarters, so that it appeared to me as if the infernal regions had broke loose."[25] Other Indians who arrived later pranced and posed in British officers' dress, with sash, gorgets, and laced three-cornered hats looted from the bodies of officers. (The next day the French sent twelve canoes up the Monongahela to retrieve the abandoned British cannon and ordnance, as well as Beaujeu's body).[26]

At about sundown, Smith saw a small party coming in with about a dozen prisoners, stripped naked with their hands tied behind their backs and their faces and part of their bodies blackened. Smith feared in the pit of his stomach for these helpless countrymen, farm boys from Virginia or lads from Devon or Lancashire or Cork, barely grown men who not many years before had brought their mothers joy. The Indians burned them to death, slowly, on the banks of the Allegheny River within sight of the fort, its ramparts crowded with French soldiers. Smith remembered:

> I stood on the fort wall until I beheld them begin to burn one of these men; they had him tied to a stake and kept

touching him with firebrands, red-hot irons, &c, and he screamed in a most doleful manner; the Indians, in the mean time, yelling like infernal spirits.

As this scene appeared too shocking for me to behold, I retired to my lodging both sore and sorry.[27]

Chapter Nineteen

Helter Skelter

WASHINGTON AND THE REMNANTS OF the two Grenadier companies marched through the night toward Dunbar's camp. It was not an easy task for the exhausted Washington, who was still weak from his fever. He later wrote: "The shocking Scenes which presented themselves in this Night's March are not to be described. The dead, the dying, the groans, lamentations, and crys along the Road of the wounded for help . . . were enough to pierce a heart. The gloom and horror of which was not a little encreased by the impervious darkness occasioned by the close shade of thick woods which in places rendered it impossible for the two guides which attended to know when they were in, or out of the track but by groping on the ground with their hands."[1]

Left on the small rise on the west side of the Monongahela River and with Washington and the remnants of the two Grenadier companies scrambling in desperation back to Dunbar's camp for help, Braddock realized that he and the remaining troops with him were exposed and vulnerable. He therefore ordered an immediate march through the night to try to take them out of striking range of the French and Indians. Covering the same ground as Washington and marching all through the night and next day, they reached Gist's at ten o'clock the next night.

Although unknown to Braddock or even Washington, the wagoneers who had cut loose their horses and fled during the battle had galloped into Dunbar's camp early on the morning of July 10 with fragmentary news of the defeat. The names of these dubious mercuries were Michael Houber, Jacob Novre, and Matthew Laird–to judge from the German names of the first two wagoneers, some of Franklin's Pennsylvania teamsters. Dunbar immediately sent up supplies to the retreating soldiers. From Dunbar's camp, riders or perhaps a runaway wagoneer carried the news to Fort Cumberland. Charlotte Browne wrote "It is not possible to describe the Distraction of the poor Women for their Husbands."[2] It was not long before the news was seeping throughout all the Middle Atlantic colonies, carried by post riders from town to town and tavern to tavern. Slaves also reportedly played a major role in disseminating the news in the southern colonies, as they visited neighboring plantations to court their lovers in the dark.[3] Indeed, one of the first thoughts to strike the southern leaders was that the defeat might lead to a rebellion by the slaves. Dinwiddie wrote shortly after the defeat: "The negro slaves have been very audacious on the news of the defeat on the Ohio. These poor creatures imagine the French will give them their freedom. We have too many here; but I hope we shall be able to keep them in proper subjection."[4]

After sleeping the night at Gist's plantation, the retreating column resumed its march, retracing its steps through the line of encampments that had marked its westward march only days before. From Gist's, on Braddock's orders, deposits of flour were left along the road for any stragglers who might need food. Several men who subsequently made it into camp said they would have died had it not been for the wounded Braddock's presence of mind, not to mention attention to detail under duress, in leaving the flour. The batman recorded that "This day there was a wounded Soldier Came up who says there was seven more Came from the place of the Ingagement together but they all dyed on the Roade and he says there was several dead as he marched along, he not being Able when Arrv'd here hardly to speeke for want of Nourishment, he living on Raw flower and water when he Came to it, which was left for them."[5]

On Friday, July 11, the column reached Dunbar's camp. Braddock, carried in a litter because he could not tolerate the pain caused by a jarring wagon, was still in charge and issuing orders. The next day he tried to restore at least minimal structure to the mauled band by having the troops parade at the evening retreat at the head of their respective regiments and companies. His first thought, however, was to provide for the wounded, ordering that they be placed in wagons for the continuation of the retreat.

Then came the most controversial decision. The same day the army, under Braddock's order and Dunbar's execution, destroyed or buried all its ammunition and provisions in order to free up more wagons to transport the wounded.[6] They smashed and buried more than fifteen hundred artillery projectiles and shells, as well as cannon balls, muskets, bullets, and even the pioneers' axes and tools.[7] The soldiers destroyed the remaining artillery, keeping only two 6-pounders. They stove in casks with 50,000 pounds of gunpowder and poured them into a spring. The horses were dying so fast that the soldiers burned one hundred wagons for lack of horses to pull them and to keep them out of enemy hands. The intent was to strip the army of encumbrances for a faster retreat.[8]

What was remarkable about the decision was that the army was not even being chased. The drunken French and Indians had failed to pursue the fleeing British and Americans. The garrison at Fort Duquesne was actually fearful that Dunbar's troops would reunite with the survivors from the battlefield and advance on the fort. In fact, what was left of Braddock's army, survivors and baggage train alike, was fleeing pell-mell from nothing.

Altogether, the value of the hastily destroyed equipment was significant, perhaps in excess of £300,000. Dunbar destroyed stores that had been assembled over the course of months in London and Ireland and shipped across the Atlantic and which would have been invaluable for the defense of the frontier had the army stood rather than fled.

A persistent rumor later arose that the contents of the pay chest, up to £25,000 in gold coins, were poured into the barrel of a cannon and buried.[9] Treasure hunters have searched for it ever since. Equally likely, the pay chest never left Fort Cumberland or, if it did, was looted by the French or Indians on the battlefield, along with the general's papers, including the diagram of Fort Duquesne and all the Anglo-American plans for the assaults on Fort Niagara and other northern French positions, which was an even greater loss. In any event, the destruction of the supplies later drew intense criticism from those who like to second-guess decisions made in the field. Perhaps the only bonus from the abandoning of provisions was a sudden influx of food into the soldiers' hands. The batman got six or eight hams, the most that he could carry on his horse.[10]

Still fearful of pursuit by the enemy, the officers resumed the tight line of march, complete with pickets and sentries, on Sunday, July 13, as they retraced their steps over Chestnut Ridge toward the Great Meadows. However, Braddock's strength was waning. Carried in his litter along the march, he grew increasingly silent except to give the necessary occasional orders. He knew his loss was utter and his reputation in shreds. He retreated into himself as much as to Fort Cumberland. He fell silent for hours at a time, muttering only several times as evening fell that Sunday, "Who would have thought it?"

As his life slowly slipped from his body, he turned to the severely wounded Orme and said, "We shall better know how to deal with them another time." These were his last words. He died at eight in the evening on Sunday, July 13.

The next morning the remaining officers who could still walk buried Braddock, with military honors, in two blankets and a

General Braddock was buried following a brief ceremony, left, in an unmarked grave in the middle of the Braddock Road so that it would remain hidden from possible Indian discovery. (*New York Public Library*) A sign, right, now marks the original gravesite of General Braddock under Braddock's Road.

crude "coffin" fashioned of pieces of bark. Washington later wrote that he had officiated at the burial.[11] They buried the general in the middle of the road that his pioneers had cut only days before on the eastern slope of Chestnut Ridge, not far from Jumonville and the Great Meadows. The gravesite was just yards from a small creek as the road began to rise toward the top of a hill. Then they ordered all the wagons and soldiers to march over and obscure Braddock's gravesite to protect his body from desecration by the Indians. The Indians subsequently did try to find Braddock's grave in order to dig him up and scalp him. But they never succeeded.

Before he died, Braddock gave Washington his war horse and the services of his cook Bishop, who in fact served Washington for many years afterward as major domo at Mount Vernon. Either before or after Braddock's death, Washington also obtained the general's sash, leopard skin saddle pad, and one or both of his pistols.[12]

The retreat to Fort Cumberland continued without delay, with Dunbar now in command. The condition of the wounded grew worse. Maggots began to infest their wounds in the heat.[13] A full accounting of the dead, wounded, and surviving was not undertaken until July 15, when the army reached camp on the east side of the Youghiogheny. On the 16th, they reached the Little Meadows in the rain. They made Fort Cumberland the next day. The surgeons immediately went to work on the wounded, removing "many Sluggs & other ragged pieces of lead" from those who had not died en route. Many of the balls were identified by their caliber as being British, further evidence of the devastating effect of "friendly fire" throughout the engagement.

At the fort, the officers, wounded and well, penned dispatches to their superiors. Orme, though much weakened by the wound to his thigh and able only to dictate, composed letters to Napier, Fox, and Dinwiddie on the 18th. Washington also wrote Dinwiddie, as well as his brother, the same day. St. Clair, though wounded, wrote to Commodore Keppel. All of these letters described the "unhappy affair," as Orme put it, albeit from differing angles.

The finger-pointing and recriminations had started. Orme, in his report to Napier, was careful to protect the reputation of His Excellency, while blaming the disorder of the enlisted men, and to a lesser degree St. Clair, for the disaster. Other officers, wrote Orme to Dinwiddie, "were sacrificed by their unparalleled good behaviour."[14] Orme commended the conduct of the Virginia officers (but not Washington by name) to Dinwiddie: "I have the pleasure to acquaint you that Captain Polson (who was killed) and his company behaved extremely well, as did Captain Stuart and his light horse, who I must beg leave to recommend to your protection and to desire you will be so kind to use your best endeavors to serve him as he has lost by the death of the general the rewards he really deserved by his gallant and faithful attendance on him."[15] In fact, Captain Stewart had two horses shot out from under him, and separate balls grazed his brow and forehead and another shot away his sword and scabbard. His Virginia light horse lost twenty-five of its twenty-nine members killed.[16]

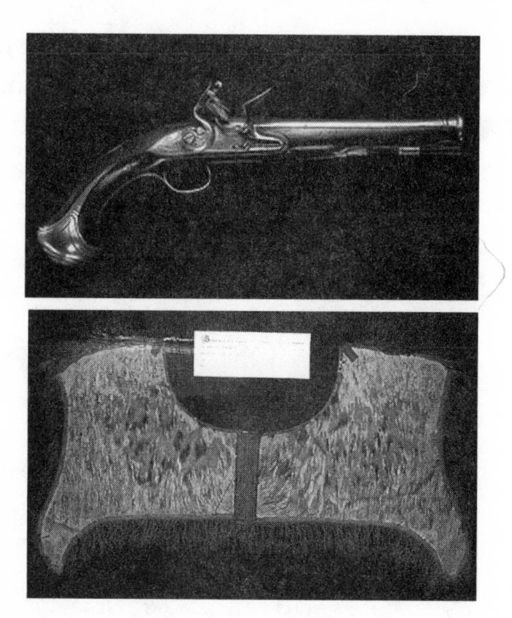

George Washington obtained both Braddock's pistols and his leopard-skin saddle pad. This pistol, .71 caliber, is one of a pair manufactured by Gabbitas of Bristol, England, and is now in possession of the Smithsonian Institution. (*Smithsonian Institution*) Braddock's leopard-skin saddle pad is now part of the American Heritage Library and Museum, Sons of the Revolution, Glendale, California. (*AHLM*)

Orme concluded: "As the whole of the Artillery is lost and the Terror of the Indian remaining so strongly in the men's minds, as also the Troops being extremely weakened by Deaths, Wounds and Sickness, it was judged impossible to make any further attempts; therefore Col. Dunbar is returning to Fort Cumberland [behind 1,200 men with the wounded and artillery who arrived the 17th], with everything he is able to bring along with him. I propose remaining here till my wound will suffer me to remove to Philadelphia, from thence I shall make all possible Dispatch to England."[17]

Orme's letter to Fox was different, however. It stands out from the others. First, Braddock expressly ordered him to write it on the day before he died, a point made clear in the opening sentence of the letter. Second, although Fox was Secretary at War and properly might have had an interest in the outcome of the battle, Fox was also a close friend of George Anne Bellamy. The letter thus was also possibly intended for her consumption. Third, Braddock dictated to Orme most of the content of the letter. It describes the action in only the most cursory terms, at least in comparison to the letters to Napier and Dinwiddie. It mentions the conduct on the battlefield of only two officers: Burton (Bellamy's "darling friend") and Braddock. The thrust of the letter was to report on these two officers (in fact, Burton's bravery and role in the battle had arguably been secondary to those of Halkett and Gage, among others). The letter reports the mortal wound of Braddock and sums up the brief description of the battle by stating: "I had the Generals Order to Inform You, Sir, that the behavior of the Officers deserved the very Highest Commendation." Braddock wanted Fox, and possibly by extension Bellamy, to know that he died as an officer in the Coldstream Regiment of Foot Guards. This parting sentence summarizes much about Braddock's character and system of values. The final sentence of the letter reports the wounds suffered by Morris and Orme and the death of Shirley and states "all the papers are lost."[18] At one level, this ostensibly refers to the military plans that were lost to the French. At another level, it also might mean personal correspondence between Braddock and Bellamy, if such existed. Perhaps it refers to both.[19] The fact that Braddock, knowing he was dying, would order Orme to write such a letter, which he probably knew would ultimately arrive in the hands of George Anne Bellamy, suggests that their relationship was indeed close.

In contrast, Washington's dispatch to Dinwiddie focused, not unnaturally, on the conduct of the Virginia troops. "The Officers in gen'l behavd with incomparable bravery, for which they greatly suffer'd. . . . The Virginia companies behav'd like Men and died like Soldiers; for I believe that out of 3 companys that were on the ground that day, scarce 30 were left alive . . . the dastardly behavior of the Regular troops (so called) (English soldier) expos'd all those who were inclin'd to do their duty to almost certain Death; and at length, in spite of every effort to the contrary, broke and ran as Sheep before the Hounds. . . . Col. Dunbar, who commands at present, intends as soon as his men are recruited at this place, to continue his march to Phila. into Winter Quarters, so that there will be no Men left here, unless it is the poor remains of the Virginia troops, who survive and will be too small to guard our frontiers."[20] Washington himself limped back to Mount Vernon to recover from his illness and the exhaustion of the campaign.

In camp at Fort Cumberland, the rote of military life reasserted itself, but this time tainted by blame, especially by the officers of the common soldiers. A court-martial was convened, and fifty-six prisoners were tried for their conduct during the engagement, most probably for cowardice or desertion. On Monday, July 28, mass floggings were carried out against the enlisted men.[21] On August 1, Dunbar received a letter from Commodore Keppel asking that the surviving seamen (only five of them were not killed or wounded) return to Hampton. On August 3, they left the army and proceeded down through Virginia, where they ultimately boarded the HMS *Garland* at Hampton for the long voyage home.

Dinwiddie wanted Dunbar to remain at Fort Cumberland and make another attempt to take Fort Duquesne. However, a council of war decided that the scheme was not feasible in light of the overwhelming losses suffered. On August 2, Dunbar marched from Fort Cumberland for Philadelphia.[22] For this decision, for his hasty retreat, and for destroying the artillery and supplies, Dunbar immediately began to attract criticism.

Orme attacked St. Clair as well. Writing to Washington, with whom he remained on friendly terms, Orme stated: "I know the ignorant and rascally C____ D____ [Colonel Dunbar] is one promoter [of criticism of Braddock] through resentment and malevolence and the thick headed baronet [St. Clair] another, intending to build his character upon the ruins of one much more amiable than his can be. For my part I judge it a duty to vindicate the memory of a man whom I greatly and deservedly esteemed. . . . It is very hard the bluntness and openness of a man's temper should be called brutality and that he who would hear opinions more freely than any man should be accused of obstinacy and peremptoriness."[23]

St. Clair also must have gotten wind of Orme's finger-pointing early on, for on July 22, he wrote another report to Napier which detailed his repeated attempts to warn Braddock of the danger, to reunite the two columns into one more powerful force and, once the battle was on, to urge Braddock to take the high ground, most of which initiatives the general had brushed aside. He told Napier that even if the British had won the battle, he was determined to ask leave to be recalled, "finding I could be of little use being never listen'd to."[24]

Gage reported to Napier on why the common soldiers fought so badly, blaming it on the American locals: "no officers ever behaved better, or men worse. I can't ascribe their behavior to any other cause than the talk of the country people, ever since our arrival in America–the woodsmen and Indian traders, who were continually telling the soldiers, that if they attempted to fight the Indians in a regular manner, they would certainly be defeated. These discourses were prevented as much as possible, and the men in appearance seemed to shew a thorough contempt for such an enemy; but I fear they gained too much upon them. I have since talked to the soldiers about their scandalous behavior, and the only excuse I can get from them is, that they were quite dispirited, from the great fatigue they had undergone, and not receiving a sufficient quantity of food; and further that they did not expect the enemy would come down so suddenly."[25]

Orme's accusations in particular next assumed the form of public letters as he retreated to Philadelphia to recuperate from his wound before embarking for England in November. The colonial press picked up his accusations and magnified them. As early as August 30, Gates, back in New York, responded that "there has not been one true account publish'd as yet a great deal of pro & con in the news papers and yesterday Col. Gage and the officers of the Van Guard contradicted Captn: Orme's publick letter by an advertisement which you will see in the Philadelphia Gazette. A few who were the General's favourites gratefully strive to save his fame by throwing the misfortune of the day on the bad behaviour of the troops, but that was not the case."[26]

News of the defeat reached London in late August via the frigate HMS *Seahorse*, which raced homeward from Virginia carrying Commodore Keppel.[27] The news was greeted by a mixture of shock and langor. Most of the aristocracy were in the country enjoying the late summer holidays and the start of the shooting season. Besides, given the pace at which armies and news moved in the eighteenth century, the war had for months been out of sight and out of mind. It was no longer *popular*. The government held no high-level inquiry, perhaps because the defeat was *too* embarrassing.[28] Cumberland, the godfather of the expedition, was also the son of the king and may well not have wanted an inquiry. The attitude in London is perhaps best summed up by Walpole's remark: "Braddock's defeat still remains in the situation of the longest battle that ever was fought with nobody."[29]

Nonetheless, Braddock, being dead, of course came in for the most criticism. One British officer who participated in the action wrote: "In the time of the Action, the General behaved with a great deal of Personal Courage, which every body must allow–but that's all what Can be said–he was a Man of Sense and good natur'd too tho' Warm and a little uncouth in his manner–and Peevish–with all very indolent and sem'd glad for any body to take business off his hands, which may be one reason why he was so grossly imposed upon, by his favourite [Orme]–who realy Directed every thing and may justly be said to've Commanded the Expedition and the Army."[30]

Scaroyady also had an acerbic assessment: "It was the pride and ignorance of that General that came from England. He looked upon us as dogs, and would never hear anything what was said to him. We often tried to tell him of the danger he was in with his soldiers, but he never appeared pleased with us, and that was the reason that a great many of our warriors left him and would not be under his command."[31]

Franklin rendered a more balanced judgment in his *Autobiography*: "This General was, I think, a brave man, and might probably have made a figure as a good officer in some European war. But he had too much self-confidence, too high an opinion of the validity of regular troops, and too mean a one of both Americans and Indians."[32]

But Washington offered what is perhaps the truest assessment of Braddock, both as a commander and as a man: "Thus died a man, whose good and bad qualities were intimately blended. He was brave even to a fault and in regular Service would have done honor to his profession. His attachments were warm, his enmities were strong, and having no disguise about him, both appeared in full force. He was generous and disinterested, but plain and blunt in his manner even to rudeness."[33]

Thus, His Excellency Major General Edward Braddock remains one of those simple people fated to leave behind a complex, mixed reputation because of their very limitations. There can be little question that his struggle to overcome adversity, as well as his personal behavior on the battlefield, did "deserve the highest commendation."

At the end of the day, Braddock was done in not only by his French and Indian enemies but also by a confluence of adverse circumstances: formidable geography, almost nonexistent intelligence, colonial assemblies which would not pay, colonial governors who dissembled, Americans who failed to provide logistical support, Americans with their own agendas, Quakers who did not lift a finger, Indian allies who failed to materialize, bad weather, drunken and ill-humored troops, and conniving staff officers. Braddock never stood a chance.

However, neither judgments on Braddock's character nor his staff's efforts to assign and avoid blame were of account to the inhabitants of the Middle Atlantic colonies. By August 1755, with Dunbar marching to Philadelphia at the head of the surviving troops and a skeleton force of Virginians holding Fort Cumberland, the frontier lay open to hordes of pro-French Indians sallying forth from Canada and Fort Duquesne.[34] By mid-August, colonial reconnaissance patrols had reported four to five hundred Indians and French at Great Meadows. In response, Fort

Cumberland prepared for a siege and transferred its hospital, including Nurse Charlotte Browne, to Frederick, Maryland. The Virginia House of Burgesses voted £40,000 to increase Virginia troop levels to twelve hundred, and Dinwiddie commissioned Washington as colonel of the reactivated Virginia Regiment.

Within three months of Braddock's defeat, the entire frontier was aflame with French and Indian attacks, which came to be known simply as "the Outrages."[35] Thousands of families abandoned their homes and farms and fled back into the Piedmont and Tidewater, terrified. So severe were the depredations that it was said that no English settlers would be left west of Virginia's Blue Ridge. With Fort Cumberland all but abandoned, the new frontier line was drawn at Frederick, Maryland. Raids penetrated to within a hundred miles of Philadelphia. Perhaps fifteen hundred settlers were murdered and many more taken captive. According to one estimate, the frontier counties of the three middle Atlantic colonies of Virginia, Maryland, and Pennsylvania lost between a third and a half of their populations between 1755 and 1758, with some four percent of their prewar inhabitants murdered or captured.[36] The French and their Indian allies killed civilians, women and children indiscriminately. They gloated at the sufferings of their victims. The impact on the psyche of Americans at the time was devastating.

Moreover, there was a premeditation to the Outrages that chilled the soul. One large raid in Pennsylvania consisted of 1,400 Indians and French divided into scalping parties of forty each. A week before, they had sent out numerous small scouting parties. The attack groups were targeted on carefully chosen settlements on the Pennsylvania frontier, such as Shamokin, Juniata, and Harris's Ferry (today's Harrisburg), until the whole frontier was blanketed. Each party thoroughly scouted its target for several days, and then all attacks were launched at the same time to achieve complete surprise.[37]

Like other aspects of the Braddock expedition, the horrors of the Outrages can only be comprehended by peeking into the lives of common people long buried by history. Two lives will suffice.

The consequences of Braddock's defeat came home to Thomas Jemison on his prosperous farm near Gettysburg. Jemison and his family had lived in central Pennsylvania for a dozen years after emigrating from Ireland. He was concerned about the Indian depredations, but none had taken place as far east as Gettysburg. He believed that if he could get safely through one more year the Anglo-American forces would drive the Indians back. (He had lost a brother serving under Washington at Fort Necessity.)

One morning he and his wife and six children were sitting down to breakfast with a visiting family of neighbors. Twelve-year-old Mary later recalled that "Father was shaving an axe-helve at the side of the house; mother was making preparations for breakfast; my two older brothers were at work near the barn; and the little ones, with myself, and the [neighbor] woman and her three children, in the house."[38] The neighbor had just left on horseback for some supplies.

> There was a sudden, appalling crash of gunfire, a glimpse of the neighbor and his horse lying dead in the yard, and then a rush of bronze bodies. 'They first secured my father, and then rushed into the house, and without the least resistance made prisoners' of them all. The raiders, 'six Indians and four Frenchmen,' grabbed all the food they could carry and, 'in great haste, for fear of detection,' drove the little herd of frightened humanity into the woods. All day long they hurried westward, the captives offered nothing to eat or drink. 'Whenever the little children cried for water, the Indians would make then drink urine or go thirsty.' That night they slept, hungry, exhausted and afraid, on the ground, and before dawn were forced to march on. They were given some breakfast at dawn, and some supper that night when they camped in a swamp.
>
> After supper the Shawnees tore the shoes from Mary's feet and replaced them with moccasins, and did the same

> for one of the neighbor boys. Mary's mother knew what that meant and hugged her, urging her to be brave and careful, to remember her English and her prayers. Her father could not speak; he had been 'sunk in silent despair' since the attack. The Shawnees led the two children away from the rest of the captives, whom they then tomahawked, scalped and dismembered. Mary was spared the sights and sounds of the killings, but the next day was forced to watch as the warriors stretched, cleaned and cured the scalps. 'My mother's hair was red, and I could easily distinguish my father's and the children's from each other.'[39]

Mary was adopted by a Seneca family at Logstown, married to a Delaware warrior, widowed in a Cherokee raid, and later moved to western New York's Genesee River country, where she chose to spend the rest of her eight decades of life as a Seneca wife, mother of eight, and matron.[40]

Or the case of Jacob Fisher:

> 1758 was the worst year yet. The outrages resumed along Mill Creek, near Woodstock [Virginia], when fifty Shawnees and four Frenchmen surrounded a congregation of several families seeking refuge in George Painter's large log house. When Painter tried a desperate run for help, they shot him down in the yard. The others surrendered, hoping in vain for mercy.
>
> The warriors fired the house and tossed George Painter's body into the flames. They burned the barn and laughed at the screams of the burning animals trapped inside. They snatched four babies from their mothers' arms, strung them up in trees, and used them for target practice until they dangled, quiet and bloody, before the horrified eyes of the families. Then they drove forty-eight surviving prisoners, men, women and children, on a hellish, six-day march over the western mountains to their village.

> There, after consultation with the matrons, they told Jacob Fisher, a pudgy twelve year-old, to gather a large pile of dry wood. He burst into tears. "They're going to burn me, father," he sobbed.
>
> "I hope not, son, do as they say," said the helpless father. Jacob, weeping, brought the wood, which the warriors and the women arranged in a circle around a sapling. They tied the howling Jacob to the sapling with a long rope cinched to his wrist and set the wood afire. Then, while Jacob's father and brothers watched, the Shawnees poked him with sharpened sticks, forcing him to run around the sapling, first winding himself tight to it, then spiralling outward, into and out of the flames. It took him hours and hours to die.[41]

Three years earlier, soon after the defeat of Braddock, and as the Outrages were just starting, Captain Charles Lewis of the Virginia Volunteers happened upon a similar scene of scalping and massacre of innocent women and children. He wrote in his journal: "This horrid scene gave us a terrible shock, but I hope with the leave of God we shall still overcome the cruel, barbarous and inhuman enemy."[42]

BRADDOCK'S MARCH WAS THE OPENING CHAPTER in a long and complicated struggle for the continent of North America. Three years after Braddock's defeat another general, John Forbes, battling fatal cancer and carried in a litter along a different route, captured the citadel of French power on the Forks of the Ohio and stopped the Outrages, but not before many more Americans, Scots Highlanders, and Englishmen died and had their heads impaled before the ramparts of Fort Duquesne.

But that is another story.

CHAPTER TWENTY

Sic Transit Gloria

BRADDOCK'S DEFEAT AND ITS IMMEDIATE aftermath was an inflection point in the American psyche the profundity of which, in its own time and place, rivaled that of September 11, 2001. Its effects, entirely unintended, reverberated throughout the colonies, throughout the British army, and throughout the lives of those who survived it.

The collapse of the British army, one of the premier fighting forces of its day sent to rescue the American people, caused panic and horror as French and Indians poured over the mountains from New England and New York to South Carolina murdering and terrorizing the populace. For their part, the victorious French positively gloated. Captain Jean Daniel Dumas, the hero of the battle, wrote to the ministry in Paris requesting that the Cross of St. Louis decoration that he received for his valor be "doubled" with a promotion. In his request he proclaimed his victory at the Monongahela "the salute of an entire colony" and noted that "incursions have multiplied against Pennsylvania, Maryland and Virginia." He boasted that the "war had been carried even into

South Carolina and to the seacoast."[1] The ensuing collapse of the social order all along the frontier and well into the interior of the entire eastern seaboard lasted from Braddock's defeat until at least 1758–59. The residue of that period on the national consciousness was an aversion to terror and anarchy and a renewed determination to restore order, safety, and predictability–in short to reconstruct a civil society, albeit on different terms than those that prevailed prior to the disaster.

The seeds of that different solution were planted in the very planning of the campaign. Thus, Braddock's expedition was the first time Britain sent regular troops in force to North America.[2] The Crown committed those troops without an effective plan for paying for them. When Braddock placed before the colonial governors the king's order to the colonies for a "common fund" to pay the cost of the expedition they balked because they knew their assemblies would not agree. The congress of the colonial governors at Carlyle House and the resulting consensus among the governors on strategy and refusal to fund the expedition was the first successful step toward a unity of policy on the part of the colonies.[3]

Braddock's defeat also was the birth throughout the colonies and subsequent American republic of the persistent myth that irregular warfare, preferably by citizen soldiers, was superior, both practically and morally, to formal warfare waged by professional troops.[4] This hubris is perhaps most tellingly caught by Ralph Waldo Emerson's "Concord Hymn":

> By the rude bridge that arched the flood,
> Their flag to April's breeze unfurled,
> Here once the embattled farmers stood
> And fired the shot heard round the world.[5]

Although American militia had fought successfully against the Pequots in the 1630s, against the Narragansetts in King Philip's War of 1676, and at the taking of Louisburg in 1745, untrained

American citizen-soldiers had never before fought in such self-conscious contrast to their British cousins. A month after the defeat at the Monongahela, a rumor ran through the colonies that the wounded Braddock had sighed from his litter, "my dear Blues (which was the Colors the Virginians wore) give 'em tother Fire, you Fight like Men, & will die like Souldiers . . . [he] could not bear the sight of a red Coat, whenever one came in his view, he raved immoderately, but when one of the blues, he said he hop'd to live to reward 'em."[6] The story is probably apocryphal. However, the important point is not whether Braddock said it but that *Americans* said it.

Moreover, the myth that was born on July 9, 1755, in rapid turn produced a milestone in military history. The slaughter of the British regulars at the Monongahela directly caused the formation of the first American special operations forces. The Americans quickly realized that the irregular tactics deployed in the battle, if only sporadically, by George Washington and his countrymen were more effective than the set piece tactics of Sir Humphrey Bland, and, starting with the veterans of the battle themselves, they did not hesitate to say so.[7] A mere eight months later Governor-turned-General William Shirley, who succeeded Braddock as Commander-in-Chief in North America, was still grieving over the loss of his son, Braddock's secretary, to the French and Indians. In response to the lessons learned at the Monongahela, and perhaps motivated in part by his own personal tragedy, Shirley commissioned Captain Robert Rogers, a tough New Hampshire veteran of the Crown Point expedition, to form an independent company of Rangers to take the war to the enemy through irregular operations. Rogers's Rangers were a mixed lot of Americans, British, and Europeans, and they were populated by no small number of veterans of the 44th and 48th Regiments who had fought under Braddock, as well as by veterans of St. Clair's old 22nd Foot.[8] Thus, Braddock's defeat directly led to the creation of Rogers's Rangers and what is generally conceded to be the birth of special operations in the American military tradition. Rogers was the author of a famous twenty-eight-point "Plan of Discipline" that reads like a guide to how *not* to fight like Braddock.[9] This epiphany and its subsequent elaboration in the ensuing broader French and Indian War through units like Rogers's Rangers instilled a reverence for flexibility, speed, and daring tactics in the American military. In short, the lesson from Braddock's battlefield became the core of how Americans fight to this day.

However, a secondary lesson drawn by the Americans was also to have a more immediate consequence. Braddock's loss provided the first proof to the Americans of the vincibility of the vaunted British redcoats. It emboldened them to strike militarily at His Majesty's forces twenty years later. The cadre of American leadership who were veterans of the engagement gained the courage to meet one of the best armies in the world on the battlefield. The battlefield at the Forks of the Ohio gave the Americans a hero, George Washington, who bravely did his duty and was seemingly impervious to bullets. It also gave the Americans a core of officers and enlisted men whose shared experiences under Braddock were to credential them as veterans and who were to serve as a nucleus of the Continental Army in the Revolution.

The effects of the battle were felt not only in America. The British army drew its own constructive conclusions from the engagement. Notwithstanding the evident lack of a formal post mortem, Whitehall in its own quiet and bumbling way began to take corrective action in response to the defeat. In particular, by 1758, the army had assembled companies of "light infantry" drawn from the regimental marksmen. These troops were sharpshooters, inured to fatigue and experts in forest warfare. They operated as skirmishers with dash and cunning. Examples included Gage's own Light Armed Foot 80th Company mustered in 1758.[10] Such mobile, lightly armed troops even attempted amphibious landings and other types of irregular warfare. Although temporarily disbanded after the Seven Years' War on the grounds that they were antisocial brigands, they were resuscitated, operated throughout the Revolution, and came into full maturation in the Peninsular campaigns of the Napoleonic Wars.

Finally, the engagement at the Monongahela profoundly affected the individual lives of those who participated in it. In analyzing this last series of consequences it is worth bearing in mind that people make events, sometimes grand events, that in turn may change people. If events had not conspired as they did and if Braddock had not been delayed so long at Alexandria or Fort Cumberland, the likelihood is that he would have swept the French from Fort Duquesne and dealt a body blow to their designs on English North America.[11] Within weeks he would have marched against Niagara and, with the momentum of victory behind him, may well have taken it and, in conjunction with Shirley and Pepperell, secured the northern frontier.[12] The high cost of the protracted French and Indian War in North America might have been avoided with New France contained at Quebec. There would have been no siege of Quebec City, no *annus mirabilis* of 1759, no patriotic prints of General James Wolfe expiring in the arms of his comrades, no birth of British Canada, no arguing between Britain and America over the war debt. Braddock might have been rewarded with the governorship of New York, a position he supposedly coveted. George Washington might have obtained a commission from the king through Braddock's influence and spent his life serving garrison duty in the colonies or Canada. The American colonies might in all probability have remained part of the British empire, slowly evolving into commonwealth status.

However, the "what ifs" are speculative at best. In fact, history worked out quite differently. When the French read the captured secret plans to roll up their forts in Canada, Paris reacted with shock and dismay. It would now be impossible, the French government concluded, to reach an understanding with Britain.[13] Thus, the mere existence of the plans damaged relations further—but with little ensuing benefit to Britain because the grand plan had fizzled. In fact Shirley and his colonial troops abandoned the attempt on Niagara because Braddock and his British regulars were not there to support them. Forewarned by the captured plans, the French reinforced Crown Point on Lake Champlain and held off William Johnson's attempt to seize that objective. Despite successfully blunting a French offensive and capturing the French commander at the Battle of Lake George, an exhausted Johnson, after receiving a musket ball in the buttocks, abandoned the effort and led his troops into a defensive position at Fort William Henry on Lake George.

Of the four-pronged grand plan, only one prong succeeded. Even as Braddock was slogging through the wilderness in early June, Monckton's men invested and took Fort Beauséjour and a smaller ancillary fort in Nova Scotia. It remained for Shirley and his New England regiment to round up and deport the French-speaking Acadians to Louisiana and the mainland colonies. Although some escaped to Quebec or Prince Edward Island, well over five thousand–entire families–were herded aboard ships, their land declared forfeited, and removed forever from their homes to make room for English-speaking settlers from New England and Great Britain. Henry Wadsworth Longfellow later immortalized the "Grand Derangement" in his epic poem *Evangeline*. At the time, the operation, which was carried out with almost chilling precision, was viewed by the English and Americans as humane and hugely successful. If history has rendered a different verdict, it must be remembered that the French and Indians were engaging in a far bloodier relocation campaign in the Ohio valley and Appalachian Mountains.

Beyond these immediate consequences, it is clear that Braddock's loss led to more determined efforts to oust the French from the Forks of the Ohio and ultimately not just to secure the northern border of the American colonies but to expel France entirely from North America. If the results for New France were disastrous, they were equally so for the pro-French Indians, whose power the British broke and whose existence the Americans ultimately all but annihilated east of the Mississippi. Braddock's defeat raised the stakes and made the war a long,

The Braddock gravesite monument erected by the Coldstream Guards in 1913. Located at Fort Necessity National Park, the obelisk marks the spot where Braddock's remains were reinterred from their original site discovered below the nearby Braddock's Road. (*National Park Service*)

costly enterprise. Notwithstanding the eventual British victory, the very cost of that war led directly to the Revolution and its consequences.

Braddock's march had further unintended consequences as well. The route that St. Clair cut following Nemacolin's trail became the basis for the later National Pike and the single major route for westward expansion into Ohio and the Midwest. One historian of the road wrote: "Few roads ever cost so much, ever amounted to so little at first, and then finally played so important a part in the development of any continent."[14]

Adventurers and settlers poured over this road within less than twenty years after Braddock's rout. Indeed, when Washington revisited the road in 1774 he was amazed to find people emigrating over it "in shoals."[15] With the frontier eventually secured, America was primed for westward expansion. An entire culture developed along the road, complete with teamsters, settlers, emigrants, mile posts, toll houses, and taverns whose front stoops were scented with peppermint to lure travelers.[16] (The National

Pike survives today as U.S. Route 40.) Many of its mileposts, taverns and toll houses still stand. As the wagons rolled and the itinerant population–farmers, shoemakers, coopers, potters, weavers, gamblers and gunslingers–walked along the National Pike toward new lands and new destinies they became the new pilgrims through the wilderness. Each passing foot, each rolling wheel, impacted the earth over Braddock's grave so that the man who would have saved North America and his legions were forgotten.

Around 1804 (the accounts vary as to the exact date) workmen repairing the road disturbed a skeleton. Legend has it that Tom Fausett, who lived nearby, pointed them to the spot. From the buttons and military insignia, they identified the remains as those of Braddock. A passing merchant took some of the bones to the Peale Museum in Philadelphia, where they were destroyed in a fire. However, the workmen reinterred most of the skeleton a few yards from where they found it, on a small rise beside the new National Pike. There the "bluff old soldier," the snuff-dipping toast of the gaming rooms of Mayfair and Picadilly, lies to this day, marked by a stone obelisk erected in 1913 by his fellow Coldstream Guardsmen. The site is on U.S. Route 40 west from the Great Meadows an hour south of Pittsburgh. The obelisk stands, as if at perpetual attention, the lone sentinel still guarding the line of Braddock's March.[17]

SO OBSCURED HAVE THE EVENTS DESCRIBED in this story become in the last two and a half centuries that there is not even agreement on the name of the battle at which Braddock suffered defeat. It is variously called the Battle of the Wilderness, Braddock's Field, the Battle of the Monongahela, the Battle of Turtle Creek. Consensus has somewhat coalesced around the name Battle of the Monongahela.

The site of the Battle of the Monongahela is in the township of Braddock, Pennsylvania, just seven miles from downtown

The town of Braddock, Pennsylvania, as it appears today, with the tree-lined ridge in the background where the French and Indians hid while attacking Braddock's forces. (*Author*)

Pittsburgh.[18] Today much of the site is occupied by the defunct U.S. Steel Edgar Thompson Monongahela Valley Steelworks. At the entrance, a sign proudly proclaims "Last Slab Rolled October 31, 1992," as if another, recent defeat is more worthy of memorial. Adjacent to the steelworks, north and west, on a sloping hillside huddles the town of Braddock. Tumbledown, abandoned redbrick buildings march rank on rank. In the few buildings that still host human life, window signs advertise the Powerball lottery and "Terrible Towels" proclaim support for the Steelers football team. The Paradise Lounge presides, oblivious to the irony of its name.

Yet the hill is still there. Beyond the boarded-up storefronts and empty houses, one can see the ridge on which the French and Indians hid. Trees still soften its crest, descendants of the forest that covered the slope. In the town, in the vicinity of the railroad tracks and Braddock Avenue, paved and cobbled, one can walk where Gage formed his square and his troops fell dead by the hundreds. One can imagine where Halkett rode up and took a bullet and his son crumpled on top of him. One can picture where Braddock, with his hat bound in a white handkerchief, raged and stormed at his faltering troops on his great English charger and where he too received his mortal wound. One can know that on the very ground one walks Washington exhorted his troops and pleaded with the general to unleash his Virginians to fight Indian-fashion. Somewhere along the pavement is the spot where St. Clair spoke to Braddock in Italian and passed out from his wounds. And where Shirley fell, shot through the head.

Today, however, the battlefield is empty. It is utterly forgotten except by the few pilgrims who each year go out of their way to walk the deserted streets. On a bleak winter morning the cold wind slices in from the Monongahela, and on a humid summer night hundreds of ghostly fireflies recall the lost souls buried beneath the surface. Today's pilgrim finds scant evidence of the day the swells of Mayfair ended their own pilgrimage before a deluge of barbarism and of the day America grew up.

EPILOGUE

The Fates of the Pilgrims

THE STORY OF BRADDOCK'S MARCH fittingly ends with a review of the fates of the pilgrims who originally walked with Braddock in life or marched with him to destiny or death.

Following its defeat at the Monongahela and the scourging of its enlisted men, the 44th Regiment was moved to the New York theater, where in late 1755 it reinforced Oswego. Subsequently, under acting commander Major William Eyre, it saw heavy service, defeat, and retreat at Fort Ticonderoga in July 1758. It remained in service in America throughout the French and Indian War until the outbreak of Pontiac's rebellion, when many of its men were drafted into other regiments to meet the crisis. The regiment was subsequently disbanded.

The 48th Regiment fared worse. After its loss under Braddock and ensuing punishments, it also moved to New York under the new command of Colonel Daniel Webb as Halkett's replacement. Although it remained below strength following the rout at the Monongahela, it supplemented its numbers with American recruits and acquired a distinctly American character.[1] At the Battle of Quebec, September 13, 1759, General James Wolfe placed the veteran 48th to hold the crucial center of the British line facing the French, where it saw heavy fighting and losses. The unit later transferred to the West Indies to lay siege to Havana, Cuba, in 1762. However, heat and disease proved fatal. When the regiment mustered to return to England on December 11, 1762, only one officer, one sergeant, a single drummer, and four privates remained standing.[2] So ended the saga of the 48th Regiment's long service in America.

WILLIAM AUGUSTUS, THE DUKE OF CUMBERLAND (1721–1765). Braddock's defeat was also a political defeat for the duke. However, he survived in his position because of his royal blood and erstwhile competence. His luck did not hold for long. In July 1757, the French defeated him at the Battle of Hastenbeck, in Hanover, one of King George II's possessions. Because Cumberland signed the Convention of Klosterzeven promising to evacuate Hanover, his father dismissed him and repudiated the agreement. Later, in 1765, Cumberland briefly headed a ministry at the request of his nephew, King George III. However, he suffered a brain clot and died on October 31, 1765, aged 44.

GEORGE ANNE BELLAMY (1727? 1729? 1733?–1788). When news of Braddock's death reached George Anne Bellamy, she lamented the fact that he had died, "leaving me only the plate which he had received as the usual perquisite from the government on his nomination."[3] In fact, he left her indirectly half of his estate. Apparently she had expected more, which is yet further evidence of a special relationship. In the event, the treasury sued to try to repossess the plate. She resisted in court and won.

The remainder of Bellamy's life was a mix of successes on the stage and affairs too numerous and convoluted to sort out. In addition to her recorded affairs with Lord Byron, Sir George Metheun, and "Honest Jack" Calcraft (who never married her), she married West Digges, an actor who was already married to another woman, and an actor named Woodward. She was renowned for her beauty (small in stature, fair, and with blue eyes), and in her early years consorted with all the luminaries of the London stage, as well as powerful men in government, like Fox, and top-ranking generals and diplomats. However, her looks began to fade after Braddock's death when she was in her thirties, and her extravagance caused her to wallow continually in debt. Her flair for the dramatic found expression in her posting herself on more than one occasion atop Westminster Bridge over the Thames and threatening to jump unless rescued physically and financially by an appropriate member of her aristocratic circle of admirers. Fortunately, she was rescued each time, but the attempts were the source of gossip and even inspired a print. If the wealthy Lord Tyrawley were her father, he did nothing to alleviate her poverty in his lifetime, which lasted until well into the 1770s. Nor did her ostensible half-brother Charles O'Hara, himself a lieutenant general and a man of considerable wealth. In 1785 Bellamy wrote a five-volume autobiography, *An Apology for the Life of George Anne Bellamy*, which is a surprisingly entertaining read by a bright lady two and a half centuries ahead of her time. She died February 16, 1788, in destitution, aged fifty-five, fifty-nine, or sixty-one, depending on whom one chooses to believe.

"The despair of Mrs. Bellamy on the steps of Westminster Bridge," a French print. (*Bibliothèque nationale de France*)

George Anne Bellamy lay forgotten for 140 years. On April 21, 1928–St. George's Day and Bellamy's birthday–the composer Jerome Kern briefly resurrected her in a musical entitled *Blue Eyes* (book and lyrics by Guy Bolton and Graham John; music by Jerome Kern). The play opened at the Piccadilly Theatre in London, with the building unfinished and the star, Evelyn Laye, in the throes of a painful divorce. Laye felt unable to give herself to the story of the eighteenth-century "Scottish" actress George Anne Bellamy (whose name was changed, "more sensibly," to "Nancy" for the production). *Blue Eyes* was mainly acclaimed for its abundance of kilts rather than its music. Although panned by the London *Times*, it lasted a heroic 276 performances.[4]

George Anne Bellamy might have smiled.

DANIEL BOONE (1734–1820). Boone married in 1756 and settled in Rowan County, North Carolina. From there, he explored and hunted across the Appalachians in Kentucky, as well as in Florida. By the 1770s he was leading parties of settlers into Kentucky and fighting the Shawnees. At various times during the Revolution he was captured by the Indians and the British but either escaped or was released. His exploits inspired James Fenimore Cooper, who used material from his life in *The Last of the Mohicans* and *Leatherstocking Tales.* In 1781 he was elected to the Virginia assembly. At the end of the war, he settled on the Ohio River and took up tavern keeping, surveying, and land speculating. In the 1790s, he moved to what is now Charleston, West Virginia, then on to Kentucky. In 1799, he led his family on a migration to Missouri, where the Spanish governor appointed him a district "syndic" or magistrate. He died in 1820 in Missouri.

LIEUTENANT COLONEL RALPH BURTON (?–1768). In January 1758, Burton was given the local rank of colonel in North America and commanded the right wing at the capture of Quebec. For his efforts, he was rewarded with the lieutenant governorship of Quebec and, subsequently, governorship of Trois Rivières, Canada, from 1760 to 1762. On July 10, 1762, seven years and a day after Braddock's defeat, he was elevated to brigadier general. He subsequently served as governor of Montreal and, finally, as Commander of the Northern Department, in charge of all Quebec. He chose to remain in Canada and died there. He remarried (after the death of his first wife, a friend of George Anne Bellamy) and had two children, Richard and Mary, who, with his widow Margaret, survived him.[5] In 1784, his daughter Mary Burton married Napier Christie in Montreal. In 1763 Napier Christie's father Gabriel Christie[6] had purchased from Captain Beaujeu's estate his landholdings at Lacolle, Quebec, known as the Seignory of Beaujeu. Napier Christie took the Burton name, becoming Napier Christie Burton and acquired title to the Burton family seats at Hotham Hall in York and Hall Bank in Beverley, Yorkshire. Napier Christie Burton eventually inherited the Seignory of Beaujeu and was instrumental in arranging the emigration of many settlers from the Burton estates in Yorkshire to the Beaujeu Seignory at Lacolle, Quebec. Thus, Ralph Burton's daughter became the mistress of the estate of the man who destroyed Braddock and helped settle it with her family and countrymen.

ROBERT DINWIDDIE (1693–1770). Governor Dinwiddie grew disheartened after the defeat of Braddock and lost interest in the Ohio Company. The Outrages forced him to retire. He returned to England in 1758 and died there in 1770.

COLONEL THOMAS DUNBAR (c. 1700–1767). Dunbar's reputation never recovered from the controversy surrounding his retreat and destruction of supplies. In November 1755, he was relieved of command of the 48th Regiment, and it was given to another colonel. However, Dunbar received honorable retirement as lieutenant governor of Gibraltar, a post similar, if not identical, to the one held by Braddock before his North American commission. Thus, Dunbar effectively replaced Braddock. Although Dunbar was never again employed in command, he rose to the ranks of major general in 1758 and lieutenant general in 1760.

TOM FAUSETT (1713?–1822). Fausett, who claimed to have killed Braddock, settled near the line of Braddock's march after the war. For years he haunted the local taverns dressed in his buckskin shirt and bear hat. He was known as "Whistling Tom" for the imitation he did of a fifer playing the "Grenadiers' March" and other martial airs.[7] He often told the story of how he killed the general for having murdered his brother during the battle. He branded Braddock a "madman" for insisting that the men fight in formation and not Indian-style. Several participants in the battle corroborated the story that Braddock was killed by one of his own men, and Fausett's claim was largely accepted for the first hundred years after the battle until Sargent tried to discredit it. Fausett never recanted his story. He died at age 109, the last surviving pilgrim of note along the road.

LIEUTENANT COLONEL THOMAS GAGE (1721–1787). Gage served extensively during the French and Indian War under James Abercrombie and Jeffery Amherst. He was appointed governor of Montreal from 1760 to 1763 and then promoted to Commander in Chief of British Forces in North America (Braddock's old position). He was married to an American woman who had divided loyalties and was long rumored to be an American spy. In 1774 he was made governor of Massachusetts, at a time of increasing tension. He tried to stamp out dissent and signed arrest orders for Samuel Adams and John Hancock. In April 1775, he ordered British troops to seize the magazine at Concord, thereby triggering the Battles of Lexington and Concord and starting the American Revolution. In light of the failure of his policies, he resigned in October 1775 and was succeeded by a split command of General William Howe as commander in America and General Guy Carleton as commander in Canada. He died in England.

LIEUTENANT HORATIO GATES (1727–1806). Gates was wounded during Braddock's defeat, shot in the chest, but his life was saved by one Private Francis Penfold, who carried him off the battlefield. Gates, who had been humbly born in England, subsequently served in various capacities in the French and Indian War, including as aide to Robert Monckton, royal governor of New York in 1763. However, like Washington, he struggled to find an appropriate commission, and he made a number of trips back to England before resigning from the army in 1769 and eventually settling in Virginia. He became involved in the Patriot cause through his friendship with Charles Lee. With the outbreak of hostilities in 1775, he was appointed a brigadier general in the Continental Army. The next year he was promoted to major general and named Commander of the Canadian Department, a post in which he never actually served. In 1777, he was named Commander of the Northern Department. In that capacity he suffered defeat by General John ("Gentleman Johnny") Burgoyne at the Battle of Freeman's Farm, New York, on September 19, 1777. However, he subsequently bested Burgoyne at the Battle of Bemis Heights on October 7, 1777, and decisively defeated him at the crucial Battle of Saratoga on October 17, 1777. By 1780, Gates was Commander of the Southern Department, where he lost the Battle of Camden to Lieutenant General Charles Cornwallis on August 17, 1780. Inquiries followed and his career never recovered, although he served on Washington's staff until the end of the war. In 1790, he moved to New York City, where he died on April 10, 1806.

SIR PETER HALKETT (1703–1755). Halkett's elder son Francis, the Third Baronet Pitfirrane, and a major in the 42nd Highland Regiment, accompanied the British expedition which seized Fort Duquesne in 1758 primarily to ascertain the fate of his father.[8] With the area swept of hostile French and Indians, he was free to return to the battlefield. In October 1758, he did so in the company of Indian guides, officers of the 42nd, and a company of the Pennsylvania Rifles commanded by Captain West, the painter Benjamin West's elder brother. The scene was vivid: "Captain West and his companions proceeded through the woods and along the banks of the river, towards the scene of the battle. The Indians [who had actually fought with the French in the battle] regarded the expedition as a religious rite, and guided the troops with awe and in profound silence. . . . They frequently found skeletons lying across the trunks of fallen trees–a mournful proof . . . that the men who sat there had perished of hunger, in vainly attempting to find their way to the plantations. Sometimes their feelings were raised to the utmost pitch of horror by the sight of bones and skulls scattered on the ground–a certain indication that the bodies had been devoured by wild beasts; and in other places they saw the blackness of ashes among the relics–the tremendous evidence of atrocious rites . . . one of his tawny guides had already told Halkett, that he recollected during the combat to have seen an officer fall beneath such a remarkable tree as he should have no difficulty in recognizing; and that at the same moment another rushing to his side was instantly shot down, and fell across his comrade's body. . . . Suddenly and with a shrill cry, the Indian . . . sprang to the well-remembered tree. While the troops rested on their arms in a circle around, he and his companions searched among the thick-fallen leaves. In a moment two gaunt skeletons were exposed lying together, the one upon the other, as they had died. . . . At the moment Sir Peter remembered him of a peculiar artificial tooth which his father bore. The bones were then separated, and an examination of those which lay undermost at once solved all doubts. 'It is my father!' exclaimed the unhappy youth, as he sunk into the arms of his scarce less affected friends."[9]

The son and his companions then buried the father and brother in a common grave on the spot, wrapped in a Highland tartan and with the discharge of muskets as a salute.

COMMODORE AUGUSTUS KEPPEL (1725–1786). Keppel rose to become an admiral and had a highly distinguished career. However, in 1778, he led the Channel Fleet in an indecisive battle with the French off Ushant, Brittany, allowing the French fleet to slip off to America and to challenge British forces fighting the Americans in the Revolution. Keppel was court-martialed as a result of this action, but he alleged that his second-in-command, Sir Hugh Palliser, gave him inadequate support. Keppel was acquitted, but not before the resulting squabble divided the Navy.

The National Maritime Muesum in Greenwich has several portraits of Keppel at various stages of his life, including one that features his flagship *Centurion* in the background. Keppel died in 1786 without issue. However, his collateral family has given us Camilla Parker Bowles, the duchess of Cornwall and the present-day wife of Prince Charles.

LIEUTENANT CHARLES LEE (1732–1782). Charles Lee was an obscure lieutenant, born the same month and year as George Washington, who played no noteworthy role in the Braddock expedition. This was odd, for the rest of his life Lee attracted notice. Shortly after the Braddock campaign he married the daughter of a Mohawk chief, who rewarded him with the name "Boiling Water." He fought at the siege of Montreal but then in 1762 removed to the European theater, where he served as a Colonel under General "Gentleman Johnny" Burgoyne in Portugal. Later, he acted as aid de camp, with rank of major general, to King Stanislas II of Poland. Returning to Britain, he sought an appropriate position in an audience with King George III. When the King started to explain that there was no posting available, he cut the King short and resigned his commission.

Lee returned to America, where he made friends with Gates, Washington, and the unrelated Richard Henry Lee. With the advent of the Revolution, Lee expected to be named commander in chief but was in fact appointed second major general of the Continental Army after Artemas Ward. However, the British had a high estimation of Lee and, regarding him as superior to Washington, viewed him as their greatest enemy within the American senior ranks. Lee commanded the city of Charleston during the British siege of June 1776. Later that year, the British captured Lee at White's Tavern in Basking Ridge, New Jersey, and held him prisoner for two years. Following his release, Lee was a sub-commander under Washington at the Battle of Monmouth. He disobeyed orders, leading to an American loss, and was subsequently court-martialed. On January 10, 1780, the

Congress released him from the Continental Army. On October 2, 1782, he died at Philadelphia unkempt and surrounded by his habitual pack of dogs.

DANIEL MORGAN (1735?–1802). Morgan settled in Virginia with a common-law wife after the war. He volunteered early in the Revolution and led the only rifle company in the Continental Army, made up of Kentucky backwoodsmen armed with long rifles. The unit served under Gates. He was a hero at Saratoga. Later, after Gates's defeat at Camden, he joined the Southern Department and was promoted to brigadier general. He defeated Lieutenant Colonel Banastre Tarleton at the Battle of Cowpens. After the Revolution Washington appointed him a major general of the Virginia militia and deployed him in the suppression of the Whiskey Rebellion. He later served in the U.S. Congress.

CAPTAIN ROGER MORRIS (1727–1794). Captain Morris went on to fight under Wolfe at Quebec. After the war he settled in New York City with his American wife, Mary Philipse, who at one point had been courted by George Washington. Her family's extensive landholdings in Putnam County, New York, gave Morris great wealth. At the outbreak of the Revolution, Morris refused to fight against the Patriots even though he was sympathetic to the British. The New York legislature confiscated his property during the war, and George Washington used his house as his headquarters for a period. In 1783 he, his wife and his four children removed to England. Later his children sold some reversionary interests in the confiscated property to John Jacob Astor. Morris died in England in 1794.

CAPTAIN ROBERT ORME (1725–1790). Captain Robert Orme recovered from his wound and returned to England, where he remained on friendly terms with Washington, addressing him on a first-name basis ("Dear George") in correspondence, one of the few people ever to do so.

The National Gallery in London has a magnificent portrait of Robert Orme by Sir Joshua Reynolds. It was painted in 1756, soon after Reynolds established his London studio. It shows Braddock's aide-de-camp as a dashing, sharp-featured officer of the Coldstream Regiment of Foot Guards with a dispatch in his hand, ready to mount his impatient horse–a mixture of romance, fire, rage, and patriotic ardor. "The thunderous sky and extravagant lighting, Orme's windswept hair, the highlighted dispatches in his hand, his foaming steed, the red coat pushed open by the ready sword–all suggest a heroic and transient moment in the life of the young officer."[10]

Orme never took possession of the painting. Instead, he resigned his commission in 1756 and eloped with Audrey Townshend, the daughter of George Anne Bellamy's friend Charles Townshend, third Viscount Raynham (1700–1764), and sister of George Townshend (1724–1807) who, as a brigadier general, assumed command when James Wolfe was killed taking Quebec City in 1759. Another brother, Colonel Roger Townshend (1732–1759) was killed by a cannonball at Fort Ticonderoga.[11] The elopement caused a scandal because Orme apparently was already married to another woman and was a father. Washington never corresponded with him again. Orme reportedly lived for years with his bigamous wife in the Netherlands. He later resided in Topsham, Devon, near Exeter, and after the death of his wife, with his son the Reverend Robert Orme, the vicar of Hertford, Hertfordshire, where he died in 1790.[12] Captain Robert Orme is not to be confused with the more famous Robert Orme (1728–1801) who wrote histories of India and Central Asia.

PONTIAC (17??–1769). After the fall of French power in the French and Indian War, the former French Indians were displeased with their new English masters. Pontiac hatched a scheme to massacre all the English garrisons and settlers in Virginia, Pennsylvania, and the Great Lakes. On a certain day in June 1763, to be determined by a change of the moon, the Indians were to attack every English post simultaneously and drive the settlers east of the Appalachians. Almost every tribe of the Algonquin nation, plus the Senecas of the Six Nations, joined in the rebellion. The plan was to approach the forts on a pretended friendly visit and amuse the soldiers with games. However, each warrior concealed weapons beneath his cloak and at the given signal was to fall upon the English and massacre them to a person. The plan miscarried at Detroit, where the garrison got word of the plot from an Indian girl the day before it was to occur. Instead, the Indians attacked and besieged the fort, but it held out. So also did Fort Pitt, formerly Fort Duquesne. The remainder of the English forts fell to Pontiac. The fighting, led in part by Gage, continued for three years. Ultimately Pontiac acceded to a peace treaty. He moved to Illinois and was murdered by another Indian at the site of present-day St. Louis, Missouri in 1769.

SIR JOHN ST. CLAIR (17??–1767). St. Clair recuperated from his wound, first at Fort Cumberland and, later, Boston. On March 20, 1756, he was made lieutenant colonel of the 60th Foot. Two years later he was given the local American rank of colonel and participated in the final and successful British assault on Fort Duquesne in 1758. He argued with his commanding officer, who accused him of "ignorance" and "treachery."[13] On February 19, 1762, he was promoted to full colonel. He was last seen on the stage of history toward the end of the French and Indian War. A sympathetic friend described him thus: "his appearance was somewhat grotesque, a long beard, blanket coat, and trousers to the ground. But he gave so good an account of what he went about, that I could have kissed him, and freely forgave his oddities, as who is without. He carried our artillery and wagons smoothly along, although in very broken sentences, intermixed with full stops, and sometimes stares, that in faith I was once or twice afraid that he was going to leave them back. But at length on he went, making every difficulty disappear."[14] In short, St. Clair had gone native, become American.

Other records bear out this conclusion. Toward the end of the French and Indian War, St. Clair moved to Philadelphia to settle the accounts of various expeditions. While there, he met and married Betsy Moland, the daughter of a prominent lawyer. They had one son, also John St. Clair. In the final few years of his life, St. Clair settled with his family on an estate called Belville near Elizabeth, New Jersey, where he lived in some style "indulging his taste for landscape gardening and collecting books."[15] St. Clair died at Belville on November 26, 1767, and was buried with full military honors at St. John's Church in Elizabeth, an American.[16]

Major Adam Stephen (1721–1791). Adam Stephen recovered from his wounds at the Battle of the Monongahela and took command of Fort Cumberland in August 1755 with a skeleton force as the Americans and British abandoned the frontier to the marauding Indians and French. Hunkered down, Stephen and his men celebrated Christmas 1755 by taking roles in Nicholas Rowe's then-popular play *Tamerlane*. Stephens joined Washington as part of the Forbes expedition in 1758 that eventually ousted the French from Fort Duquesne. He spent the next five years in almost constant fighting against the Indians along the frontier, interrupted only by a failed run against George Washington for the Virginia House of Burgesses. Through his military service he assembled significant tracts of land in western Virginia and was instrumental in convincing former British officer Horatio Gates to buy land and settle near him in Berkeley County. Promoted to brigadier general shortly after the start of the Revolution, Stephen led one of the columns that crossed the Delaware River and advanced on Trenton in the fabled Christmas Day gamble by Washington. He also fought at the ensuing Battle of Princeton and won promotion in early 1777 to major general, one of five division commanders in the Continental Army. Stephen was drunk at the Battle of Germantown on October 3, 1777, and ordered his men into an attack on General "Mad Anthony" Wayne's fellow American troops, leading, at least in part, to

Washington's retreat. At Stephen's request, Washington convened a court of enquiry and subsequent court-martial which found Stephen guilty of "unofficer-like behaviour." Washington approved Stephen's dismissal from the army and on November 20, 1777, he was quietly cashiered out, thus sadly ending a stellar career of over twenty years' service.

CAPTAIN ROBERT STEWART (17??–1809). Captain Stewart continued in service on the frontier and was eventually promoted to lieutenant colonel of the Virginia troops. He became a fast friend with Washington, with whom he corresponded extensively. After the French and Indian War ended, Stewart returned to Britain (he was a native of Scotland) and later took up the position of comptroller of customs in Jamaica. With the outbreak of the American Revolution, Stewart endeavored to "remove the very erroneous opinions the Ministers of that day had formed of the General's [Washington's] Character and military abilities." He failed. Toward the end of the war, the government brought him from Scotland to London to be sent to Washington with overtures for peace, but the plan was shelved. In 1783 he wrote his old friend Washington seeking a post as ambassador or attaché at a European court. However, Washington had to decline Stewart because such posts were reserved for those who had fought on the American side in the Revolution. Stewart died at Hampstead in 1809 and is buried in the vaults of St. James's Chapel, Tottenham Court Road, London.

GEORGE WASHINGTON (1732–1799). Directly after Braddock's defeat, Washington allied with Orme in trying to defend the general's reputation. At the most practical level, he expressed regret over the death of Braddock because, had he lived, in his view the general surely would have secured him a "preferment" in the British army. Thus Braddock's death changed history in unseen ways. However, there was more to the relationship than cold calculation. There is little question that Washington's bond with

Braddock was intense, tangible, and personal. It was reflected in Washington's stepping forward to conduct the burial service for Braddock and falling "heir" to many of Braddock's personal possessions, from his sash to his saddle pad to his servant. Washington kept the flame for Braddock alive as he matured and aged, as illustrated by a letter to Captain Charles Morley dated July 2, 1777, on losing Braddock's pistol: "His Excellency is much exercised over the loss of this pistol, it being given him by Gen. Braddock, and having since been with him through several campaigns, and he therefore values it very highly."[17] Moreover, Washington's admiration for Braddock persisted throughout his life. One of the first things Washington did after standing down from his duties as commander during the Revolution was to embark upon a visit in the autumn of 1784 to his lands in western Pennsylvania during which he searched in vain for His Excellency's grave by Braddock's Run. Washington was "desirous of erecting a monument over it."[18]

In the absence of the desired "preferment," was there an influence of the Braddock campaign on George Washington, both as a soldier and as a man? The question may seem impertinent given Washington's long, variegated, and in many ways elusive career. Moreover, Washington knew Braddock personally only for a few months and in fact spent a total of forty-three days directly with him on campaign. However, it must be remembered that Washington's exposure to Braddock and his staff was only one of two intimate encounters Washington had with senior professional British military officers until he faced them as enemies as commander in chief of the American forces in the Revolution (the other being his participation in the Forbes campaign which took Fort Duquesne three years after Braddock's defeat). Further, that exposure came at a critical and impressionable stage in his development, at age twenty-three, and, though short, was a harrowing and crucial apprenticeship. It therefore is possible to discern certain threads of influence. At least six stand out.

First, throughout his career Washington exercised a hierarchical concept of military and political leadership. While his predisposition to such a model may have derived in part from his plantation upbringing, it also accorded with how Braddock, his early role model, comported himself. Discipline was the linchpin that held an army together in both men's view. When Washington commanded the reconstituted Virginia Regiment in the immediate aftermath of Braddock's defeat and later the Continental Army in the Revolution, the influence of General Braddock on Colonel, and later General, Washington was manifest. Like his mentor, he became a stern disciplinarian, even seeking and obtaining from the Virginia assembly the right to execute his own soldiers. Concomitant with this hierarchical view of command was a certain cultivated combination of manifest personal presence and aloofness. Much as Braddock was everywhere directing his campaign in person but at the same time not deigning to talk to his perceived inferiors, so Washington was everywhere personally present with his troops during the Revolution, including most especially at Valley Forge, but always aloof. He extended this style of leadership into his presidency, when he traveled the country from Maine to Georgia so that people could see him but typically on public occasions held a sword in one hand and a book in another so that no one would be tempted to try to shake his hand.[19]

Second, consistent with a philosophy of hierarchical leadership, Washington, like Braddock, remained throughout his life a fervent advocate of a regular professional army. The model of the tightly disciplined redcoats–and ironically the lesson of how the crumbling of that discipline at the Monongahela led to disaster–inspired Washington in his efforts to forge something approaching American equivalents out of the Virginia provincial forces in the immediately ensuing years and the Continental Army later. Although Washington later expanded his repertoire to include use of semi-flexible tactics, his "sense of how to fight regular troops remained thoroughly orthodox."[20] Thus, Washington believed in

George Washington, now President of the United States, returned to Fort Cumberland in 1794 to review troops assembled to quell the Whiskey Rebellion. The rebellion centered in the same area of Western Pennsylvania where he fought alongside General Braddock thirty-nine years earlier. (*Metropolitan Museum of Art*)

the superiority of American soldiers but was convinced they fought best in an army modeled on European standards and discipline. So much was this the case that shortly after Braddock's defeat Washington bought a copy of Sir Humphrey Bland's classic *Treatise of Military Discipline* and referred to it constantly "throughout his lifelong quest to create a trained, professional American army."[21] Braddock would have approved.

Third, Washington throughout his career shared Braddock's disdain of militia. Despite the myth of superiority of the American militia spawned at the Battle of the Monongahela, Washington, like Braddock, had a jaded view of the utility of militia, and he sought to keep his Continental Army separate from its tainting influence.[22] At one point Washington told Congress that placing "any dependence upon Militia, is, assuredly, resting upon a broken staff."[23]

Fourth, notwithstanding his hierarchical nature of command, Braddock on numerous occasions pursued a style of "open leadership" through the convening of councils of war among his senior officers who voted on important decisions. He listened to their recommendations and was on occasion overruled by their views. It is notable that Washington adopted exactly the same approach, holding councils of war, listening and adhering to the collective wisdom in contravention of his occasional initial impulses.[24] Among those, at least early in the Revolution, whose professional advice he particularly sought were the former British regulars, and Braddock veterans, Gates and Lee. Washington almost certainly learned this approach from Braddock.

Fifth, whether or not one views Washington as a "Fabian" general in terms of overall performance, it is clear that in specific instances Washington emulated Braddock in aggressively taking the fight to the enemy. Washington engineered the successful surprise attack at Trenton, even at the cost of dividing his force (but with a more felicitous result than Braddock achieved with his divided force). He drove this aggressive soldiering home with the ensuing victory at Princeton. Also like Braddock, Washington made use of special mobile units or "flying camps" in the Continental Army to project force with celerity and in greater concentration. Although Braddock's column was a lumbering affair, Washington advocated breaking off a flying column for the advance, which was a lesson he digested and deployed in other contexts later in his career. Indeed, in temperament Washington shared with Braddock an innate impatience with inactivity and little tolerance for delay or obstruction.[25]

Sixth, Washington, like Braddock, was a micromanager. However, here the fruits of their talents differed. Washington was indefatigable in the service of the well-being of his soldiers and their cause, day in and day out. Nowhere was this more telling than at Valley Forge. As observed by one biographer, "No detail was too small."[26] He was rewarded with loyalty and affection. Washington also devoted significant time and effort to cultivating relations with the national and various state governments, which relations were on the whole good. He was rewarded with trust and supplies.[27] Braddock also micromanaged but with far more mixed results. His management was not so much for the welfare of his soldiers as for the good of the expedition. He was rewarded with respect but not affection. His also devoted considerable and detailed attention to relations with the colonial governments, but the results were little short of disastrous. He was rewarded with acrimony and defaults.

Finally, there are a handful of areas in which Washington seemed to have learned how to improve on what he observed in Braddock's performance. As noted above, he was mindful of the need for successful logistics and mastered them as Braddock never did. While perhaps equally neglectful of reconnaissance,[28] Washington–unlike Braddock–had a fascination with intelligence and went out of his way to run networks of spies. One also suspects that Washington, because of his early service in the Ohio Valley, had a greater strategic sense than Braddock, albeit one that at times was tinged with self-interest, such as in his repeated advocacy for the Virginia route to Fort Duquesne.

There is, however, another and perhaps ultimately more important area in which Washington chose not to emulate Braddock. As observed by Washington's biographer James Flexner, Washington "did not regard his military eminence as an excuse for self-indulgence, but rather as the opposite. In this, he was very different from the highborn British generals with their mistresses, their hangovers and gaming tables. Washington asked nothing of his men that he was unwilling to do himself."[29] The tone set by Washington survives in the U.S. military to this day.

At the very least, Washington emerged from the Braddock fiasco with his reputation intact and enhanced by the bravery with which he fought. His service erased the blot of Fort Necessity on his own career and was the beginning of a maturation process that produced a very different and much greater man than embarked upon the march.

Twenty-six years later, on October 19, 1781, as a British military band played "The World Turned Upside Down," George

Washington directed American Major General Benjamin Lincoln to receive the surrender of the British army at the Battle of Yorktown, ending hostilities in the Revolutionary War. With Washington looking on and Lord Cornwallis avoiding the surrender ceremony because of "ill health,"[30] the sword of surrender was personally presented by Brigadier General Charles O'Hara. O'Hara was George Anne Bellamy's ostensible half-brother. That evening a "very social and easy" O'Hara dined with Washington. O'Hara undoubtedly knew that Washington had served with Braddock. One can only speculate whether their conversation touched on mutual acquaintanceships and events twenty-six years earlier.

Notes

Prologue

1. Sargent, *History of an Expedition Against Fort Du Quesne,* 126, footnote 1, citing Voltaire, *Précis du Siècle de Louis XV*, c. xv.

2. The primary materials that tell this story consist largely of letters and journals kept by the men and women who made the march. Of these materials, four journals are of particular importance and are quoted extensively herein: the Journal of Captain Robert Orme, one of Braddock's aides-de-camp ("Orme's Journal"), the diary of an unidentified batman or servant to Captain Robert Cholmondeley ("Batman's Journal"), the diary of an unidentified sailor who accompanied the expedition as part of a detachment of seamen ("Seaman's Journal"), and the journal of Matron Charlotte Browne, a head nurse ("Browne's Journal"). In addition, two orderly books and one letter book are of major importance: the orderly book of Colonel Sir Peter Halkett, commander of the 44th Regiment, maintained by Lieutenant Daniel Disney, adjutant ("Halkett's Orders"), Braddock's orderly book ("Braddock's Orders"), and the letter book of Sir John St. Clair, deputy quartermaster general to the campaign ("St. Clair Letters"). These primary sources, together with many other letters and lesser diaries, are collected in Wahll, *Braddock Road Chronicles,* which is an invaluable compendium of first-hand source material for both the scholar and interested layperson. In cases where I cite primary material in Wahll's collection, there also is a corresponding reference to that material in Wahll.

Chapter One: The Proximate Cause

1. Sargent, *History of an Expedition Against Fort Du Quesne,* 58–59.

2. Dinwiddie was de facto governor of Virginia. The actual governor, the Earl of Albemarle, was titular only and resided in Paris as British ambassador to France.

3. Fort Ligonier Association, *War for Empire in Western Pennsylvania*, 20. When used in conjunction with the colonial seal, the Latin phrase reflects Virginia's support of Charles II's claim to the throne and the restoration of the English monarchy under Charles II in 1660 following the republican Commonwealth. The motto

originally read *En Dat Virginia Quintum* ("Behold! Virginia Yields the Fifth"), meaning the fifth kingdom in support of Charles after England, Scotland, Ireland, and France (England still had claims to the French throne at that point). It was shortened to "the Fourth" following the union of England and Scotland in 1707.

4. Ibid., 16.

5. Ibid., 19.

6. Besides advancing the interests of the Ohio Company and combating the French, Dinwiddie's other preoccupation during this period was a spat with the House of Burgesses in Williamsburg over whether he could charge fees for signing and sealing patents for crown land. Eventually, the matter was referred to London for settlement. See documents T1/353/46 (Opposition of House of Burgesses to his claim for a fee for signing and sealing patents for crown land) and T1/358/45 (Act for settling the differences between Dinwiddie and House of Burgesses), UK Public Record Office. In America, as in England in this period, public service paid.

7. Sargent, *History of an Expedition Against Fort Du Quesne,* 39.

8. Fort Ligonier Assocation, *War for Empire in Western Pennsylvania,* 16.

9. Ibid., 20.

10. Tanacharison was called the "Half King" by the Iroquois to show his subordinate status, and that of the Mingo, to the Six Nations' central council at Onondaga. I thank Glenn F. Williams for this observation.

11. The Half King died not long after the Washington expedition, probably in the autumn of 1754 and allegedly of acute alcoholism. See, generally, Lewis, *For King and Country,* 64ff.

12. Anderson, *Crucible of War*, 56–57. The story may be apocryphal. Anderson acknowledges that there were no eyewitness accounts of the Half King's washing his hands in Jumonville's brains, although he deems the sole second-hand account to be credible.

13. See generally, Sargent, *History of an Expedition Against Fort Du Quesne,* 43–55.

14. Fort Ligonier Association, *War for Empire in Western Pennsylvania,* 20.

15. Sargent, *History of an Expedition Against Fort Du Quesne,* 45.

16. National Archives of Canada, Fond des Colonies, MG 1- Serie C11A, orders from Contrecoeur to Coulon de Villiers, June 28, 1754.

17. Washington also anxiously awaited reinforcements from Rutherford's and Clarke's Independent Companies of Foot. The commanders of the Independent Companies held their commissions from the King rather than from a colonial government. They were small garrison forces maintained by the Crown in two exposed colonies, South Carolina and New York. Dinwiddie had ordered the

Independent Companies from New York to Virginia, where they arrived on June 8 by ship. However, they could not reach Fort Necessity in time to relieve Washington. On September 1 they marched to Wills Creek, where they were joined by Captain Demerie's Independent Company from South Carolina. Together, they began the construction of a fort at that place. By the time of the visit of St. Clair and Sharpe in January 1755, they had completed a fortification with several large magazines and barracks to receive the anticipated army. The fort was armed with ten 4-pound cannon and swivel guns. It was christened Fort Cumberland in honor of the Duke of Cumberland and gave its name to present-day Cumberland, Maryland, which grew on its site. Braddock, however, had a low opinion of the New York Independent Companies. He was later to write that they were "good for nothing." Braddock letter to Sir Robert Napier, March 17, 1755, quoted in Wahll, 84.

18. Van Bramm and Stobo initially had the run of Montreal but, as the war intensified, were placed under closer confinement. Both eventually obtained their freedom.

19. Sargent, *History of an Expedition Against Fort Du Quesne,* 54–55, citing *Enquiry into the Causes of the Alienation of the Delaware and Shawanese Indians, &c.* (London, 1759), 80.

Chapter Two: Weaving a Web

1. St. Clair's claims to a baronetcy were never proven.

2. Netherton, *Braddock's Campaign and the Potomac Route West*, vol. 1.

3. If he did not, he was negligent. His French adversaries possessed and used the map.

4. The Allegheny Mountains are a sub-chain of the Appalachian Mountains and run from Pennsylvania to Georgia.

5. Christopher Gist, who accompanied Washington on his 1753 mission to Rivière aux Boeufs, was an agent of the Ohio Company.

6. Darlington, *Christopher Gist's Journals*, 31–32.

7. Hulbert, *Braddock's Road and Three Relative Papers*, preface, 32.

8. These are merely the principal forts. New France was in fact sustained through a network of close to one hundred forts and outposts throughout Canada and the interior of America. See, e.g., the list of French forts of the French and Indian War period at http://fiwar.virtualave.net/forts/french.html.

9. Parkman, *Montcalm and Wolfe*, 20, 37.

10. Sargent, *History of an Expedition Against Fort Du Quesne,* 24, citing I. Entick, 126.

11. These included the Pottawotami, Chippewa, Sauk-Fox, Illinois, Kickapoo, Miami, Shawnee, and Delaware.

12. Sargent, *History of an Expedition Against Fort Du Quesne,* 64.

13. Shetrane, "The Indian in Ohio," 332; Parkman, *Montcalm and Wolfe*, 41. Note that many tribes, and the Great Lakes area Indians in particular, practiced ritual cannibalism.

14. Sargent, *History of an Expedition Against Fort Du Quesne,* 33.

15. Doddridge, *Notes on the Settlement and Indian Wars,* 102ff.

16. Some 500 slaves, including captured Americans, labored with 200 miners in the lead mines. See O'Meara, *Guns at the Forks*, 13. Galena later became famous as the Illinois hometown of General Ulysses S. Grant.

Chapter Three: His Excellency's Secret

1. For example, the *Cambridge Biographical Dictionary* entry for Braddock begins: "Braddock, Edward (1695–1755) Scottish soldier, born in Perthshire." The notion that Braddock was a native of Perthshire, Scotland, has gained particular currency without any apparent basis in fact. McCardell, *Ill-Starred General,* places his birth in London based on actual parochial baptismal records. Also arguing in favor of London are the facts that: Edward Braddock is an English, not a Scottish, name; Scots were not generally integrated into the highest levels of the British army until after the 1740s (and even then not into Guards regiments); Braddock's father was a major general in the socially connected Coldstream Regiment of Foot Guards, which in 1694–95 was on guard duty in London and on campaign in the Low Countries but not in Scotland; and Braddock's personal circle of associates, both in London and on campaign, as described below, were English and in fact arguably excluded Scots.

2. For Braddock's London background, see, generally, the well-researched and informative McCardell, *Ill-Starred General,* 3ff.

3. See SP 34/13/62 in the UK Public Record Office ("Major General Edward Braddock to Lord Dartmouth desiring to know the Queen's pleasure with regard to certain commissions in the Coldstream Regiment of Foot Guards, 10 October 1710").

4. The sash is in the collection of the Mount Vernon Ladies Association at Mount Vernon. The pistol, manufactured by a Bristol gunsmith Gabbitas and with a brass butt plate engraved with the initials "EB," is now in the collection of the Smithsonian Institution. Braddock's leopard skin saddle pad is now in the collection of the Sons of the Revolution in the State of California Museum in Glendale, California. Washington evidently took possession of all of these items

on Braddock's death. Why none of these personal effects passed into Braddock's estate consistent with his will is unclear.

5. McCardell, *Ill-Starred General,* 57–60.

6. However, the death of Fanny Braddock made the rounds of the gossip mill in Bath and was eventually part of the impetus for an attempt by Parliament to pass legislation to curb excessive gambling. Ibid.

7. Officers who held appointments in one of the three regiments of foot guards had dual commissions. They were purchased at a higher price but had perquisites. An officer with an appointment as a subaltern (ensign or lieutenant) in the Guards also held a commission as a captain in the British army and wore the trappings of the higher rank when on duty outside the regiment. I thank Glenn F. Williams for this information.

8. According to Horace Walpole and others, Braddock's relationship with Mrs. Upton was the inspiration for the character Captain Bilkum in Henry Fielding's satire *The Covent Garden Tragedy*, which premiered June 1, 1732. Fielding, who was the son of one of the Duke of Marlborough's officers, set the play in a brothel and in Captain Bilkum created a bullying cheapskate that was instantly recognizable by the cognoscenti as Braddock. Fortunately for Braddock, the play folded after a single performance.

9. When Braddock advanced to captain in the Guards, he most likely advanced to the grade of lieutenant colonel in the army at the same time (by purchase, not merit). The rank of colonel was a purely honorific one in the British army at this time. Officers advanced from lieutenant colonel to brigadier as a matter of course. I thank Glenn F. Williams for this clarification.

10. Historical Manuscripts Commission, *Report on the Manuscripts of Mrs. Frankland-Russell-Astley of Chequers Court, Bucks.* (London: Mackie & Co., 1900) (hereinafter "Frankland Manuscripts"), 350.

11. Ibid., 352.

12. Ibid., 354.

13. Ibid., 358.

14. Ibid., 364.

15. Ibid., 366.

16. Ibid., 367.

17. Ibid., 392.

18. Ibid., 364.

19. Ibid., 388.

20. Russell and Braddock took particular delight in a small, fast yacht called in

Dutch a "scoot." The verb "to scoot" entered the English language in the mid-eighteenth century. One wonders if it might have been introduced by soldiers returning from the Low Countries campaigns.

21. Frankland Manuscripts, 363.

22. Ibid., 367.

23. Ibid., 378.

24. Ibid., 366.

25. Ibid., 366.

26. Ibid., 381.

27. Ibid., 394.

28. Ibid., 400. Emphasis added.

29. Walpole's house still stands, as do one or two townhouses of similar vintage, as well as an old carriage arch at the foot of Arlington Street. However, Arlington Street was severely damaged by German bombs during World War II, and most of the buildings on the street date from after the war. The east side of the foot of Arlington Street, where Braddock's house reportedly stood, is currently of twentieth-century construction. It therefore is doubtful that Braddock's house survives. The two-block-long street is intersected by Bennet Street. During the eighteenth century the Blue Posts public house graced the southeastern corner of Arlington and Bennet Streets, and the latter served as an assembly point for waiting sedan chairs. Today the far northwestern corner of Arlington Street hosts the Ritz Hotel.

30. Bellamy, *Apology,* vol. 2, 15.

31. McCardell, *Ill-Starred General,* 110.

32. Ibid., 109.

33. Bellamy, *Apology*, vol. 1, 186–88.

34. Ibid., vol. 1, 242.

35. Ibid., vol. 1, 168, and vol. 2, 1.

36. Parkman, *Montcalm and Wolfe*, 94. However, Parkman's sentence, viewed in more complete form, allows for a whiff of doubt: "his *present* relations *seem* to have been those of an elderly adviser and friend" (emphasis added). Thus Parkman hints that their relationship may at one time have been of a different nature.

37. At about the time Braddock knew him, Tyrawley kept a fourteen-year-old mistress, whom he had spirited out of a Quaker boarding school. She later went on to act under the name of Mrs. Bellamy on the stages of Dublin and London. Purportedly on St. George's Day, April 21, 1733, but perhaps as early as 1727,

she bore a daughter, ostensibly by Tyrawley. The child was christened George Anne in honor of the day, which coincidentally is the official anniversary date of the Coldstream Regiment of Foot Guards. Her mother refused to acknowledge her for years. Braddock, who knew the child since infancy, became a second father to her. The evidence on the true relationship between Braddock and George Anne Bellamy is inconclusive. Certainly Braddock was her kindly benefactor. He possibly was her lover, at least at one point. The evidence, other than the known personalities and predilections of the principals themselves, is elusive. However, the *Oxford English Dictionary* defines Braddock's term of endearment for Bellamy–"Pop"–to mean, among other things, "a mistress, a kept woman" (the word is short for "poplet," meaning a "female favourite; a wench"). Certainly there was ample precedent for British brass mingling with Drury Lane greasepaint. For example, Braddock's Arlington Street neighbor Horace Walpole related an affair between Bellamy's contemporary and archrival Peg Woffington and Colonel (later Major General) Julius Caesar, one of Braddock's fellow officers of the Coldstream Foot Guards (and acquaintance from the Flanders campaign) whose improbable name derived from an ancestor who was an Italian-born court physician to Elizabeth I. Lord Tyrawley, who happened to be nearby when Walpole heard of the affair, sparred, "I suppose she was reduced to aut Caesar aut Nullus" (either Caesar or nothing). Even more intriguing are the hints that Braddock, not Tyrawley, possibly might have been her biological father. McCardell accepts Tyrawley's paternity as a given, as asserted by George Anne herself in her autobiography, *An Apology for the Life of George Anne Bellamy*, although a question lingers. She relates in her autobiography that she was born at Fingal, Ireland, after her mother's marriage to an unsuspecting ship's captain named Bellamy whom she had met in Lisbon when she was already pregnant with George Anne by Lord Tyrawley. The story of her birth in the *Apology* is altogether too convenient, as well as uncorroborated. Because of the uncertainty over the year of her birth, Lord Tyrawley (1690–1773) would have been between 37 and 43 when she was born, a not impossible age to be sowing wild oats. Braddock, in contrast, would have been between 32 and 38. Both George Anne and her mother actively sought Tyrawley's acknowledgment of her paternity. They had a motive to do so: he was a wealthy peer who could provide for them. Although George Anne assumed the surname Bellamy in honor of the witless stepfather with whom she briefly lived, Tyrawley ultimately and with reluctance acknowledged George Anne as a daughter, and she was brought up in Tyrawley's Catholic faith. Tyrawley paid for her brief education at a convent in Boulogne, France, her leading memory of which was observing a nun being immured alive in the walls of the convent for having breached her vow of chastity with a *chevalier* (a lesson evidently lost on George Anne). She soon returned to England. However, with Tyrawley serving as British ambassador to Portugal from 1728 to 1741 and to Russia from 1743 to 1745, she was farmed out to one of his former servants, a wig maker who kept a shop in St. James's Street, a mere block or two from Braddock's house in Arlington Street. George Anne occasionally later lived with Tyrawley when he was in London between diplomatic assignments and on every possible occasion took pains to assert her familial relationship with him. However, she was constantly under the watchful eye of Braddock.

Tyrawley's household was a ménage of mistresses and illegitimate children. (Walpole observed that he returned from Portugal "with three wives and fourteen children" and that he was considered "singularly licentious, even for the courts of Russia and Portugal.") He therefore might indeed have been her father. However, several hints suggest otherwise. First, when George Anne's supposed husband, the parvenu army agent John Calcraft (see below) devised a coat of arms for himself and Bellamy, he appropriated both the three lions from Tyrawley's crest and the greyhound from Braddock's for his and George Anne's "borrowed crest" (*Apology*, vol. 1, 313). This would have been odd behavior in the absence of a known or suspected blood relationship. Second, Bellamy's reactions on the deaths of the two men were studies in contrast. She describes her hearing of Braddock's death thus: "During my confinement . . . I met with one of the severest losses I had ever felt. Mr. Calcraft coming one day into my room to enquire after my health, I took notice that he seemed uncommonly thoughtful. Upon which my second sight instantly visited me, and I cried out with emotion, 'Bad news from America!' To this he only replying with a shake of the head, I exclaimed, 'My fears are too prophetic, and I have lost a second father.' He then informed me of the defeat and death of my much-beloved friend General Braddock. I had no sooner received the heart-rending intelligence, than I gave way to the most unbounded grief; which brought on a fever, and I lay for some time in a dangerous situation from these complicated oppressions" (*Apology*, vol. 1, 288). Contrast this scene with her reaction on the death of Tyrawley: "About this period Lord Tyrawley died. An incident which did not much affect me at the time it happened, as his Lordship's faculties had been so much impaired for a long while before he departed this life, that his dissolution was rather to be wished for than dreaded." George Anne went into formal mourning on his death but did not even attend his funeral (*Apology*, vol. 2, 192–93). Third, Tyrawley neither acknowledged nor provided for George Anne in his will. In contrast, he left express bequests to "my natural [i.e., illegitimate] daughters Anne O'Hara and Jemima O'Hara." See Will of The Right Honorable James O'Hara Lord Tyrawly or James Lord Tyrawly, July 17, 1773, UK Public

Record Office, PROB 11/990. Tyrawley died without legitimate issue, his title lapsed, and George Anne spent the remaining fifteen years of her life in destitution, finally dying in 1788. In contrast to Tyrawley, Braddock did indirectly provide for George Anne in his will, leaving her, in effect, half of his total estate of £7,000. His total estate exceeded the £5,000 that was the then-going rate for purchase of a commission as a lieutenant colonel in the Coldstream Regiment of Foot Guards, and half of the estate would have been a not inconsiderable legacy. Finally, there are extant etchings of Braddock and Bellamy, executed after the deaths of both but based on lost paintings made during their lifetimes. The etchings show a strong facial resemblance, especially in the eyes, upper lips, chin, and general physiognomy of a round and somewhat plump face. Both Braddock and Bellamy were short of stature and full-figured and shared a voluble, enthusiastic personality; they lived on the margins of complete acceptance, as defined by their same class. In contrast, the early (1712) portrait of Tyrawley in the National Portrait Gallery in London bears little discernible resemblance to Bellamy. It is hard to conjecture why a bachelor of Braddock's background and disposition would have shown a sustaining interest in the girl if he had not been either her father or her lover. Calcraft's appropriation of both the Braddock and Tyrawley coats of arms possibly hints at one interpretation: George Anne may have been the daughter of either Braddock or Tyrawley, and neither she nor her mother nor either man knew for certain which. The matter inevitably remains speculative at best.

38. Bellamy, *Apology,* vol. 1, 252.

39. Buying a "colonelcy" was a sinecure, not a promotion. I thank Glenn F. Williams for this clarification.

40. Hulbert, *Braddock's Road and Three Relative Papers*, quoting a letter from the duke's aide, Colonel Napier, to Braddock.

41. George Anne Bellamy was aware of Braddock's reputation but defended him. She relates the following incident in the *Apology*: "This great man having been often reproached with brutality, I am induced to recite the following little accident, which evidently shews the contrary. As we were walking in the Park one day we heard a poor fellow was to be chastised; when I requested the General to beg off the offender. Upon his application to the general officer, whose name was Dury, he asked Braddock, How long since he had divested himself of brutality and the insolence of his manners? To which the other replied, 'You never knew me insolent to my inferiors. It is only to such rude men as yourself, that I behave with the spirit which I think they deserve.'" Bellamy, *Apology,* vol. 1, 288.

42. McCardell, *Ill-Starred General,* 126.

43. McCardell, *Ill-Starred General,* 129. One of Braddock's duties at Gibraltar apparently was keeping an eye on the French Mediterranean fleet. In April 1754 he reported to Whitehall on French ships passing through the Strait. The report was dismissed as a "mistake." See UK Public Record Office SP 78/249, April 25, 1754.

Chapter Four: Minuet

1. The Secretary of State for the Southern Department headed policy and diplomacy with Ireland, the countries in Southern or "Catholic" Europe and the Mediterranean, the Ottoman Empire, and the New World colonies. The Secretary for the Northern Department was charged with the "home islands," Scotland, the countries of Northern or "Protestant" Europe, and Russia.

2. McCardell, *Ill-Starred General,* 127.

3. Ibid., 129.

4. UK Public Record Office SP 78/249 (May 8 and May 22, 1754).

5. Ibid., June 19, 1754.

6. Ibid., June 26 and 27, 1754. Albemarle advised Robinson that his informers had reported that a Parisian tailor had been given an old suit of the Pretender's son to use as a measure for making a large order of clothes, thereby sparking a suspicion that the Pretender's son might be in Paris. Ibid., May 29.

7. Ibid., May 9 and May 15, 1754.

8. Ibid., May 23, May 29, June 6, June 12, 1754. Also SP 78/250.

9. Anderson, *Crucible of War,* 67. Because of the frequency of transatlantic crossings between America and England it is likely that London learned of the events before Paris. However, by this time the French court would have learned of the developments through its ambassador and other agents in London and may possibly have had its own independent reports via ship from Canada.

10. McCardell, *Ill-Starred General,* 122, citing British Museum Additional Manuscript 32850, f 289.

11. See, generally, Anderson, *Crucible of War,* 67ff.

12. Ibid.

13. McCardell, *Ill-Starred General,* 129.

14. UK Public Record Office, SP 78/250, February 19, 1755.

15. Ibid.

16. Entick, *History of the Late War*, vol, 1, p. 124, quoted in Hulbert, *Braddock's Road and Three Relative Papers*, 33.

17. UK Public Record Office, SP 78/250, January 13, 1755.

18. UK Public Record Office, SP 78/250, January 18, January 22, and February 5, 1755.

Chapter Five: Sweet William's Revenge

1. After suppressing the Jacobites, the Butcher of Culloden or Sweet William, depending on one's viewpoint, returned to the Low Countries for further campaigning. Once again Braddock served under him but saw no combat.

2. When General Ligonier raised with Newcastle the need to defend Annapolis, he replied "Annapolis! Annapolis! Oh! Yes, Annapolis must be defended; to be sure, Annapolis should be defended–where is Annapolis?" Smollett observed, "He was generally laughed at as an ape in politics, whose office and influence served only to render his folly the more notorious." On another occasion, at the beginning of the war, he was thrown into panic by a rumor that 30,000 French troops had marched from Acadia to Cape Breton. Someone asked, "Where did they find transports?" "Transports!" Newcastle exclaimed. "I tell you they marched by land." "By land to the island of Cape Breton?" his interlocutor inquired. "What, is Cape Breton an island? Are you sure of that? Egad! I will go directly and tell the King that Cape Breton is an island!" Sargent, *History of an Expedition Against Fort Du Quesne,* 104, note 1.

3. McCardell, *Ill-Starred General,* 136.

4. Some historians place his birth at 1695, the same as Braddock.

5. Burrows, *The Essex Regiment (1st Battalion).*

6. See, generally, Brumwell, *Redcoats,* 227ff.

7. Wahll, 10.

8. Darling, *Red Coat and Brown Bess,* 6, footnote 9.

9. Sargent, *History of an Expedition Against Fort Du Quesne,* 134–35.

10. *Gentleman's Magazine* 75 (1755), 389.

11. Hulbert, *Braddock's Road and Three Relative Papers,* 58.

12. McCardell, *Ill-Starred General,* 128.

13. Judging from his exact choice of words, Cumberland's knowledge appears to have been derived from a certain letter written May 16, 1754, by an "Officer of Distinction" from Great Meadows and reported in the October 22, 1754, edition of the *Maryland Gazette.* One might surmise that this officer was Washington. See *Maryland Gazette,* October 22, 1754; Wahll, 26.

14. Hulbert, *Braddock's Road and Three Relative Papers,* 57.

15. Whitehall justified these assaults during a time of at least technical peace on the grounds that the forts were all located in English territory. Niagara was the most questionable candidate for this thesis.

16. Bellamy, *Apology,* vol. 1, 242.

17. Ibid.

18. Almost nothing is known of Mary Yorke. Her husband went on to command a battery of light artillery at the Battle of Quebec in 1759. She was not the Mary Yorke who owned a house in Arlington Street in 1768 who was the subject of an Act of Parliament (see House of Commons Parliamentary Papers 1768 item c.61).

19. The HMS *Centurion* was a warship which rivaled the later HMS *Victory* in fame. Rated at 400 men and 60 guns, she had circled the globe under Anson and later covered Wolfe's landing at Quebec. When she was eventually broken up, her figurehead of a lion was preserved at the royal hospital for naval pensioners at Greenwich, just down river from London. Sargent, *History of an Expedition Against Fort Du Quesne,* 139.

20. Not surprisingly, Braddock and Commodore Keppel got along famously.

21. The complete fleet consisted of the following vessels. Keppel's Squadron: *Centurion* (Commodore Keppel); *Norwich* (Captain Barrington); *Syren* (Captain Proby). Transports: *Anna* (Captain Nevin); *Terrible* (Captain Wright); *Osgood* (Captain Crookshanks); *Concord* (Captain Boynton); *Industry* (Captain Miller); *Fishburn* (Captain Tipple); *Halifax* (Captain Terry); *Fame* (Captain Judd); *London* (Captain Brown); *Prince Frederick* (Captain Burton); *Isabel and Mary* (Captain Hall); *Molly* (Captain Curling); *Severn* (Captain Rawlings). Ordnance Ships: *Whiting* (Captain Johnson); *Newall* (Captain Montgomery); *Nelly* (captain unknown).

Chapter Six: The Generalissimo Comes to Town

1. Bonner-Smith, ed., *The Barrington Papers,* 113; Harrison, "With Braddock's Army," 306; McCardell, *Ill-Starred General,* 138–39.

2. McCardell, *Ill-Starred General,* 140.

3. Exactly how "indefatigable" St. Clair was is illustrated by his January 15 report from Williamsburg to Napier. After describing his efforts to set up hospital facilities, arrange provisions for the troops once landed, secure horses for the officers, find floats for transport of the artillery, recruit men, coordinate with the colonial governors, and cut firewood, he added as a postscript: "P.s. If a large quantity of Iron is not brought out with the artillery, it will be necessary that a Dozen of Quintal should be brought [bought?] at Hampton to make portable Ovens." Letter from St. Clair to Napier, January 15, 1755, in Wahll, 39–41. Similarly, in letters a month later he wrote Napier of a "proposal for getting some Croats to settle on the Ohio." Letter from St. Clair to Napier, February 15, 1755,

in Wahll, 51. St. Clair must have known Croats from his Italian campaigning days in the Austrian Empire. Over a hundred years later Croats did in fact settle on the Ohio, lured by the steel mills of Pittsburgh.

4. McCardell, *Ill-Starred General,* 144.

5. Stobo's French "hosts" eventually discovered his perfidy. The sketch was found by the French in Braddock's baggage on the battlefield because the Governor of New France Vaudreuil reported to his ministry in Paris on July 24, 1755, that Stobo and Van Braam "had informed their governors about the forces and plans of the French." See National Archives of Canada, Fonds des Colonies, MG 1- Serie C11A, 6283, dated July 24, 1755. In his subsequent interrogation, Stobo justified his actions on the grounds that the French had failed to respect the articles of capitulation of Fort Necessity by destroying the fort, taking its munitions, and pillaging the effects of the Americans, including the papers of George Washington. See National Archives of Canada, Fonds des Colonies, MG 1-Serie C11A, 6490, dated November 8, 1756. The French tried Stobo for espionage, but he escaped before he could be executed. The apparent original sketch is on display at the Chateau Ramezay Museum in Montreal.

6. Ibid.

7. Braddock's Orders; Wahll, 57.

8. Orme's Journal; Wahll, 63.

9. See Braddock's Orders; Wahll, 58; also letter from Major John Carlyle to his brother George Carlyle dated August 15, 1755, in Abbot, "General Braddock in Alexandria," 208–14.

10. Braddock's Orders; Wahll, 58.

11. Braddock's Orders; Wahll, 60; Orme's Journal, cited in Wahll, 64. Whoever prevailed upon Braddock to drop St. Clair's scheme was correct. It was an impractical plan.

12. A naval 12-pounder of the type provided to Braddock sits today in Waterfront Park on the Potomac River at Alexandria, Virginia. The piece bears the royal insignia "GR" for Georgius Rex and the king's broad arrow signifying naval property. Its nine-foot length suggests that it was cast before artillery reforms in the Royal Navy in 1756 shortened the length of 12-pounders to five and a half feet.

13. Barbero, *The Battle, A New History of Waterloo.*

14. Wahll, 75, citing Pargellis, *Military Affairs in North America 1748–1765.*

15. Orme's Journal; Wahll, 75.

16. McCardell, *Ill-Starred General,* 150.

Chapter Seven: The Opportunity of a Lifetime

1. Lewis, *For King and Country,* 162.

2. March 15, 1755 letter from Washington to Orme; Wahll, 81.

3. March 21, 1755 letter from Washington to Orme; Wahll, 90.

4. March 22, 1755 letter from Orme to Washington; Wahll, 90–91. It is unclear whether these letters were exchanged at Williamsburg or Alexandria. Wahll suggests Alexandria. However, the fact that Orme responded the day after to the specific points in Washington's letter argues that the two men were close by one another. Moreover, the clear references to Braddock's instructions in Orme's letter, on a day Braddock was known to be in Williamsburg, suggest that all three men might have been in Williamsburg on March 21–22.

5. For a much more charitable, and possibly naïve, view of Washington's motives see Freeman, *George Washington, A Biography, Volume Two, Young Washington,* especially chapters 1 and 2 (pp. 1–35). In the author's view, Washington's correspondence speaks for itself and manifests a consummate and far from reluctant stratagem by Washington to work his way into Braddock's adventure. Despite this difference in interpretation, the first four chapters of Freeman's biography provide a good introduction to the Braddock expedition and Washington's role in it.

6. Alberts, "Braddock's Alumni," 82.

Chapter Eight: An Army in Alexandria

1. Letter dated August 15, 1755 from Major John Carlyle to his brother at Abbott, "General Braddock in Alexandria." However, Braddock appointed Carlyle as commissary for the expedition for his troubles, an honor that Carlyle acknowledged was worth at least £500.

2. Batman's Journal; Wahll, 79.

3. Batman's Journal; quoted in Wahll, 86.

4. McCardell, *Ill-Starred General,* 154–55.

5. Alexandria residents have long debated the location of the British encampment. On the one hand, a distinct possibility is the area northwest of the edge of present-day Old Town, Alexandria, approximately where the Braddock Road Metro Station and Braddock Field are located today and perhaps extending as far west as the present Russell Road. Arguing in favor of this location is the fact that Braddock Road, which farmers used to carry provisions to the troops and on which the troops eventually marched out of Alexandria, terminates there. On the other hand, a more logical and healthier campground would have been on

Shuter's Hill, site of the present-day Masonic Temple. The troops could have marched from there to nearby Braddock Road as well. Both locations were sites of Civil War encampments.

6. Browne's Journal; Wahll, 91.

7. Braddock's Orders; Halkett's Orders; Wahll, 92–93.

8. The field officer of the day was the busiest officer in the camp, for he had charge of the whole encampment during his tour of duty. In case of alarm he took command of all officers and men in the vicinity of the disturbance. All detail of troops destined for drill, work or guard duty were first drawn up on the Grand Parade at the head of the senior regiment before marching off to their particular mission. The two lieutenant colonels and majors of the regulars took turns at this post. The parole or password changed daily and was normally the name of an English town. See Nichols, "The Braddock Expedition," quoted in Wahll, 95.

9. St. Clair observed that "A great number of the levees brought up by Mr. Dick [the Assistant Commissary] have a very bad look, some of them were brought to me in changes [chains]." St. Clair's Letters, 94; Wahll, 124.

10. Wahll, 159, citing Nichols, "The Braddock Expedition." Apparently it did not matter if they were criminals, provided they fit the profile.

11. See entries from the May 9, 1755 *Virginia Gazette,* quoted in Wahll, 184. The army offered a reward of three pistoles for each deserter apprehended.

12. Orme's Journal, cited in Sargent, *History of an Expedition Against Fort Du Quesne,* 358. A public whipping of this magnitude probably would not have alarmed the citizens of Alexandria, although it would have the frontier people the British had come to defend. The lash was common in Tidewater Virginia. One roughly contemporaneous backwoodsman who went to Tidewater Maryland described his disgust at the endemic cruelty to slaves and servants he found there: "I had not been long in my new habitation, before I witnessed a scene which I shall never forget. A convict servant, accused of some trivial offense, was doomed to the whip. Tied with his arms extended upwards to the limb of a tree, and a bundle of hickories thrown down before him, he was ordered to look at them and told that they should all be worn out on him, and a great many more, if he did not make a confession of the crime alleged against him. The operation began by tucking up the shirt over his head, so as to leave his back and shoulders naked. The master then took two of the hickories in his hand, and by forward and back-handed strokes, each of which sounded like a wagon whip, and applied with the utmost rapidity and with his whole muscular strength, in a few seconds lacerated the shoulders of the poor miserable sufferer, with not less than fifty scourges,

so that in a little time the whole of his shoulders had the appearance of a mass of blood, streams of which soon began to flow down his back and sides; he then made a confession of his fault. A fault not worth naming; but this did not save him from further torture. He had put his master 'to the trouble of whipping him and he must have a little more.' His trousers were then unbuttoned and suffered to fall down about his feet, two new hickories were selected from the bundle, and so applied that in a short time his posteriors, like his shoulders, exhibited nothing but lacerations and blood. . . . A basin of brine and a cloth were ordered to be brought; with this his stripes were washed or salted as they called it. During this operation the suffering wretch writhed and groaned as if in the agonies of death. . . . From this scene of torture I went home with a heavy heart, and wished myself in the backwoods again; nor did the frequency of witnessing such scenes lessen, in any degree, the horror which they first occasioned in my mind."

It frequently happened that torture was inflicted upon slaves and convicts in a more protracted manner than in that above described. When the victim of cruelty was doomed by his master to receive the lash, several of his neighbors were called on, for their assistance. They attended at the time and place appointed. A jug of rum and water were provided for the occasion. After the trembling wretch was brought forth and tied up, the number of lashes he was to receive was determined on, and by lot, or otherwise, it was decided who should begin the operation; this done, the torture commenced; at the conclusion of the first course, the operator, pretending great weariness, called for a drink of rum and water, in which he was joined by the company. A certain time was allowed for the subject of their cruelty *to cool*, as they called it. When the allotted time had expired, the next hand took his turn, and in like manner ended with a drink, and so on until the appointed number of lashes were all imposed. This operation lasted several hours, sometimes half a day, at the conclusion of which the sufferer, with his hands swollen with the cords, was unbound and suffered to put on his shirt. His executioners, to whom the operation was rather a frolic than otherwise, returned home from the scene of their labor half drunk. Another method of punishment, still more protracted than this, was that of dooming a slave to receive so many lashes, during several days in succession; each of these whippings, excepting the first, was called "tickling up the old scabs." Doddridge, *Notes on the Settlement and Indian Wars,* 136–37. It should be pointed out that the lash in the British army was administered by sober men and that the recipients were neither convicts nor slaves but free Britons like their punishers.

13. Halkett's Orders for April 2, quoted in Wahll, 108–9.

14. Halkett's Orders for April 1, quoted in Wahll, 106.

15. Ibid., April 2, quoted in Wahll, 108.

16. Sargent, *History of an Expedition Against Fort Du Quesne,* 297.

17. Wahll, 120, citing a letter from Washington to Sally Fairfax dated May 14, 1755.

18. *Extracts of Letters from a (British) Officer in one of those Regiments to his friend in London,* Letter I, quoted in Wahll, 119ff.

19. Reported in McCardell, *Ill-Starred General,* 157. Charles Lee was tall, rail thin and unkempt in appearance. In his later years at least he habitually surrounded himself with a pack of hounds. The British captured Lee just before the Battle of Trenton, and he spent more than a year as a prisoner of war. Upon his release, he resumed field command, disobeyed orders and fled at the Battle of Monmouth. He resigned in disgrace.

20. Alan Houston, in his "Benjamin Franklin and the 'Wagon Affair' of 1755," quotes two letters from a John Hamilton among the contents of Benjamin Franklin's quire book that he discovered in the British Library. Houston attributes the letters to "Rev. Hamilton" but states that the identity of "Rev. John Hamilton remains obscure because there were two chaplains in Braddock's army." Houston, "Benjamin Franklin and the 'Wagon Affair' of 1755," 175, n. 88. Houston's John Hamilton might in fact have been the local physician.

21. Letter from A. Hamilton to G. Hamilton, August 1755; Wahll, 446ff.

22. Sargent, *History of an Expedition Against Fort Du Quesne,* 193.

Chapter Nine: The Carlyle House Congress

1. No relation to Braddock's aide-de-camp Roger Morris.

2. Letter from A. Hamilton to G. Hamilton, August 1755; Wahll, 447.

3. During the interim, on April 8, Lord Tyrawley–Braddock's old gaming companion and putative father of George Anne Bellamy–was named colonel of the Coldstream Regiment of Foot Guards, replacing the Earl of Albemarle who had died the previous December 22. It is not known whether news of his friend's appointment ever reached Braddock in the field.

4. Netherton concluded "Never before had such an influential group of leaders gathered, face to face, to plan such a grand strategy. . . . One would have to wait twenty years to see another so grand in its participants, objectives or results–in 1775, in Philadelphia, at Independence Hall." Netherton, *Braddock's Campaign,* 68. It is possible that Washington met with Braddock while he was in Alexandria, but there is no conclusive evidence that Washington attended the congress of the governors at Carlyle House. The Carlyle House congress was in fact the second pan-colonial conference. It was preceded by the June 1754 Albany Conference which was called at the instigation of the Board of Trade to hammer out a peace

treaty between the colonies and the Six Nations. However, largely at the inspiration of Benjamin Franklin, a committee appointed by the colonial commissioners assumed a larger mandate and drafted and approved a plan of union which the various colonial assemblies subsequently rejected. The Albany Conference at the end of the day failed both to conclude a treaty with the Six Nations and to forge colonial unity.

5. Letter dated August 15, 1755 from Major John Carlyle to his brother at Abbott, ibid.

6. Orme's Journal; also Sargent, *History of an Expedition Against Fort Du Quesne,* 302.

7. O'Callaghan, *The Documentary History of the State of New York*, 649.

8. Sargent, *History of an Expedition Against Fort Du Quesne,* 153, citing letter from Braddock to Lord Halifax and Sir Thomas Robinson. The notion of direct taxation by Parliament of the virtually untaxed American colonies had been gaining currency for at least several months and was also favored by Dinwiddie and in a variant form by Shirley. See generally, Beer, "British Colonial Policy, 1754–1765," 30–31.

9. Sargent, *History of an Expedition Against Fort Du Quesne*, 303–5.

10. McCardell, *Ill-Starred General,* 168.

11. Netherton, *Braddock's Campaign,* 8, 13.

12. Fitzpatrick, *The Writings of George Washington,* vol. 1, 118; Netherton, *Braddock's Campaign*, 12.

13. St. Clair's Letters, 87; also Wahll, 101.

14. St. Clair's Letters, 93; Wahll, 113.

15. St. Clair's Letters, 96; Wahll, 130. Emphasis added.

16. Orders by Sir John St. Clair, Deputy Quarter Master General to his Majesty's forces in America, April 21, 1755, St. Clair's Letters, 110; also Wahll, 149.

17. McCardell, *Ill-Starred General,* 170. Indeed, Braddock shared St. Clair's frustrations. On April 19 he wrote to Sir Robert Napier (and thus to the Duke of Cumberland): "I have met with infinite difficulties in providing carriages etc., for the train nor am I as yet quite relieved from one, a great part still continuing here which has delayed me for some time. . . . I am impatient to begin my march over the mountains. . . . I am to expect numberless inconveniences and obstructions from the total want of dry forage, from the being obliged to carry all our provisions with us which will make a vast line of baggage and which . . . will . . . retard me considerably. . . . I have been greatly disappointed by the neglect and supineness of those assemblies of those provinces with which I am concerned; they

promised great matters and have done nothing whereby instead of forwarding they have obstructed the service . . . the people of this part of the country laying it down for a Maxim, never to speak Truth upon any account." Ibid., 171. Similarly, Orme shared St. Clair's concern. Writing on April 16 to the deputy quartermaster, the aide-de-camp stated: "Sixty wagons are absolutely necessary on the Maryland side. I have applied by the general direction to Governour Sharp who has improved [*sic*] some but any short of the compliment he is expected here tomorrow and his Excellency will again urge him to use every method to procure more. . . . For God's sake my dear Sir John prepare everything as fast as possible for our march. I own I fear no thing but the want of horses and carriages, I wish you may be able to provide a sufficient number, I am convinced if there is any deficiency we shall owe it to the impossibility of procuring horses and carriage." St. Clair's Letters, 102; Wahll, 137–38.

18. St. Clair's Letters, 105; Wahll, 139.

19. Benjamin Franklin's son William Franklin, later royal governor of New Jersey and a Tory during the Revolution, writing to his father a few weeks later, makes clear how deleterious the impact of the expeditionary force was: "'Tis scarcely to be believed what havock and oppression has been committed by the army in their march. Hardly a farmer in Frederic County has either Horse, Waggon or Servant to do the business of his plantation. Many are intirely ruined, being not able to plat their Corn, or do any thing for their subsistence. . . . The abuse they gave the people, at whose houses they stopped is scarce to be paralleled. They have not paid any of the Tavern-keepers much above one half of their bills. . . . And when they are shewn an authentic Copy of those rates, they grow immediately inraged, swearing that they are the Law during their stay in this Country; and that their Will and pleasure shall be the rule. . . . Several of the Farmers who made opposition to some of these outrageous doings have been sent for by a file of Musketeers, and kept along time confined, and otherwise mal-treated. . . . However, all those, who have given me these Informations, agree, that the General, and others of the superior officers have acted in quite a different manner; and that it is by the subaltern officers chiefly that they have been so scandalously insulted. Methinks, that if anything can add to the reproach of the British Americans for having these petty tyrants sent amongst us, it will be tamely submitting our selves to their arbitrary and unwarrantable insults. What must Posterity think of us, when history tells them, that such an infatuation prevailed in the Counsels of America, as to render it necessary for 1000 Men to be sent over to defend 3 or 400,000 against one quarter of their number? But enough on this head: I can scarcely think of it with patience." Houston, "Benjamin Franklin and the 'Wagon Affair' of 1755," 271–72.

20. Halkett's Orders; Wahll, 146.

21. Braddock was still underestimating the length of the route.

22. McCardell, *Ill-Starred General,* 171.

Chapter Ten: The Maryland March

1. Today the landscape has changed markedly. Cutting and landfill have extended the river's edge far from Braddock's Rock. However, between the Lincoln Memorial and the Kennedy Center for the Performing Arts, to the left of an access ramp to the Theodore Roosevelt Bridge, a remnant of the rock still exists some fifteen feet below the surface encased in a surrounding well.

2. The April 21, 1967 edition of the *Alexandria Gazette* reported in its "100 Years Ago" column that workmen excavating for a sewer on the upper portion of High Street (Wisconsin Avenue) in Georgetown in 1867 discovered the remains of a corduroy road some eight feet below the surface. It was made of "cedar bush, trees and large stones" and was attributed to the Braddock expedition.

3. Batman's Journal; Sargent, *History of an Expedition Against Fort Du Quesne*, 367; Wahll, 135.

4. Seaman's Journal; Sargent, *History of an Expedition Against Fort Du Quesne*, 368; Wahll, 138.

5. Batman's Journal; Sargent, *History of an Expedition Against Fort Du Quesne*, 368; Wahll, 140.

6. Batman's Journal; Sargent, *History of an Expedition Against Fort Du Quesne*, 368; Wahll, 146.

7. Braddock's Orders; Wahll, 161–62.

8. Ecker, *A Portrait of Old Georgetown*, 3. For the more complete version of Braddock's letter quoted above, see Laver, *Records of the Columbia Historical Society*.

9. Orme's Journal in Sargent, *History of an Expedition Against Fort Du Quesne*, 307; Wahll, 147.

10. See Wahll, 142.

11. Pargellis, *Military Affairs in North America, 1748–1764,* 82; McCardell, *Ill-Starred General,* 172.

12. Franklin, *Autobiography of Benjamin Franklin*, 213.

13. Ibid., 213–14, 219.

14. Ibid., 223.

15. Ibid., 218–19.

16. McCardell, *Ill-Starred General*, 178.

17. Houston, "Benjamin Franklin and the 'Wagon Affair' of 1755," 274.

18. Ibid.

19. For an enlightening discussion of the wagons deployed see Wahll, 156–57. In all, the expedition hired about 300 wagons with four horses each, plus six hundred packhorses. The rate for the wagons was 13 shillings American money or 10 shillings English money per day (there being about a 25 to 30 percent devaluation of American against English currency). The packhorses went for two shillings a day. The claims for these rentals quickly added up and were not settled until long after the expedition.

20. Franklin, *Autobiography of Benjamin Franklin*, 221.

21. Fitzpatrick, *Writings of George Washington*, vol. 1, 70. It appears that by then Washington had sorted out the issues of estate which had caused him to ask Braddock's permission to join the expedition in progress. He also had used the time to test the waters for running for the House of Burgesses. See Lewis, *For King and Country,* 171.

22. Batman's Journal; Wahll, 158.

23. Seaman's Journal; Sargent, *History of an Expedition Against Fort Du Quesne*, 370; Wahll, 163–64.

Chapter Eleven: The Virginia March

1. Letter from St. Clair to Orme, April 13, 1755; St. Clair's Letters, 97; also Wahll, 130–31. The ever-diligent St. Clair added as a "P.S." to his letter to Orme a request that "all the smiths at Frederick," Maryland, be put to work making 100 felling axes, 10 horse shoes, 12 whip saws and three sets of miners' tools for "breaking and blowing rock."

2. The site today is a residential neighborhood of Alexandria at the intersection of Braddock and Russell Roads.

3. What was a fork in the road in 1755 is today a five-way intersection in suburban Alexandria boasting a shopping center, an automobile dealership, and the eastern edge of the grounds of Episcopal High School.

4. The route was as follows: 18 miles to Fairfax courthouse; 12 miles to Mr. Coleman's on Sugar Land Run "where there is Indian corn"; 15 miles to Mr. Miners; 12 miles to Mr. Thompson "ye Quaker" with 3000 wt corn (at present-day Hillsboro, Virginia); 17 miles to the ferry at the Shenandoah (via Keyes or Vestal's Gap in the Blue Ridge); 23 miles to Winchester.

5. Letter from unidentified British officer, April 30, 1755; Wahll, 165–66.

6. Ibid., 166–67.

7. Fitzpatrick, *Writings of George Washington,* vol. 1, 72; Wahll, 173. See also May 6 letter from George Washington to his brother John Augustine Washington that references his meeting Braddock at Frederick. Fitzpatrick, 72; Wahll, 175.

8. Fitzpatrick, *Writings of George Washington,* vol. 1, 120.

9. Batman's Journal; Sargent, *History of an Expedition Against Fort Du Quesne,* 370; Wahll, 168.

10. Some scholars appear to place the Widow Barringer's in West Virginia, near present-day Charles Town. See, e.g., Hough, *Braddock's Road Through the Virginia Colony,* Vol. VII: cited in Wahll, 172. The author's view is that a location nearer Clear Brook, Virginia, is more likely.

11. Seaman's Journal; Sargent, *History of an Expedition Against Fort Du Quesne* 371; Wahll, 171.

12. Halkett's Orders; Wahll, 173.

13. Seaman's Journal; Sargent, *History of an Expedition Against Fort Du Quesne,* 371; Wahll, 174.

14. Seaman's Journal; Wahll, 176.

15. Seaman's Journal; Sargent, *History of an Expedition Against Fort Du Quesne,* 372; Wahll, 179.

16. Letter from unidentified British officer, May 8, 1755; Wahll, 180–81.

17. Ibid., 180.

18. Charlotte Browne, following the same route in a wagon one month later, found that the horses could not keep on their feet and that the wagons broke down. She got out and walked until her feet were blistered. Harrison, "With Braddock's Army," 315; Wahll, 266.

19. An ancient log cabin, attributed to Michael Cresap, stands today at Old Town. It is probably not the same cabin that was at Old Town in Braddock's day.

20. Seaman's Journal; Sargent, *History of an Expedition Against Fort Du Quesne,* 372; Wahll, 182.

21. Sargent, *History of an Expedition Against Fort Du Quesne,* 194.

22. It was noted above that three sets of armor were included in the expedition's supplies sent from the Tower of London.

Chapter Twelve: The Noble Savages of Fort Cumberland

1. The site today hosts Emmanuel Parish Episcopal Church.

2. Seaman's Journal; Sargent, *History of an Expedition Against Fort Du Quesne,* 373; Wahll, 185–86. From the seaman's description, it would appear that the Indians

were better armed with modern rifles than the British soldiers were with traditional muskets. This observation is important because in the later battle the Indians outgunned the English and Americans. It is also interesting to note his observation about the effect of alcohol on the fertility and/or lifespan of the Indians. His conclusion about the spiritual life of the Indians is more suspect.

3. Seaman's Journal; Sargent, *History of an Expedition Against Fort Du Quesne,* 376; Wahll, 192.

4. McCardell, *Ill-Starred General,* 190–91.

5. Braddock's Orders; Wahll, 187.

6. Parkman, *Montcalm and Wolfe,* 26–27; McCardell, *Ill-Starred General,* 186.

7. McCardell, *Ill-Starred General,* 114. In fact, Gist's son had recruited some Cherokees, but they were later dissuaded from traveling north by a trader who challenged Gist's authority because he bore no letter from the king.

8. Seaman's Journal; Sargent, *History of an Expedition Against Fort Du Quesne,* 375; Wahll, 191.

9. Seaman's Journal; Sargent, *History of an Expedition Against Fort Du Quesne,* 377; Wahll, 199.

10. Seaman's Journal; Sargent, *History of an Expedition Against Fort Du Quesne,* 379; Wahll, 200–201.

11. Letter from unidentified British officer, May 23, 1755; Wahll, 209–10.

12. Lewis, *For King and Country,* 172. The eight Indians who remained with Braddock appear to have been (i) Scaroyady, who always spoke for the group, (ii) Aroas or Silver Heels, Scaroyady's son or son-in-law, (iii) Kash-wughdanionto, White Thunder or Belt of Wampum (the father of Bright Lightning and the keeper of the wampum), a Seneca who had rivaled Scaroyady to succeed the Half King, (iv) Cashuwayon or Captain Newcastle, (v) Froson, (vi) Kahuktodon, (vii) Attscheehokatha, (viii) Dyoquario, the latter five all Iroquois. Sargent, *History of an Expedition Against Fort Du Quesne,* 310.

13. O'Callaghan, *The Documentary History of the State of New York*, 674, citing a letter from Sir William Johnson written at Albany July 21, 1755 to the Board of Trade in London. Johnson further stated that he had advised Braddock why the Indians had failed to come to his aid.

14. Letter from George Washington to John Augustine Washington, May 14, 1755, Wahll, 194. Washington had opened the letter by noting as his top priority that "wearing boots is quite the mode" among the officers in the camp and requesting his brother to send up a pair that are "good and neat."

15. Braddock's Orders; Wahll, 184.

16. The results of this review, as recorded at the time, were: "The 1st Brigade, Commanded by Sir Peter Halkett: 44 Regiment of Foot 700–700; Capt Rutherford's Indep Co NY & Capt Gates 100–95; Capt. Polson Carpenters 50–48; Capt Peronnee's Virg. Rangers 50–47; Capt Wagner's Virginia Rangers 50–45; Capt. Dagworthy's Maryl. Rangers 50–49. The Second Brigade, Commanded by Colonel Dunbar: 48th Regiment of Foot 700–700; Capt. Demerie's S.C. Detacht 100–97; Capt. Dobb's N.C. Rangers 100–80; Capt. Mercer's Co. Carpenters 35; Capt. Stevens Virginia Rangers 50–48; Capt. Hogg's Virginia Rangers 50–40; Capt. Cox's Virginia Rangers 50–43." The latter was commanded by Captain George Mercer, not to be confused with Dr. Hugh Mercer, Washington's friend, organizer of the Virginia militia and hero of the Battles of Trenton (1776) and Princeton (1777). Hugh Mercer served in Braddock's expedition too but in a subordinate capacity.

17. Braddock's Orders; Wahll, 196.

18. Sargent, *History of an Expedition Against Fort Du Quesne,* 377.

19. Braddock's Orders; Wahll, 198.

20. Hamilton, *Braddock's Defeat,* 90.

21. Sir Humphrey Bland was Governor of Gibraltar from 1749 to 1754. Braddock knew and served under him. One of his successors was James O'Hara, Lord Tyrawley. It was a small world.

22. Darling, *Red Coat and Brown Bess,* 10.

23. Ibid.

24. Sargent, *History of an Expedition Against Fort Du Quesne,* 126, footnote 1, citing Voltaire, *Précis du Siècle de Louis XV.*, c. xv.

25. Orme's Journal; Sargent, *History of an Expedition Against Fort Du Quesne,* 312.

26. Ibid.

27. Lewis, *For King and Country,* 171.

28. The apparent fact that the seaman took part in the "Captain's guard" suggests that the seaman who kept the journal might have been Spendelow himself. A lieutenant in the navy is equivalent to a captain in the army. However, the journal continued after the battle, in which Spendelow was killed, although it could have been finished by another hand.

29. Seaman's Journal; Sargent, *History of an Expedition Against Fort Du Quesne,* 377.

30. McCardell, *Ill-Starred General,* 193–94.

31. Letter of unidentified British officer, May 20, 1755; Wahll, 202–4.

32. Batman's Journal; Hamilton, *Braddock's Defeat,* 15; Wahll, 205.

33. From all accounts, Braddock was fully justified in delaying at Fort Cumberland to allow the other troops to come up, ensure supply lines and

organize the American troops. However, Captain Rutherford, one of Halkett's officers and an avowed critic of Braddock, was later to castigate Braddock for undue delay at Fort Cumberland, stating that the General "spent a month idly with his women and feasting." Sargent, *History of an Expedition Against Fort Du Quesne,* 382. Rutherford's is the sole voice to make this charge. It should perhaps be dismissed were it not for the fact that it perfectly echoed Carlyle's description of Braddock's behavior during the long delay in Alexandria.

34. Seaman's Journal; Sargent, *History of an Expedition Against Fort Du Quesne,* 379; Wahll, 206.

35. McCardell., *Ill-Starred General,* 199.

36. Braddock's Orders; Wahll, 212.

37. Braddock's Orders; Wahll, 206.

38. Batman's Journal; Hamilton, *Braddock's Defeat,* 17; Wahll, 225.

39. Batman's Journal; Sargent, *History of an Expedition Against Fort Du Quesne,* 380; Wahll, 212.

40. Orme's Journal; Wahll, 213; Hamilton, *Braddock's Defeat,* 16; Wahll, 223.

41. McCardell, *Ill-Starred General,* 199.

42. Ibid.

43. Ibid., 204.

44. Halkett's Orders; Sargent, *History of an Expedition Against Fort Du Quesne,* 312; Wahll, 216ff.

45. Sargent, *History of an Expedition Against Fort Du Quesne,* 321–22.

46. Ibid.

47. Letter of unidentified British officer, July 25, 1755; Wahll, 431.

48. McCardell, *Ill-Starred General,* 205.

49. To judge from the amended plans adopted at the second council of war, it appears that at least part of Halkett's advice was heeded, however.

50. Letter of unidentified British officer, July 25, 1755; Wahll, 430.

51. Wahll, 428.

52. I thank Glenn Williams for clarification on this point.

53. Batman's Journal; Hamilton, *Braddock's Defeat,* 16; Wahll, 210.

Chapter Thirteen: Advance Across the Allegheny Mountains

1. St. Clair's Letters; Wahll, 42.

2. Batman's Journal; Sargent, *History of an Expedition Against Fort Du Quesne,* 380; Hamilton, *Braddock's Defeat,* 17; Wahll, 229.

3. Orme's Journal; Sargent, *History of an Expedition Against Fort Du Quesne,* 323; Wahll, 230.

4. Journal of Engineer Harry Gordon; Wahll, 242–43.

5. Braddock's Orders; Wahll, 226.

6. Letters from Washington, May 28 and 30, 1755; Wahll, 234, 228.

7. Browne's Journal; Wahll, 235.

8. St. Clair's Letters, 132; Wahll, 235.

9. St.Clair's Letters, 134; Wahll, 236–37.

10. Batman's Journal; Hamilton, *Braddock's Defeat,* 17, Wahll 236.

11. Batman's Journal; Hamilton, *Braddock's Defeat,* 18; Wahll, 240.

12. St. Clair's Letters, 137; Wahll, 240.

13. St. Clair's Letters, 136; Wahll, 240.

14. Braddock's Orders; Sargent, *History of an Expedition Against Fort Du Quesne,* xlvi; Wahll, 248.

15. In contrast, the Duke of Wellington, to take but one example, shot numerous deserters from his army after taking Ciudad Rodrigo just sixty-seven years later. Hibbert, *Wellington,* 116. Washington also was a stern disciplinarian during the Revolution. Braddock may have influenced him.

16. Batman's Journal; Hamilton, *Braddock's Defeat,* 18; Wahll, 243.

17. Batman's Journal; Hamilton, *Braddock's Defeat,* 18; Wahll, 245.

18. Browne's Journal; Harrison, *Braddock's Defeat,* 312; Wahll, 245.

19. Batman's Journal; Hamilton, *Braddock's Defeat,* 19; Wahll, 246.

20. Batman's Journal; Hamilton, *Braddock's Defeat,* 19; Wahll, 248–49.

21. Bellamy took special pride in her costume. The producer, Mr. Rich, had obtained a gown of the Princess Dowager of Wales for Mrs. Woffington. "It was not in the least soiled," Bellamy wrote, "and looked very beautiful by day-light; but being a straw colour, it seemed to be a dirty white, by candle-light; especially when my splendid yellow was by it [Bellamy had ordered her gown from a couturier in Paris]. To this yellow dress I had added a purple robe; a mixture so happy, made it appear, if possible, to greater advantage. Thus accoutred in all my magnificence, I made my entrée . . . as the Persian Princess." Bellamy, *Apology,* vol. 1, 249–50.

Chapter Fourteen: To Little Meadows

1. Letter from Braddock to Napier, June 8, 1755; Wahll, 253–54. Braddock was referring to St. Clair and Orme.

2. Ibid., 254.

3. Letter from Braddock to unidentified recipient, June 9, 1755; Wahll, 256–57.

4. One study of the reconstituted 48th Regiment in 1757 shows that the rank and file were 40 percent English, 10 percent Scots, and 34 percent Irish. The same study shows the commissioned officers in the 48th in 1757 as 16 English, 5 Scots, 19 Irish, 3 American, and 1 foreign. It also shows the average age and service of British soldiers wounded on the Braddock campaign as a somewhat surprising 34 and 10.3 years, respectively. See, Brumwell, *Redcoats,* 318–19. The conclusion is that, in addition to complements of new recruits enlisted in Ireland and America, the two regiments contained a core of experienced veterans, mainly English and Irish, and were officered by similar men.

5. Kopperman, *Braddock at the Monongahela,* 177; Wahll, 261.

6. Letter from unidentified British officer; Hamilton, *Braddock's Defeat,* 40; Wahll 261.

7. Orme's Journal; Sargent, *History of an Expedition Against Fort Du Quesne,* 331; Wahll, 264–65.

8. The army moved by drum rolls. "Beating the General" was an order to assemble.

9. Orme's Journal; Sargent, *History of an Expedition Against Fort Du Quesne,* 333; Wahll, 273.

10. Orme's Journal; Wahll, 275.

11. Orme's Journal; Sargent, *History of an Expedition Against Fort Du Quesne,* 334; Wahll, 279.

12. Sargent, *History of an Expedition Against Fort Du Quesne,* 201. Alas, the Shades of Death are no more, having been cut down many years ago.

13. Journal of Engineer Harry Gordon; Wahll, 279.

14. Batman's Journal; Hamilton, *Braddock's Defeat,* 19; Wahll, 255–56.

15. Batman's Journal; Hamilton, *Braddock's Defeat,* 20; Wahll, 258.

16. Batman's Journal; Hamilton, *Braddock's Defeat,* 20; Wahll, 265.

17. St. Clair's Letters, 138; Wahll, 259. In addition to reporting to Braddock, St. Clair exercised for the first time since Braddock's arrival in America his prerogative of direct communication with the Duke of Cumberland, via Sir Robert Napier. On June 13 he wrote a report to Napier which echoed almost exactly the complaints that Braddock had made to Napier in his own letter of June 8. There was little, if any, daylight between the worldviews of the general and his deputy quartermaster.

18. Browne's Journal; Wahll, 256.

19. Browne's Journal; Wahll, 262.

20. Browne's Journal; Wahll, 266.

21. Browne's Journal; Wahll, 274.

Chapter Fifteen: The Flying Column

1. Lewis, *For King and Country,* 174.

2. Braddock's order book for Thursday, June 17, contains a complete list of the hand-picked junior officers. See Hamilton, *Braddock's Defeat,* 108; Wahll, 285.

3. Fischer, *Washington's Crossing,* 404 ("Ratios of Artillery and Infantry in the Battles of Trenton and Princeton").

4. Letter from Dunbar to Napier, July 24, 1755; Wahll, 412.

5. Letter from unidentified British officer; Wahll, 282.

6. Orme's Journal; Sargent, *History of an Expedition Against Fort Du Quesne,* 336; Wahll, 288.

7. *Maryland Gazette,* June 5, 1755; Hamilton, *Braddock's Defeat,* 10; Wahll, 290–91.

8. Orme's Journal; Sargent, *History of an Expedition Against Fort Du Quesne,* 338; Wahll, 292.

9. Anderson, *Crucible of War,* 96, citing a letter from Rutherford to Richard Peters, received August 13, 1755.

10. Lewis, *For King and Country,* 174.

11. Journal of Engineer Henry Gordon; Wahll, 296.

12. Orme's Journal; Sargent, *History of an Expedition Against Fort Du Quesne,* 340; Wahll, 295.

13. Wahll, 285, citing Nichols, "The Braddock Expedition."

14. Halkett's Orders; Hamilton, *Braddock's Defeat,* 112; Wahll, 297.

15. Orme's Journal; Sargent, *History of an Expedition Against Fort Du Quesne,* 340; Wahll, 297.

16. Batman's Journal; Hamilton, *Braddock's Defeat,* 22; Wahll, 298.

17. Letter from unidentified British officer; Hamilton, *Braddock's Defeat,* 44; Wahll, 297–98.

18. Wahll, 304.

Chapter Sixteen: Terra Incognita

1. Letter from unidentified British officer; Hamilton, *Braddock's Defeat,* 45; Wahll, 301.

2. Orme's Journal; Sargent, *History of an Expedition Against Fort Du Quesne,* 341; Wahll, 300.

3. Halkett's Orders; Hamilton, *Braddock's Defeat,* 112; Wahll, 299.

4. Orme's Journal; Sargent, *History of an Expedition Against Fort Du Quesne,* 341; Wahll, 300.

5. Journal of Engineer Harry Gordon; Wahll, 303.

6. Pierre Claude Pecaudy, Sieur de Contrecoeur, was the commander of Fort Duquesne. The inscribers were probably recording his name in his absence.

7. Orme's Journal; Sargent, *History of an Expedition Against Fort Du Quesne,* 243; Wahll, 303.

8. The Half King's Rocks still exist.

9. Batman's Journal; Hamilton, *Braddock's Defeat,* 24; Wahll, 313.

10. Batman's Journal; Hamilton, *Braddock's Defeat,* 24; Wahll, 311.

11. Orme's Journal; Sargent, *History of an Expedition Against Fort Du Quesne,* 345; Wahll, 314.

12. Halkett's Orders; Hamilton, *Braddock's Defeat,* 115; Wahll, 311.

13. Batman's Journal; Hamilton, *Braddock's Defeat,* 46, 24; Wahll, 317.

14. The first-hand accounts are conflicting and confusing as to where the flying column spent the night of July 1. Despite recent research on this phase of the march (see, e.g., Frank A. Cassell and Elizabeth W. Cassell, *A Tour of Braddock's Road from Fort Necessity to Braddock's Field* (Westmoreland Heritage) and article by Steeley, J. in *Westmoreland History* 7, no. 2, September 2002), historians and geographers will no doubt debate the exact location of the route of march and related encampments during the first days of July for years to come. For purposes of this narrative, however, it is sufficient to say that the army was in the middle of nowhere.

15. Batman's Journal; Hamilton, *Braddock's Defeat,* 24; Wahll, 319.

16. Halkett's Orders; Hamilton, *Braddock's Defeat,* 118; Wahll, 319.

17. Orme's Journal; Sargent, *History of an Expedition Against Fort Du Quesne,* 346; Wahll, 320–21.

18. Letter from unidentified British officer; Hamilton, *Braddock's Defeat,* 25; Wahll, 332.

19. Orme's Journal; Sargent, *History of an Expedition Against Fort Du Quesne,* 349; Wahll, 329.

20. Wahll, 330, citing Nichols, "The Braddock Expedition."

21. It was apparently on this scouting expedition that St. Clair approached close enough to the Forks of the Ohio to see Fort Duquesne. The ever-imaginative St. Clair spotted a small eminence within cannon shot of the fort and imagined it to

be the ideal place to position cannon that could lob hot shot into the fort and set it afire. See "Progress of the War in America", *Gentleman's Magazine,* 378.

22. Orme's Journal; Sargent, *History of an Expedition Against Fort Du Quesne,* 352; Wahll, 339–40.

23. Halkett's Orders; Hamilton, *Braddock's Defeat,* 120; Wahll, 338.

24. Seaman's Journal; Sargent, *History of an Expedition Against Fort Du Quesne,* 384; Wahll, 341.

25. Sargent, *History of an Expedition Against Fort Du Quesne,* 214–15.

Chapter Seventeen: Captain Beaujeu's Prayer

1. The "Troupes de la Marine" were regular soldiers who constituted an army to defend and police French colonies, in this case, New France. All of its officers were "gentlemen" or aristocrats, many if not most from metropolitan France, while the men were largely recruited from among the habitants of French North America. They should not be confused with French marines, who were the companies of seagoing soldiers assigned to warships of the French navy. The confusion for modern readers is compounded by the fact that the French ministry of the navy (the French word for navy is *marine*) administered France's overseas colonies, as well as performed admiralty functions of the fleet. I thank Glenn F. Williams for this information.

2. McCardell, *Ill-Starred General,* 240–244.

3. Measures of a league varied depending on the period and location, but it is generally reckoned to be between three and three and one-half miles.

4. Kopperman, *Braddock at the Monongahela,* 266; Wahll, 333.

5. Sargent, *History of an Expedition Against Fort Du Quesne,* 221.

6. See ibid., 222.

7. "Praying Indians" in this context means the bands of Iroquois who converted to Catholicism and allied themselves with the French, thus breaking away from the Six Nations.

8. Sargent, *History of an Expedition Against Fort Du Quesne,* 223.

9. Account of M. Roucher, a French Canadian; Kopperman, *Braddock at the Monongahela,* 267; Wahll, 344; also Sargent, *History of an Expedition Against Fort Du Quesne,* 409–11 .

10. Account of Ensign Godefroy, a French officer; Kopperman, *Braddock at the Monongahela,* 266; Wahll, 333; also Sargent, *History of an Expedition Against Fort Du Quesne,* 409–11.

11. McCardell, *Ill-Starred General,* 244.

12. Account of James Smith, American captive; Wahll, 344.

13. The estimates of the size of the French and Indian force vary. Smith himself put the Indian element at no more than 400. One French account puts the Indians at 641 and the combined French and Canadians at 250. Washington, who witnessed the force on the receiving end, put their total number no higher than 300. See Sargent, *History of an Expedition Against Fort Du Quesne,* 223, note 1. The best guess is that the total combined force was between 600 and 900, a figure not so wide of Braddock's own 1,200 combatants in the flying column.

Chapter Eighteen: The Trampling of the Vineyard

1. Batman's Journal; Hamilton, *Braddock's Defeat,* 27; Wahll, 359.

2. Letter from unidentified British officer; Hamilton, *Braddock's Defeat,* 49; Wahll 350.

3. Orme's Journal; Sargent, *History of an Expedition Against Fort Du Quesne,* 353; Wahll, 345.

4. See, e.g., Seaman's Journal; Sargent *History of an Expedition Against Fort Du Quesne,* 384; Wahll, 355.

5. McCardell, *Ill-Starred General,* 246–47.

6. See letter from unnamed British officer in Wahll, 424. Kopperman identifies this officer as "British E," an officer close to St. Clair and an eyewitness to the fighting who prepared his account long after the engagement (and thus may have been less reliable than those who wrote earlier, although his observation on the use of rifles is first-hand and unequivocal). Wahll identifies the officer as most likely Captain Gabriel Christie. See also Bailey, *British Military Flintlock Rifles,* 11–12, recounting and confirming the incident.

Additional evidence that the French and/or Indians were using rifles is suggested by Croghan's observation that the enemy was firing from far off, at least 200 yards (Wahll, 380), while at the same time individually targeting British and American officers who suffered inordinately high casualties (see, e.g., Wahll, 349), which would have been unlikely with massed musket firing. A number of participants commented on the apparently deliberate targeting of officers. For instance, Lieutenant William Dunbar, whose account Kopperman deems to be among the most accurate, wrote "The officers . . . soon became the mark of the Enemy, who scarce left one, that was not killed or wounded." See Wahll, 349. See also letter dated July 16, 1755, from John Hamilton to Benjamin Franklin stating: "The Officers were all picked out, as marks, as you may judge from those of our Regiment" (Houston, "Benjamin Franklin and the 'Wagon Affair' of 1755," 280). Moreover, the distance at which the French and Indians held themselves, together with concealment behind trees, may help account for the observation, made by several participants in the battle, that the British and Americans rarely saw more than three or four enemy at a time.

Further, O'Meara reports in *Guns at the Forks* (146) that many of the balls removed from British and American soldiers by surgeons after the battle appeared "chewed." While this might have been caused, as O'Meara supposed, by carrying the bullets in the mouth (apparently the oxidation of the lead had a sweet taste that attracted the soldiers) or deliberate biting to create a dumdum effect, it is also plausible that the soft lead balls were in fact scored by their being rammed or pounded into the barrels (common practice at the time) or by their subsequent discharge through the crudely rifled barrels.

In the siege of Louisburg in 1745, Americans used some fifty British-manufactured and supplied rifles. The French inventory of booty taken at Braddock's defeat included a "large quantity of rifles, serviceable and out of service" (Wahll, 386). Apparently these rifles were part of the same stock commissioned for the Louisburg expedition, later stored in the Tower of London and requisitioned by St. Clair for protection of his engineers (Bailey, *British Military Flintlock Rifles,* 11–12). If Braddock's troops were supplied with rifles, there is no evidence that they actually used them in the battle. As noted above, American-produced long rifles had been coming into use for at least twenty years prior to the battle, so the Americans, especially the Virginians, may have carried and used some in the battle.

If rifles were deployed, the next question is whether the French or Indians or both were using them. Presumably, it would have made little sense to have armed untrained Indian allies with the new weapons, which were both slower firing and more complicated to load than muskets (most issues of arms to Indian allies during this period were smoothbore trade arms). However, note the British observation of Indians' facility with rifles cited above. If indeed the French, or French and Indians, were fighting with rifles, it is unclear where they obtained them because French armories are not known to have produced rifles during this period. According to most experts, rifle-making in America first became significant in the 1730s and 1740s and was a skill imparted largely by German immigrants and an industry located principally in German-settled areas. See e.g., Shumway, *Rifles of Colonial America,* vol. 1, 16, 63. It is not hard to imagine that Indian raids in the years leading up to 1755 throughout Pennsylvania, with its large German population, might have produced at least a modest stock of weapons whose use the Indians had quickly mastered. Indians also undoubtedly obtained rifles from settlers through regular trading. The fact that the surgeons in Braddock's army noted the smaller caliber of many balls removed from the wounded also is consistent with the reduced caliber of the so-called

Kentucky rifles developed in America by the mid-eighteenth century, .40 to .55 inches versus over .70 for the muskets from which they were derived. See Sheppard, *Arms and Armour 1660 to 1918,* 70.

Finally, there is nearly contemporaneous confirmation that Indians were armed with rifles. Colonel Henry Bouquet, who played an instrumental role in the subsequent Forbes campaign which dislodged the French from Fort Duquesne, wrote in a letter to Forbes dated June 3, 1758 that "There are 37-1/2 barrels of very good powder at Harris's Ferry, intended for Fort Augusta. Half of it is *fine powder for rifles, and Indians,* and it is no longer possible to buy it" (emphasis added). Stevens, Kent, and Leonard, *The Papers of Henry Bouquet,* vol. 2, 17. Lest there be any question as to Bouquet's meaning, he wrote again on June 7, 1758: "A large part of the provincials are armed with grooved rifles and have their molds. Lead in bars will suit them better than bullets–likewise the Indians–, but they also need fine powder FF." Ibid., 50. "FF" grade black powder was an especially fine powder with a faster burn rate that was used in .36 to .50 caliber rifles. Although Bouquet's remarks were made three years after the Braddock expedition, it is nearly contemporaneous affirmation that the Indians allied with the English were armed with, and adept in the use of, rifles. There is little reason to think that the Indians allied with the French three years previously were not as well.

Taking all of the above factors into account, the weight of the evidence suggests that at least some the Indians allied with the French fighting Braddock used rifles, probably obtained through trade or stolen in earlier raids against settlers, and that they deliberately and effectively targeted British officers, thereby affecting the outcome of the battle.

7. See the Seaman's Journal, quoted in Sargent, *History of an Expedition to Fort Du Quesne,* 374: "The [Indian] men are . . . very dexterous with a rifle barreled gun, and their tomahawk."

8. Sargent, *History of an Expedition Against Fort Du Quesne,* 230.

9. Perhaps St. Clair was trying to communicate with the general so that others standing nearby could not understand.

10. Apparently the fighting was so violent that Washington lost his signet ring on the field of battle. It was later found and currently resides in the New York State Library at Albany, New York. See Society of the Cincinnati Library catalogue, mss. 546.

11. Wahll, 476.

12. See Sargent, *History of an Expedition Against Fort Du Quesne,* 244ff.

13. See, e.g., Ritenour, *Old Tom Fossit,* 233–35. However, the fact that various wit-

nesses in close proximity to Braddock, including Washington, did not report the incident and that Braddock was hit first through the arm, with the bullet passing into his lung, suggests that the lucky shot came from in front of him and possibly at a higher elevation (remember he was mounted when hit), which would be consistent with the field of fire being laid down by the enemy from their position on higher ground to the north of the road.

14. Faragher, *Daniel Boone*, 36–38.

15. Boone later named one of his sons after Morgan, Daniel Morgan Boone. Morgan was a wagoneer, originally from Pennsylvania but more recently had worked as a plantation overseer in Virginia. He served with Gates's company. Once an officer reprimanded him for being late with his wagon. Morgan replied with an insolent remark, and the officer drew his sword. Morgan turned his whip on him, knocked the sword from his hand, and beat him. As a result Morgan received a sentence of five hundred lashes, but he fainted after four hundred and fifty and the remainder were remitted. Such is the stuff of which American generals were made. See Sargent, *History of an Expedition Against Fort Du Quesne,* 240, note 1.

16. One of the functions of the officer's sash was to be used as a litter to carry a wounded or dead officer off the field.

17. *Leslie to a Merchant of Philadelphia,* July 30, 1755, in *Hazard's Pennsylvania Register*, V. 191, cited in Parkman, 112. Leslie was a lieutenant in the 44th.

18. There are various lists, with differing counts and spellings. See, e.g., Wahll, 438.

19. If anything, this estimate of casualties is conservative. One contemporary estimate placed the total casualties at 977 out of 1,459 present. Breslaw, *A Dismal Tragedy*, 126.

20. Freeman, *George Washington, A Biography*, vol. 2, *Young Washington*, 86.

21. Only 195 of the total 673 men in the Light Brigade were neither killed nor wounded–a casualty rate of approximately 71 percent. In contrast, the 877 casualties at Braddock's defeat (using Sargent's count) should be measured against the total number of actual combatants on the field, which was approximately 1,200 (the noncombatant wagoneers and drovers were unarmed, did not fight, and fled at the first opportunity). The approximately 877 combatants killed or wounded represents a casualty rate of 73 percent. The figure would be even higher if the larger casualty count noted above is used.

Indeed, perhaps the closest historical analogy to Braddock's loss occurred almost two millennia earlier, in 9 A.D., when three Roman legions (the LVII, LVIII, and LXIX) under Publius Quintilius Varus were ambushed and annihilated by Arminius in the German forest at the Battle of Teutoburgerwald. Varus, like Braddock, was a conservative headstrong general with no prior combat experience. His legions, marching through a thick forest, were surprised by a barbarian enemy and could not deploy into fighting formation. As events were to show, in both cases the defeated army burned its wagons and the victorious enemy committed shocking atrocities against the defeated soldiers. Aware of the totality of his defeat, Braddock tried to emulate Varus in attempting suicide. The Romans buried Varus's body to prevent its desecration even while the battle raged. Compare the treatment of Braddock's body in the next chapter.

22. Account of M. Roucher; Kopperman, *Braddock at the Monongahela,* 271; Wahll, 379.

23. Letter from Contrecoeur to Count de la Galisonnière, July 20, 1755; Wahll, 403.

24. The description of the battle and retreat in this and the ensuing chapter are a collage of various eye witness reports taken from journals and letters of Orme, Washington, four British officers, the batman, the seaman, and Private Duncan Cameron, as well as several French officers and Canadians, and supplemented by Sargent, Lewis, McCardell, Kopperman and other authors. See generally Wahll, 345–71 for a compendium of the first-hand accounts. The most vivid and complete account is that of an unidentified British officer (Wahll 350–52, identified as "British A" by Kopperman). Kopperman's work is the most meticulously researched on the battle itself, and he goes the extra step of assessing the credibility of the various eyewitness accounts.

25. Account of James Smith; Wahll, 362–63.

26. According to one French report, the captured guns brought into the fort on July 11 included four brass 12-pounders, two brass 6-pounders and four brass mortars with a diameter of seven and a half inches, together with great quantities of ammunition and powder. There were also brought in about eighty head of "horned Cattle with which the Indians made as great Slaughter as they had done with the English." See report of M. Roucher in Kopperman, *Braddock at the Monongahela,* 271; Wahll, 378; see also English report on lost brass ordnance in Wahll, 391. A separate report on the battle and captured artillery by Contrecoeur describes the cannon as being of "cast iron," which was almost certainly true of the naval 12-pounders. See Wahll, 385. It is unclear if any of the naval guns actually accompanied the flying column, although St. Clair early on ordered carriages to be specially constructed from wagons for the big guns.

27. Account of James Smith; Wahll, 363. Miraculously, Smith survived his ordeal. He was held captive for four years by the Caughnawagas, a branch of the

Mohawks allied with the French. Eventually he was adopted into the tribe and spent his captivity in Ohio. Although he was well treated and empathetic to the Indians, he escaped in 1759. He returned to Pennsylvania, married, and took up farming. However, with the outbreak of Pontiac's rebellion, his neighbors turned to him as an expert in Indian warfare. He organized a successful company of Rangers who dressed and fought Indian-fashion. At the time of the American Revolution, Smith was commissioned a colonel in the American forces. He later explored and settled in Kentucky, where he served in the state legislature. He was a religious man and acted as a missionary to the Indians in his later years. In the War of 1812, at age seventy-five, he offered his services once again to his country and published a treatise on Indian warfare. Some forty years after his escape from captivity he wrote of his experiences in *An Account of the Remarkable Occurrences in the Life and Travels of Col. James Smith* (Lexington, Ky., 1799).

Chapter Nineteen: Helter Skelter

1. Account of George Washington; Sargent, *History of an Expedition Against Fort Du Quesne,* 637; Wahll, 376.

2. Browne's Journal; Wahll, 378. Browne received a double blow: six days later her brother the commissary died at the fort from fever. ("Oh! How shall I express my Distraction. This unhappy day at 2 in the after Noon deprived me of my dear Brother in whom I have lost my kind Guardian and Protector and am now left a Friendless Exile from all that is dear to me." Wahll, 390. However, despite grief, illness and eventual evacuation to Frederick, Maryland, Charlotte Browne recovered sufficiently to attend a ball in that town on Saturday September 20 "which was compos'd of Romans, Jews and Hereticks who in this Town flock together." She observed that "The Ladys danced without Stays or Hoops, and it ended with a jig from each Lady." Wahll, 466–67.

3. Spencer, "Carlyle House and Its Associations."

4. Parkman, *Montcalm and Wolfe,* 117, citing letter to Lord Halifax.

5. Batman's Journal; Hamilton, *Braddock's Defeat,* 34; Wahll, 434.

6. The order was given in Braddock's name. See letter of anonymous British officer, Wahll, 427. Although Dunbar was severely criticized for the action after the fact, Braddock was still conscious and giving orders on the day the supplies were destroyed.

7. Artillery projectiles came in two varieties, exploding shells for the howitzers, and solid shot (i.e., "cannon balls") for the guns–hence the expression "shot and shell." Mortars fired "bombs" and "carcasses." I thank Glenn F. Williams for this information.

8. Sargent, *History of an Expedition Against Fort Du Quesne,* 235.

9. This rumor has achieved even greater currency in recent years. See, e.g., Michael Paul Henson, "Braddock's Field of Dreams," *Treasure Cache* (January 2000), 30. Variants on the buried treasure theme include a rumor that Washington and Braddock buried the money before the battle or that a wagoneer made off with it. The buried Braddock treasure has even become the subject of websites on the Internet. See, e.g., www.losttreasure.com/newsletter/11-1-2000.html.

10. Batman's Journal; Hamilton, *Braddock's Defeat,* 32; Wahll, 381. For a more sober and reasoned assessment of what happened to Braddock's treasure chest (it stayed with Dunbar and was never lost), see Kershaw, "The Legend of Braddock's Gold Reconsidered."

11. Washington may well have officiated. The chaplain was wounded. Some accounts placed the burial at midnight.

12. Braddock carried two fine brass-barreled flintlock pistols manufactured by Gabbitas, with "EB" engraved in the butt plates. The location of the second pistol today is uncertain, but it may have been in a private collection in recent years.

13. Batman's Journal; Hamilton, *Braddock's Defeat,* 32; Wahll, 383.

14. Orme's Journal; Wahll, 396.

15. Ibid.

16. Letter from Captain Robert Stewart, July 19, 1755; Kopperman, *Braddock at the Monongahela,* 229; Wahll, 402.

17. Letter from Orme to Dinwiddie, July 18, 1755; Wahll, 397.

18. Letter from Orme to Fox, July 18, 1755; Wahll, 395.

19. The loss of the military plans was of sufficient concern to the British that on July 22 they sent an Indian to Contrecoeur at Fort Duquesne to request their return. See Hamilton, *Braddock's Defeat,* 34; Wahll, 406. Apparently, his mission was not successful.

20. Letter from Washington to Dinwiddie, July 18, 1755; Kopperman, *Braddock at the Monongahela,* 231; Wahll, 398–99.

21. Batman's Journal; Hamilton, *Braddock's Defeat,* 34; Wahll, 435.

22. Letter from Washington to Dinwiddie, July 18, 1755; Wahll, 399.

23. Hamilton, *Braddock's Defeat,* 83; McCardell, *Ill-Starred General,* 271.

24. Letter from St. Clair to Napier, July 22, 1755; Wahll, 405.

25. Letter from Colonel Gage; Kopperman, *Braddock at the Monongahela,* 191; Wahll, 416–17.

26. Letter from Captain Horatio Gates, August 30, 1755; Kopperman, *Braddock at the Monongahela,* 195; Wahll, 464.

27. "Progress of the War in America," *Gentleman's Magazine,* August 26, 1755, 378. Eighteen years later Horatio Nelson was to serve as a midshipman on the *Seahorse.*

28. The closest to an official inquiry was a November 21, 1755, postmortem held by the on-the-scene army commanders at Albany, New York, taking the testimony of the likes of Dunbar and Gage. See WO/34/73 in the UK Public Record Office. However, the narrow scope and predisposition of the inquest are betrayed by its title: "Inquiry into the Behaviour of the Troops at the Monongahela."

29. McCardell, *Ill-Starred General,* 269.

30. Letter from unidentified British officer; Wahll, 428.

31. McCardell, *Ill-Starred General,* 263.

32. Franklin, *Autobiography,* 222.

33. Sargent, *History of an Expedition Against Fort Du Quesne,* 357; Wahll, 377.

34. Some of the French Indians had departed Fort Duquesne shortly after the battle. The Ottawas in particular under Pontiac had feuded with the French over the division of the spoils, and on the day after the battle threw down the war-club, saying they would join the enemies of France, and thus departed the fort. They left but never made good on their promise.

35. Lewis, *For King and Country,* 194 ff.

36. Anderson, *The War That Made America,* 153.

37. Nichols, "The Braddock Expedition," cited in Wahll, 469.

38. Lewis, *For King and Country,* 195.

39. Ibid.

40. Ibid., 195–96.

41. Ibid., 246.

42. Wahll, 479.

Chapter Twenty: Sic Transit Gloria

1. Letter from Jean Daniel Dumas at Fort Duquesne to the ministry dated July 24, 1756, Fonds des Colonies, MG 1, Serie C11A, number 6517. Dumas also noted that the ministry's failure to send requested materiel had allowed Fort Cumberland to "subsist" but that George Washington "had changed his plans judging that he didn't have enough troops to undertake anything." Dumas, the victor, was ultimately rewarded by the French king with the governorship of Mauritius, an interesting counterpoint to Braddock's reputed interest in the governorship of New York if he had succeeded.

2. The British may have recognized France as having the stronger army and as being dominant in land warfare. That is why Britain initially chose to challenge France in North America, where France was weaker and more vulnerable, than in Continental Europe. Britain used its commercial wealth to subsidize Continental allies, particularly Prussia, to hold the line against France in Europe.

3. The 1754 Albany Congress, ordered by the Board of Trade in London to improve relations with the Indians and coordinate planning for defense, was a more limited and, ultimately, abortive affair. Most of the colonial legislatures which considered the resulting Plan of Union rejected it out of hand. See generally Anderson, *The War That Made America,* 77 ff.

4. In agreement, see Anderson, *The War That Made America,* 105.

5. Bennett, *The Book of Virtues*, 713. Bennett uses the poem to illustrate the virtue of "Loyalty."

6. Lengel, *General George Washington,* 60.

7. See, e.g., letter of anonymous British officer, who stated: "one thing I must observe with regard to the method of Fighting here among our Savage Indians, who maintain a kind of Running Fight, skulking behind Trees and Bushes, That it is a Folly to Set Regular Troops to Engage them. The only Fit for them are such Forragers as are your Hussars, Hayducks, Wild Tartars or Arabs, or even our own Scots Highlanders for Foot Fighting could manage them very well. Our Backswoods-men here and Huntsmen and many of our American Militia understand better how to Smash these Fellows in their own way than any of his Majesty's Regular Troops." Wahll, 456. Even Washington, no admirer of American militia, praised how his Virginia companies "behav'd like Men and died like Soldiers." Wahll, 398.

8. Examples of volunteers appear to have included Ronald Carruthers, John Clarke, Thomas Drought and William Irwin, serving in various ranks, from the 44th Regiment; Richard Boyce, William Nicholson, Walter Patterson and Charles Perry, serving in various ranks, from the 48th; as well as Richard Elrington, Andrew Crotty, Charles Humble and Thomas Millet from the 22nd. See "Known Volunteers in Rogers's Rangers," at www.usgennet.org/usa/topic/colonial/rogers/roster.html.

9. For example, Rule 7 reads: "If you are obliged to receive the enemy's fire, fall or squat down till it is over." Similarly, Rule 10 reads: "If the enemy is so superior that you are in danger of being surrounded by them, let the whole body disperse." Unfortunately, despite his contribution to American military thinking, the New Hampshire-bred Rogers suffered a fate as ironic as those of many of the participants in the Braddock campaign. Because of Rogers's suspected Tory

sympathies and espionage activities during the Revolution, George Washington refused his offer to form a special operations unit for the American army. He later was arrested. After his release, he formed a Loyalist special operations unit to fight the Patriots which captured and executed the American spy Nathan Hale. His wife divorced him, he became an alcoholic and was hounded out of America; he died in poverty in England in 1795.

10. See Darling, *Red Coat and Brown Bess,* 30. Also Brumwell, *Redcoats,* 227 ff.

11. Contrecoeur was to write shortly after the battle: "If the enemy had returned with the 1000 fresh troops which they held in reserve a little distance from them, and of which we didn't know the distance . . . we would have been at a loss." Wahll, 385. An alternative view is that the division of the troops was not material to his defeat. If Dunbar's men had marched with Braddock, this theory holds that they would have simply added to the confusion on the battlefield, made a larger target for the French and Indians and resulted in an even more devastating defeat.

12. For a dissenting–and probably well informed–point of view, see letter from Colonel Henry Bouquet to General John Forbes dated June 11, 1758, stating: "I am told that Braddock's army went 3 days without finding grass for the horses, which made them unfit to carry provisions; *and he would have been likely to die of hunger, if he had beaten the enemy*" (emphasis added). Stevens, Kent and Leonard, *The Papers of Henry Bouquet,* vol. 2, 74.

13. See series of deciphered letters from "CH., N" to "S.d.S" from the Series Segretaria di Stato, Francia, in the Secret Archives of the Vatican available in the National Archives of Canada at MG17-A1 dated October 20 and December 22, 1755, and January 19, 1756. The author of the reports states that the orders called for "invading all of America and pillaging French ships." He concluded that, as a result, it will be "very difficult [for England] to arrive at an entente with France."

14. Hulbert, *Braddock's Road,* Preface.

15. Gutheim, *The Potomac,* 129.

16. See generally Searight, *The Old Pike.*

17. Today Braddock's grave lies within a stone's throw of a roadhouse, the Braddock Inn.

18. The land where the battle occurred was farmland during the early nineteenth century and hosted several large manor houses. The Marquis de Lafayette visited one of the manors during his 1824 tour of America. However, coal was discovered in the ravines in the 1830s. One of the earliest extractors of coal at Braddock's Field was one Thomas Fausett, a local landowner and presumably a relation to the Tom Fausett who claimed he had killed Braddock.

Coal and the river landing for its shipment provided the early impetus for development of the town of Braddock. Later urbanization was fueled by Andrew Carnegie's steel works.

Epilogue

1. Brumwell, *Redcoats,* 75.

2. Ibid., 157. There were an additional twenty-four sick men unable to stand and three invalids scheduled for retirement to the Royal Hospital at Chelsea.

3. Bellamy, *Apology,* vol. 2, at 194.

4. www.musical-theatre.net/html/recordcabinet/3blue.html.

5. Burton's will, dated 1767, is available in the National Archives of Canada. See Gerald M. Kelly Fonds, R1747-0-8-E.

6. Captain Gabriel Christie (1722–99) served as deputy quartermaster under St. Clair on the Braddock expedition and later at the siege of Quebec under Wolfe. He was the son of a wealthy Scottish merchant and eventually rose to the rank of General and Chief of Staff in North America. He made a fortune in the North American timber trade and married Sarah Anne Stevenson. Wahll thinks, based on handwriting analysis, that he probably is the unidentified British officer who wrote letters with a jaundiced view of America and who recorded the enemy's use of rifles in the battle. If so, it is ironic that a man with such a distaste for things American would have spent the rest of his life in the New World. His high-cheeked portrait resides today in the Chateau Ramezay Museum in Montreal.

7. Ritenour, *Old Tom Fossit,* 233.

8. Sargent, *History of an Expedition Against Fort Du Quesne,* says it was Peter Halkett who made the journey, while other historians argue it was Francis Halkett, who had fought with his father under Braddock. It matters little which son it was.

9. Sargent, *History of an Expedition Against Fort Du Quesne,* 276–77, quoting Galt's *Life of West.*

10. www.kfki.hu/~arthp/html/r/reynolds/captain.html.

11. The Lieutenant Robert Townshend who served in the 44th under Braddock and was killed at the Battle of the Monongahela was a very distant cousin from a Welsh branch of the family.

12. On the Townshends generally, see http://home.wordline.co.za/~townshend/1stmarquess.htm. The keeper of this website has informed the author that the archivist at Raynham Hall in Norfolk, England possesses a hand-drawn family chart that refers to "Rev. Robert Orme (a runaway marriage)." This presumably refers to the marriage of Captain Robert Orme and Audrey Townshend, not to

the marriage of their son, the divine. See also the will of Captain Robert Orme dated October 12, 1771 and probated October 13, 1790. UK Public Record Office, Catalogue Reference: Prob 11/990. Orme remained married to Audrey Townshend until her death in 1781 and had a son and daughter by her; he also appeared to have been reconciled with his Townshend in-laws because he provided for them in his will. For Orme's earlier correspondence with George Washington, see Abbott, *Papers of George Washington, Colonial Series, August 1755–April 1756*, vol. 2, 320–22.

13. Hulbert, *Braddock's Road*, 211.

14. Lewis, *For King and* Country, 168.

15. www.clansinclairusa.org/clansinclairold/ev_wor_misc.htm. Among St. Clair's horticultural accomplishments was the introduction to America of the Pipperidge pepper, also known as the Willing's Barbados. See www.sev.internet.edu/%7Ejnekola/Heirloom/PeppersUW.htm.

16. See, generally, Hildeburn, "Sir John St. Clair." Belville is sometimes spelled Belleville and, according to some sources, may have been located near Trenton, New Jersey, rather than Elizabeth. St. Clair's widow remarried within a year and a half after his death to another British officer and died in London in 1783. Her son by St. Clair became the fourth baronet. In contrast to the loyalist ties of Betsy, her father (who died in 1761) trained several lawyers who were later prominent in the Revolutionary cause, including John Dickinson, and her mother hosted George Washington for several weeks during the Revolutionary War by allowing him to use her Bucks County house as his headquarters in August 1777.

17. Smithsonian Institution, online catalogue, no. 245168.126.

18. Hulbert, *Braddock's Road and Three Relative Papers*, 211. Washington's diaries do not corroborate the search, but it was recorded and perpetuated in local tradition.

19. Unless indicated otherwise, the author is indebted for the following observations on Washington's characteristics as a soldier and leader to remarks made by the historian David Hackett Fischer at the American Enterprise Institute's Irving Kristol Award and Lecture on March 8, 2006. The observations on the effect of Braddock on Washington's characteristics are the author's.

20. Lengel, *General George Washington,* 61.

21. Ibid., 61, 79.

22. Ibid., 545.

23. Ibid., 159.

24. Flexner, *George Washington in the American Revolution,* 537.

25. Lengel, *General George Washington,* 78.

26. Ibid., 369.

27. Ibid.

28. Ibid., 365.

29. Ibid., 540.

30. Charles O'Hara led an eventful life. The illegitimate son of Lord Tyrawley by one of his three Portuguese "wives," O'Hara was born c. 1740. Like his father, he opted early on for a military career. He fought bravely as a brigadier general with Cornwallis throughout much of the southern campaign during the Revolution and was twice wounded at the Battle of Guilford Courthouse. Although expected to die, he recovered and was with Cornwallis at the siege of Yorktown. The night after dining with Washington following the surrender, O'Hara attended a banquet given by the French general Rochambeau, at which he exhibited, according to one French participant, "sang froid and gaiety even." O'Hara went on to serve in Gibraltar, command Sir John St. Clair's old 22nd of Foot regiment, rise to Lieutenant General, fight against the French, suffer capture in 1793 personally by the young Napoleon Bonaparte, narrowly escape the guillotine and end up his career in his father's old position of Governor of Gibraltar. He was a popular and successful governor, renowned for his eccentric old-fashioned manner of dress which was more appropriate to the Seven Years' War than the Napoleonic era. He was affectionately known as "Old Cock of the Rock." When he died in 1802 he left a considerable fortune of £70,000 to his four illegitimate children by Gibraltan women and £7,000 to his black servant.

Bibliography

Archives

Alexandria City Public Library, especially the Local History/Special Collections, Alexandria, Va.

Braddock Carnegie Library, Braddock, Pa.

British Museum, London

Chateau Ramezay Museum, Montreal, Canada

Fort Ligonier Museum, Ligonier, Pa.

Library of Congress, Washington, D.C.

National Archives of Canada (available online)

Secret Archives of the Vatican (available online)

The Society of the Cincinnati Library, Washington, D.C.

United Kingdom Public Record Office (available online)

Journals and Orderly Books

Available at Library of Congress and published in Wahll, Sargent, and elsewhere.

[Anonymous], *The Batman's Journal*

Braddock, Major General Edward, *Orderly Book*

Browne, Charlotte, *Diary*

Gordon, Engineer Harry, *Journal.*

Halkett, Colonel Sir Peter and Disney, Ensign Daniel, *Orderly Book*

Orme, Captain Robert, *Captain Orme's Journal,* British Museum: King's MSS., No. 212

[Anonymous], *The Seaman's Journal*

St. Clair, Colonel Sir John, *Letter Book*

Published Sources

Abbot, W. W., ed., "General Braddock in Alexandria: John Carlyle to George Carlyle, 15 August 1755," *Virginia Magazine of History and Biography,* 97 (April 1989), 205–14.

____, ed., *Papers of George Washington, Colonial Series, August 1755–April 1756, Vol. II.* Charlottesville: University Press of Virginia, 1983.

Alberts, Robert C., "Braddock's Alumni," *American Heritage* 12, no. 2, February 1961.

Alexandria Gazette, "100 Years Ago," October 21, 1967.

Anderson, Fred, *Crucible of War.* New York: Vintage Books, 2001.

____, *The War That Made America.* New York: Viking, 2005.

Bailey, DeWitt, *British Military Flintlock Rifles, 1740–1840.* Lincoln, R.I.: Andrew Mowbry Publishers, 2002.

____, *British Military Longarms, 1715–1865.* New York: Arms & Armour Press 1971.

Bailey, Kenneth P., *The Ohio Company of Virginia and the Westward Movement 1748–1792.* 1939; reprint Wennawoods, 2000.

Barbero, Alessandro, *The Battle: A New History of Waterloo.* New York: Walker, 2005.

Beer, George Louis, *British Colonial Policy, 1754–1765,* New York: Macmillan, 1922 (reprint of article in *Political Science Quarterly* 22, March 1907).

Bellamy, George Anne, *An Apology for the Life of George Anne Bellamy.* 1st ed. London: Published by the author and sold by J. Bell, 1785.

____, *An Apology for the Life of George Anne Bellamy.* 2nd ed. Dublin: published by Messrs. Moncrieff, Burnet, Jenkin, Wilson, Exshaw, Burton, Whit, Byrne and H. Whitestone, 1785.

Bennett, William J., *The Book of Virtues.* New York: Simon & Schuster, 1993.

Black, Jeremy, *Warfare in the Eighteenth Century.* London: Cassell, 2002.

Bonner-Smith, D., ed., *The Barrington Papers* (Publications of the Naval Record Society), vol. 77.

Braddock, Edward, *Major General Edward Braddock's Orderly Books.* Cumberland, Md.: W. H. Lowdermilk, 1878.

Breslaw, Elaine G., "A Dismal Tragedy: Drs. Alexander and John Hamilton Comment on Braddock's Defeat," *Maryland Historical Magazine,* 75, no. 2, 1980.

Brock, R. A., ed., *The Official Records of Robert Dinwiddie, Lieutenant Governor of the Colony of Virginia, 1751–1758.* 1883; reprint, New York: AMS Press, 1971.

Brumwell, Stephen, *Redcoats: The British Soldier and War in the Americas, 1755–1763*. Cambridge: Cambridge University Press, 2002.

Bryan, Helen, *Martha Washington: First Lady of History*. New York: John Wiley & Sons, 2002.

Burrows, J. W., *The Essex Regiment (1st Battalion)*. New edition. London: Naval & Military Press, 2005.

Chartrand, Rene, *The French Soldier in Colonial America*. Historical Arms Series No. 18. Alexandria Bay, N.Y.: Museum Restoration Service, 1984.

____, *Monongahela 1754–1755: Washington's Defeat, Braddock's Disaster*. Oxford: Osprey Publishing, 2004.

Darling, Anthony D., *Red Coat and Brown Bess*. Historical Arms Series No. 12, Alexandria Bay, N.Y.: Museum Restoration Service, 1971.

Darlington, William M., *Christopher Gist's Journals*. Bowie, Md.: Heritage Books, 2002.

Dinwiddie, Robert, *The Official Records of Robert Dinwiddie, Lieut. Governor of the Colony of Virginia 1751–1758*. Introduction and notes by R.A. Brock, Whitefish, Mont.: Kessinger Publishing, 2006.

Disney, Daniel, *Papers of Daniel Disney 1747–1757*. Library of Congress Microfilm 18,330-1P.

Doddridge, Joseph, *Notes on the Settlement and Indian Wars*. Pittsburgh: Ritenour and Lindsey, 1912; reprint, Parsons, W.Va.: McClain Printing Company, 1996.

Donehoo, George, *A History of the Indian Villages and Place Names in Pennsylvania*. Harrisburg, Pa.: Telegraph Press, 1928.

Drimmer, Frederick, ed., *Captured by the Indians, Fifteen Firsthand Accounts, 1750-1870*. New York: Dover Publications, 1985.

Ecker, Grace Dunlop, *A Portrait of Old Georgetown*. Richmond, Va.: Dietz Press, 1951.

Faragher, John Mack, *Daniel Boone*. New York: Henry Holt, 1992.

Fischer, David Hackett, *Washington's Crossing*. Oxford: Oxford University Press, 2004.

Fitzpatrick, John C., ed., *The Writings of George Washington*. Washington, D.C.: Government Printing Office, vol. 1, 1931.

Flexner, James Thomas, *George Washington in the American Revolution (1775–1783)*. Boston: Little, Brown, 1968.

Fort Ligonier Association, *War for Empire in Western Pennsylvania*. Fort Ligonier, Pa., 1993.

Franklin, Benjamin, *The Autobiography of Benjamin Franklin.* New York: Walter J. Black, 1941.

Freeman, Douglas Southall, *George Washington, A Biography*, volume 2, *Young Washington.* New York, Charles Scribner's Sons, 1948.

Gallup, Andrew, *The Celeron Expedition to the Ohio Country 1749: The Reports of Pierre-Joseph Celeron and Father Bonnecamps.* Bowie, Md.: Heritage Books, 1997.

Gutheim, Frederick, *The Potomac.* Baltimore: Johns Hopkins University Press, 1986.

Hadden, James, *Washington's Expeditions (1753–1754) and Braddock's Expedition (1755) with History of Tom Fausett, the Slayer of General Edward Braddock.* Uniontown, Pa., 1910.

Hamilton, Charles, ed., *Braddock's Defeat: The Journal of Captain Robert Cholmley's Batman, The Journal of a British Officer and Halkett's Orderly Book.* Norman: University of Oklahoma Press, 1959.

Harrison, Fairfax, "With Braddock's Army: Mrs. Browne's Diary in Virginia and Maryland," *Virginia Magazine of History and Biography*, 32, no. 4, October 1924.

Hibbert, Christopher, *Wellington: A Personal History.* Reading, Mass.: Perseus Press, 1997.

Higginbotham, Don, *George Washington and the American Military Tradition.* Athens: University of Georgia Press, 1985.

Hildeburn, Charles R., "Sir John St. Clair, Baronet, Quarter-Master General in America, 1755 to 1767," *Pennsylvania Magazine of History and Biography*, 9, no. 1, 1885.

Historical Manuscripts Commission, *Report on the Manuscripts of Mrs. Frankland-Russell-Astley of Chequers, Bucks.* London: Mackie & Co., 1900.

Hough, Walter S., *Braddock's Road Through the Virginia Colony.* Strasburg, Va.: Shenandoah Publishing House, 1970.

Houston, Alan, "Benjamin Franklin and the 'Wagon Affair' of 1755," *William and Mary Quarterly*, 66, no. 2, April 2009.

Hulbert, Archer Butler, *Braddock's Road and Three Relative Papers.* Historic Highways of America, vol. 4, Cleveland: Arthur H. Clark Company, 1903.

Hunter, William A., *Forts on the Pennsylvania Frontier 1753–1756.* Harrisburg: Pennsylvania Historical and Museum Commission, 1960.

Jackson, Major Joseph, *The Leadership Failure of Major General Edward Braddock*, unpublished monograph, U.S. Army Combined Arms Center, Ft. Leavenworth, KS, [n.d.]

Kent, Donald H., ed., *Contrecoeur's Copy of George Washington's Journal for 1754.* Eastern National Park & Monument Association, 1989.

Kershaw, Gordon, "The Legend of Braddock's Gold Reconsidered," *Maryland Historical Society Magazine,* 96, no. 1, Spring 2001.

Kopperman, Paul E., *Braddock at the Monongahela.* Pittsburgh: University of Pittsburgh Press, 1977.

Lacock, John Kennedy, "Braddock Road," *Pennsylvania Magazine of History and Biography,* 37, no. 1, 1914.

Lamb, George H., *Unwritten History of Braddock's Field.* Pittsburgh: Nicholson Printing Co., 1917.

Laver, John B., ed., *Records of the Columbia Historical Society*, vol. 22, Washington, D.C., 1919.

Lengel, Edward G., *General George Washington: A Military Life.* New York: Random House, 2005.

Lewis, Thomas A., *For King and Country: George Washington, The Early Years.* New York: John Wiley & Sons, 1993.

Lincoln, Charles H., *A List of Additional Manuscripts of the French and Indian War in the Library of the Society.* Worcester, Mass.: The Society, 1908.

Lucier, Armand Francis, *French and Indian War Notices Abstracted from Colonial Newspapers, vol. 1: 1754–55.* Bowie, Md.: Heritage Books, 1999.

Magnusson, Magnus, KBE, general ed., *Cambridge Biographical Dictionary.* Cambridge: Cambridge University Press, 1990.

Manucy, Albert, *Artillery Through the Ages.* Washington, D.C.: U.S. Government Printing Office, 1985.

Maryland Gazette, 1754–1755.

McCardell, Lee, *Ill-Starred General: Braddock of the Coldstream Guards.* Pittsburgh: University of Pittsburgh Press, 1958.

Moller, George, *American Military Shoulder Arms*, vol. 1. Niwot: University Press of Colorado, 1993.

Munson, James D., *Col. John Carlyle, Gent.: A True and Just Account of the Man and His House.* Northern Virginia Regional Park Authority, 1986.

Nester, William R., *The Great Frontier War: Britain, France, and the Imperial Struggle for North America 1607–1755.* New York: Praeger, 2000.

Netherton, Ross, *Braddock's Campaign and the Potomac Route West.* Winchester-Frederick Historical Society, Falls Church, Va.: Higher Education Publications, 1997.

Nichols, Franklin T., "The Braddock Expedition." Ph.D. diss., Harvard University, 1946.

____. "The Organization of Braddock's Army," *William and Mary Quarterly,* 1947.

O'Callaghan, E. B., *The Documentary History of the State of New York.* Albany, N.Y.: Weed, Parsons & Co., 1849.

O'Meara, Walter, *Guns at the Forks.* Englewood Cliffs, N.J.: Prentice-Hall, 1965.

Pargellis, Stanley M., *Military Affairs in North America, 1748–1765: Selected Documents from the Cumberland Papers in Windsor Castle*, n.p., Archon, 1969.

Parkman, Francis, *Montcalm and Wolfe.* New York: Modern Library, 1999.

Peterson, Harold L., *Arms and Armor in Colonial America 1526–1783.* New York: Bramhall House, 1956.

Phillips, Kevin, *The Cousins' Wars.* New York: Basic Books, 1999.

Post, Christian Frederick, *Two Journals of Western Tours.* 1798.

"Progress of the War in America." *Gentleman's Magazine,* London, August 1755.

Reid, Stuart and Chappell, Paul, *King George's Army 1740–93: (1) Infantry.* Osprey Military Warrior Series No. 285. Rushden, Northants., UK: Osprey Publishing, 1995.

Reid, Stuart, and Richard Hook, *British Redcoat 1740–1793.* Osprey Military Warrior Series No. 19. Wellingborough, Northants., UK: Osprey Publishing, 1999.

Ritenour, John Sturgis, *Old Tom Fossit.* Pittsburgh: J. R. Weldin Co., 1926.

Sallust, *The Conspiracy of Cataline.* Translated with an introduction by S. A. Handford. Harmondsworth: Penguin Books, 1975.

Sargent, Winthrop, ed., *The History of an Expedition Against Fort Du Quesne in 1755.* Philadelphia: Lippincott, Grebo & Co., for the Historical Society of Pennsylvania; reprint, Lewisburg, Pa.: Wennawoods Publishing, 1997.

Searight, Thomas B., *The Old Pike: A History of the National Road,* Uniontown Pa.: published by the author, 1894, reprinted, Bowie, Md.: Heritage Books, 1990.

Shepperd, G.A., *Arms and Armour 1669 to 1918.* London: Rupert Hart-Davis, 1971.

Shetrane, H. C., "The Indian in Ohio," *Ohio Archeological and Historical Publications,* 27. Columbus: Ohio State Archeological and Historical Society, 1919.

Shumway, George, *Rifles of Colonial America,* vol. 1. York, Pa.: George Shumway Publisher, 1980.

Sipe, C. Hale, *The Indian Chiefs of Pennsylvania.* Butler, Pa.: Ziegler Printing Co., 1927.

____, *The Indian Wars of Pennsylvania,* 2d ed. Harrisburg, Pa.: Telegraph Press, 1929.

Spencer, Richard Henry, "Carlyle House and Its Associations," *William and Mary College Quarterly Historical Magazine,* 18, July 1909.

Spendelow, Charles, *General Braddock's Expedition.* Dartford, UK: Ritchie, 1963.

Stephen, Sir Leslie, and Sir Sidney Lee, *Dictionary of National Biography,* Vol. II. Oxford: Oxford University Press, 1964.

Stevens, S. K., Donald H. Kent, and Autumn L. Leonard, *The Papers of Henry Bouquet, The Forbes Expedition,* 2, Harrisburg: Pennsylvania Historical and Museum Commission, 1951.

Volwiler, Albert T., *George Croghan and the Westward Movement 1741–1782.* New York: AMS Press, 1971.

Waddell, Louis M., and Bruce D. Bomberger, *The French and Indian War in Pennsylvania 1753–1763.* Harrisburg: Pennsylvania Historical and Museum Commission, 1996.

Wahll, Andrew J., *Braddock Road Chronicles 1755.* Bowie, Md.: Heritage Books, 1999.

Williams, Glenn F., *Year of the Hangman: George Washington's Campaign Against the Iroquois.* Yardley, Pa.: Westholme Publishing, 2005.

Internet Resources

Conspiracy of Pontiac,
www.usgennet.org/usa/topic/colonial/book/chap9_5.html

English Settlers of Lacolle, Quebec,
www.fortunecity.com/millennium/rose/1328/hist.html

Faragher, John Mack, Chronology from Daniel Boone: the Life and Legend of an American Pioneer,
http://xroads.virginia.edu/~HYPER/HNS/Boone/chronology.html

French forts in North America,
http://fiwar.virtualave.net/forts/french.html
Thomas Gage, 1721–1887, William L. Clements Library, The University of Michigan, Thomas Gage Papers,
www.clements.umich.edu/Webguides/Arlenes/G/Gage.html
Horatio Gates, www.patriotresource.com/people/gates.html
Sir Peter Halkett (1703-1755), www.ancientfaces.com/cgi-bin/displaystory.cfm?ID=227
Major General Charles Lee,
www.patriotresource.com/people/charleslee.html
Hugh Mercer, Columbia Encyclopedia, Sixth Edition (2001),
www.bartleby.com/65/e-/E-Mercer-H.html
Roger Morris, Columbia Encyclopedia, Sixth Edition (2001),
www.bartleby.com/65/mo/Morris-Rg.html
National Portrait Gallery, London, Details of NPG 2034,
www.npg.org.uk/live/room_detail.asp?mkey=mw04475
The Queen's House at the National Maritime Museum,
www.nmm.ac.uk/queens_house/qh_picture_info_01/17.htm
Rogers's Rangers, Known Volunteers www.usgennet.org/use/topic/colonial/rogers/roster.html
Shakespeare and the Globe: Then and Now, Encyclopaedia Britannica: Bellamy, George Anne,
www.britannica.com/shakespeare/micro/729/87.html
Sir John St. Clair with Braddock, www. Clansinclairusa.org/clansinclairold/ev_wor_misc.htm.
Stewart, A.I.B., Sons of the Highland Manse, www.ndirect.co.uk/~iforshaw/Mag35/page11.html
"General Townshend," George Townshend, 1724–1807,
http://home.worldline.co.za/~townshend/1stmarquess.htm
Web of English History, The Age of George III, William Augustus, Duke of Cumberland (1721-65), http://dspace.dial.pipex.com/town/terrace/adw03/c-eight/cumber.htm

INDEX

Acknowledgments

I am indebted to the scholars of Braddock's march who have gone before–Winthrop Sargent, Francis Parkman, Douglas Southall Freeman, Lee McCardell, Walter O'Meara, Paul E. Kopperman, Fred Anderson, Andrew Wahll, among others. Without their insights and inspired writing, this book may never have gotten off the ground.

Creating this particular *Braddock's March*, from first sentence to publication, has taken sixteen times longer than Braddock's expedition itself. I wish to thank all the pilgrims along the way who gave a word of encouragement or more: Bruce H. Franklin (thoughtful and intelligent publisher who made it happen), Joe Vallely (agent extraordinaire), Noreen O'Connor-Abel (whose good eye as editor improved the text), Trudi Gershenov (who created the beautiful jacket design), Tracy Dungan (who drew the maps), Glenn Williams (author and knowledgeable guide on the intricacies of British military lore of the period who provided explanations and points of clarification), Andrew Wahll (cartographer and author who helped show me the route, both literally and figuratively), John Weisman (friend and mentor in the ways of writing), Carol Boyd (my first enthusiastic reader), Ellen McCallister Clark (Library Director at the Society of the Cincinnati Library who graciously opened the collections), Alexandria historian Michael Miller, and a host of others, including Martin West, Marc Leepson, Max Gartenberg, Alex Hoyt, and the helpful staff at the Alexandria, Virginia Public Library. If I have omitted others, my apologies.

Finally, there are the "Grenadiers"–those who earned the legend "Nec Aspera Terrent"–my two sons, to whom this book is dedicated and who must have visited every French and Indian War fort in the East and Canada, and, Beth, who drove so many, many days while I scribbled.

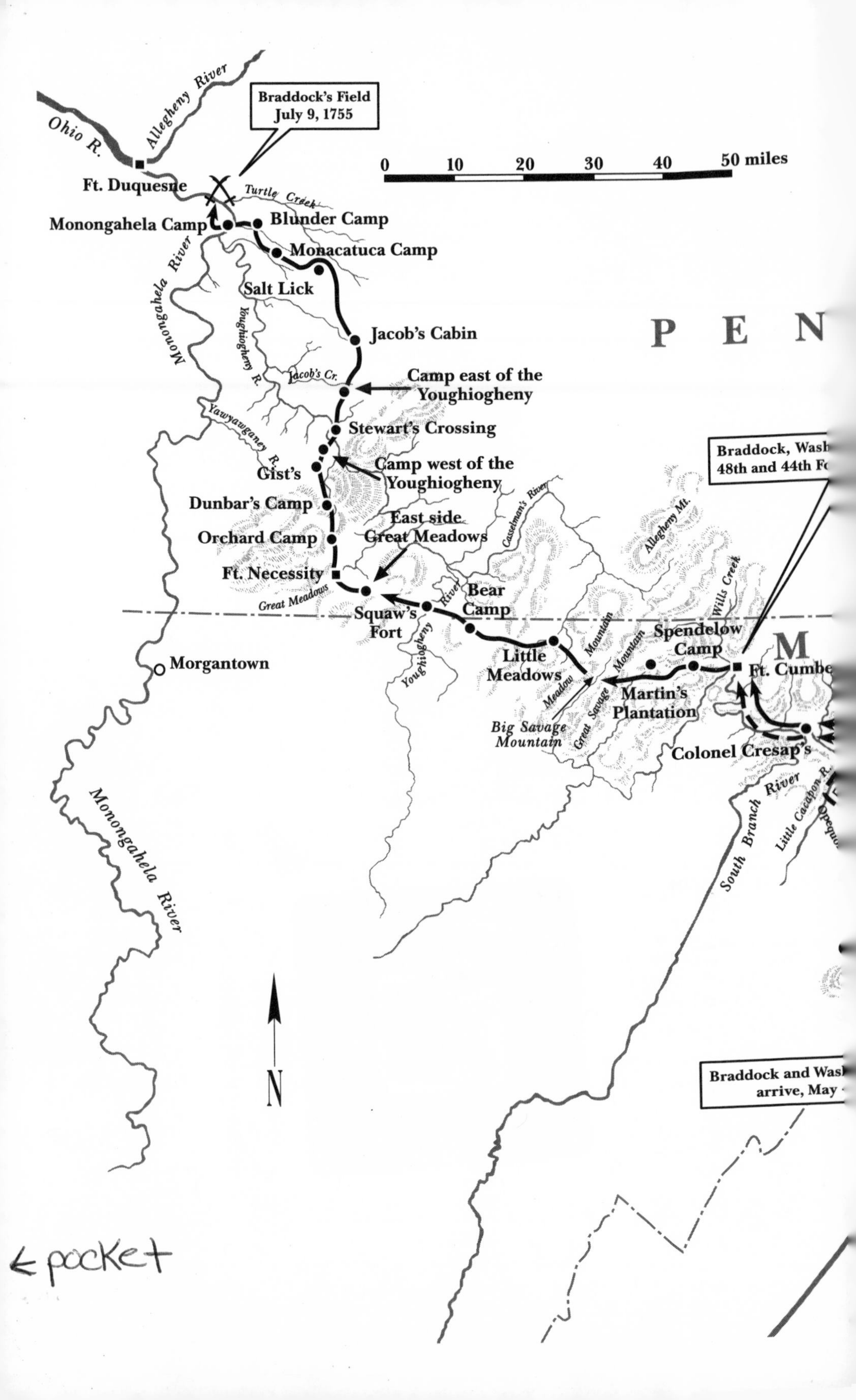

Braddock's Field
July 9, 1755
Ohio R.
Allegheny River
0 10 20 30 40 50 miles
Ft. Duquesne
Turtle Creek
Monongahela Camp
Blunder Camp
Monacatuca Camp
Monongahela River
Salt Lick
Youghiogheny R.
Jacob's Cabin
P E N
Jacob's Cr.
Camp east of the
Youghiogheny
Yawyawganey R.
Stewart's Crossing
Braddock, Wash
48th and 44th F
Gist's
Camp west of the
Youghiogheny
Dunbar's Camp
Casselman's River
East side
Great Meadows
Orchard Camp
Allegheny Mt.
Ft. Necessity
Wills Creek
Great Meadows
Bear
Camp
Squaw's
Fort
Youghiogheny River
Mountain
Spendelow
Camp
M
Little
Meadows
Mountain
Morgantown
Ft. Cumbe
Meadow
Great Savage
Martin's
Plantation
Big Savage
Mountain
Colonel Cresap's
South Branch River
Little Cacapon R.
Monongahela River
N
Braddock and Wash
arrive, May

←pocket